Pastoral Care — a training manual

Douglas Hamblin

Basil Blackwell

To the Clwyd Training Groups, especially Sue Jenkins, whose courage and charm I admire, and Martin Weeks for his energy and integrity.

© Douglas Hamblin 1984
First published 1984

Published by Basil Blackwell Ltd
108 Cowley Road
Oxford OX4 1JF
England

British Library Cataloguing in Publication Data

Hamblin, Douglas
  Pastoral care.
  1. Student counselors, Training of—Great
  Britain   2. Personnel service in secondary
  education—Great Britain
  I. Title
  373.14′042′0941   LB1731

  ISBN 0-631-13416-6

Typeset by Freeman Graphic
in Helvetica and Plantin
Printed in Great Britain

Contents

Preface

This training manual is based on my work over the last fifteen years. Training involves team work. Yet team-work within the school may be weaker than we acknowledge, in both the pastoral and the curricular dimensions of teaching. Full professional satisfaction may well depend on our ability to work as groups to provide mutual support and demonstrate proper concern for our pupils. Realistic self-evaluation leads to productive training – this book stresses that evaluation and training go hand in hand. Strong emphasis is given to the need to abandon the search for instant recipes. What works in one school will not work in another; what can be achieved in one school can be attained in another, but by different methods and organisation. To take over programmes of tutorial work blindly is to risk superficial performance in which neither tutors nor pupils are involved. Deputy heads and heads of year or house must work together to develop their own skills and ability to discharge their leadership functions. This reflects the fact that the teacher as a professional has a large part to play in developing training and monitoring within the school.

Once again I acknowledge my debt to all my past students, especially Beth Webster, Roger Roper, Madeleine O'Shea, Dewi Williams and Katie Doherty. I think they will know why. For any omissions, I apologise. My thanks are due to all those at Basil Blackwell who have made working with them a pleasure over the years. Special thanks go to Joan Morrison who saw this book through the press. Mrs Katrina Guntrip typed the manuscript with efficiency, zest and cheerfulness. I am also grateful to Maggie Bradbury for her cartoons. Her style is appreciated by adolescents, and the message strikes home. I alone am responsible for the many imperfections of this book. I am clear, however, that pastoral care of the type described helps the school to become a truly caring community, encouraging talent and creativity in a rapidly changing society.

Swansea
February 1984

Introduction

The viewpoint taken

Pastoral care helps pupils to succeed in their learning tasks and fosters their personal maturity. Critical awareness of the school's aims, methods, ideals and realities must be part of the outcome of training, whilst the perceptions and reactions of pupils are accepted as a crucial part of the data on which we act. Pastoral care is compassionate but tough minded, rejecting sentimentality as unworthy of the creative educator. It is intimately related to achievement and vigorously pursues standards of excellence – it provides no excuses for failure or evasion, for either teacher or pupil.

Pastoral heads must monitor the processes which shape pupils' development and promote initiative so that the justifiable objectives of the school are achieved. Processes as much as content of pastoral activity are highlighted, reflecting my belief that one of the greatest barriers to achieving the goals of pastoral care is inadequacy in dealing with interpersonal relationships, expectations and group pressures which perpetuate ineffectiveness and reinforce disadvantage.

The manual should help the pastoral team become its own support group, using strengths that are present within the school. Salvation is not likely to come from outside sources. Pastoral heads must therefore take the initiative by training themselves and their tutors. The reader hoping for a step-by-step plan which can be adopted unthinkingly will be disappointed. Each school is unique – what works in one will not work in another. Techniques are offered and issues explored, but those responsible for training must select what seems useful, presenting it in the sequence best suited to them, adding whatever is needed to train a particular group. The manual is not intended to undermine professional responsibilities. It takes a balanced view, discouraging premature or superficial training activity and inertia. It gives aims and objectives but the reader must also set his own. My objectives are not sacred – things set apart – but have been submitted to critical scrutiny over the years. There are no final objectives. This requires training and evaluation to interact continuously. It is tempting to see evaluation as an activity solely intended to assess outcomes. This is too restrictive. Evaluation initiates training, provides corrective feedback during the implementation, opening up new ventures as success occurs. Let us therefore welcome the opportunity for self-evaluation.

One of the fundamental assumptions behind this manual is that constructive caring links the pastoral and the curricular. Integration, however, does not destroy the role boundaries necessary for efficient task achievement. It should be clear to those who use this manual that the head of year or house should possess skills which complement those of the heads of academic departments. The problem has been that many pastoral heads lack the skills of counselling and of leading a team of tutors, and this has led to retreatism and taking ineffective disciplinary roles.

Training should lead, not only to clearer objectives but, as a necessity, to sharper values. I see pastoral care as leading to positive mental health because it helps the pupil to develop self-respect and to acquire skills for coping with life – even when unemployed he will maintain a sense of significance and take up a responsible role. Pastoral care should, I believe, be in the tradition of balanced liberal education, stimulating responsible initiative. Behind pastoral care is the ethic of stern love which requires us to give pupils good experience. There have to be criteria to assess how to do this if pastoral care is to help develop the truly morally educated person in an unpredictable world.

Wider considerations

Pastoral care is plagued by a curious history of expediency and uncertainty, sometimes coloured by vague moral justifications. In some schools this was an uneasy equilibrium between the pastoral and the curricular, in which the pastoral system – if it could be called a system – contributed little that was vital. The current, welcome development of tutorial work has corrected the balance, but this work must be based on a sound knowledge of adolescent development, on concern and on sound standards of behaviour, for the onus for discipline, as with every helping process, is on those who offer pastoral activities. Good intentions are not enough. This manual alerts us to the ways in which unjustified assumptions are made about pupils' problems. Imposing our ideas of what they *ought* to want or the problems they *should* have creates threat rather than productive interaction. We forget that pupils have expectations of teachers; we may not admit that we do not meet their expectations; yet pastoral care means that we have to examine this possibility if we are to be seen as professionals who are concerned for their clients. Much can be learned from the doctor–patient relationship!

Let me make two simple points. First, foisting tutorial activities on pupils without first explaining to them the aims of pastoral work seems oddly at variance with the concept of 'caring'. Where, at times, is the respect for vulnerability and individuality that is an inseparable aspect of care? Second, what is our model of the pupil? We ignore the possibility that pupils can be active in their own guidance, creating materials for use in tutor periods. It has appeared likely that the tutorial activities which superficially appear liberal, may be based on the conception of a pupil who has to be activated, acted upon, rather than having the capacity to interpret and shape his own world. Co-operation and maturity are more likely to result when pupils are encouraged to take responsibility for their own guidance, rather than being treated as if they were the passive recipients of the benign wisdom of the pastoral team.

Marland (1980) helpfully distinguishes between the content of tutor work and the pastoral programme. This manual makes a similar distinction in the emphasis on understanding and modifying, where necessary, processes of judging and interacting. It relates pastoral care to these factors because organisational structures and procedures incorporate assumptions about the nature of teacher and pupil roles, creating an ethos in which values related to personality and major life issues are evident.

Finally, let us recognise that the mandate for pastoral care stems from the way that care contributes to the legitimate goals of the school, developing the pupil's responsible well-being, and enhancing the teacher's job satisfaction. Pastoral care, when viewed as an attack on under-functioning and passive forms of learning, and as an activity which raises the level of performance of all pupils, resolutely promoting standards of excellence, helps provide that satisfaction. It represents the perfection of the role of the teacher.

1: Basic issues and training strategies

The structure of this chapter

This book is based on the belief that the school must take the major responsibility for the development of pastoral care. Current approaches to evaluation, e.g. Dockrell and Hamilton (1980) stress the need to understand latent as well as manifest processes. Participant observation over a period of time may be essential to understand the significance of attitudes and action within a school. System difficulties and tensions generate defensive attitudes and perceptions which obscure the problem.

Training within the school must begin with examination of the state of the pastoral system. In this, identification of strengths and areas of potential development is as important as assessment of problems. Hamblin (1974a) pointed out that change could be seen as the equivalent of surgery which cuts out diseased parts rather than building on strengths. Tyler (1965) produced the useful idea of minimal change as the basis for counselling, going on to argue (Tyler (1969)) for counselling to be a process of building on strengths, developing more of the 'good that is'. This is as true of systems as it is of individuals.

This chapter takes the same viewpoint, looking at:

1 Recent investigation and evaluation of pastoral systems.
2 The skills of innovation.
3 The relationship between discipline and the pastoral system.

What are the trends?

Best *et al* (1980) suggested that pastoral care was an amorphous activity of doubtful legitimacy. Teachers saw it as irrelevant, or as a distraction from their main task of instruction. In a later study Best *et al* (1983) showed that revisions of the pastoral system were for teachers' convenience rather than the better care of pupils. Doherty (1981) found that form tutors could see their role as unimportant, lacking in professional content and activity. Negative attitudes, confusions and contradictions must be faced, but they cannot be given an undeserved power to stifle change. The teachers' cry, 'I did not come into teaching to do this', does not give them the right to impose an out-of-date conception of teaching on a changing profession.

Recent evidence from fifty-five schools where senior teachers undertook evaluations will help those beginning training within the school. Appreciation of the integrity and care with which they approached the task must be expressed. Their contribution to understanding the causes of ineffective pastoral care is outstanding.

Job specifications and performance of head of year and house
Job descriptions in the schools stressed welfare, administration and discipline. There was welcome evidence of the responsibility for leading a team of tutors. Separation of the pastoral and curricular was equally obvious. The evaluators were asked to rank the elements in order of importance. Welfare and leading a team of teachers were strongly endorsed, but the most striking feature was the neglect of the links between pastoral care and the curriculum as an important source of concern for the middle management of pastoral care.

Most revealing was the ranking of job elements present in the day-to-day work of head of year/house, i.e. although the job specification might stress leading a team of tutors, more time is actually consumed by disciplinary activities. The results endorse the need for vigorous discussion and education within the school. Curricular links are largely ignored in daily work, and little time is given to leading the team of tutors. The heavy endorsement of discipline as a consumer of time suggests that, even in these schools, the pastoral system may still be a punitive one, despite the emphasis on welfare. Training must involve educating the teachers about the nature of pastoral care and improving the head's (of house or year) ability to argue for the professional nature of their role.

First- and fifth-year pupils' perceptions of their needs
Consumer research is an essential part of pastoral care. We may impose our definition of pupils' needs on them unquestioningly, creating resistance and the perception of pastoral care as irrelevant.

The evidence showed that first-year pupils were basically concerned with day-to-day problems, the quality of daily experience, and their schoolwork. In the field of learning their over-riding need was to explain their difficulties to subject teachers. Lack of confidence related to learning appeared to be a prime area for attention. They asked for help with study and understanding the methods of teaching. Other aspects related to learning difficulties were:

1 Homework was seen as a problem, especially uneven allocation on certain nights. There was evidence that they wanted help with this form of study. Some were unsure of ways of tackling it, whilst others felt it came before they had settled down and so was a source of stress.

2 Help was needed with examination preparation.

3 'Catching up' after illness was a source of anxiety for the first year.

4 Resentment was expressed about comparison with others. Associated with this were feelings about being held back by slower pupils or about lack of accommodation to those slower pupils.

5 Marking presented a problem for many of them. Difficulty in understanding comments could be explored. Coping with the experience of work *not* being marked was mentioned – pupils obviously had strong feelings about it.

Discipline was a source of worry in unexpected ways. We can concentrate on our expectations of pupils to the exclusion of their expectations of us.

1 First-year pupils were worried about coping in the classrooms of teachers who had inadequate control.

2 They were upset by teachers:
   a leaving the class for a long time,
   b refusing to listen,
   c not turning up on time for lessons.

3 There was some confusion about the roles of teachers, especially those in authority, e.g. deputy heads and heads of year/house.

4 Help was requested to 'avoid getting into trouble'. Differences in norms and structure of the secondary school led to reprimands for doing what was part of primary school routine, e.g. 'putting one's hand up'.

5 Unjust punishments – detention of the class for an individual's offence – created warranted resentment.

6 Staff's failure to deal with unruly pupils worried them, as did the teachers who ignored breaches of school rules.

Other sources of threat were friendship difficulties, bullying, coping with peers from different social backgrounds and lack of dinner-time supervision. Unrecognised, and probably unintended, assaults on dignity and privacy alarmed them, e.g. locked and dirty lavatories and lack of privacy in showers. Fear of going into lavatories was not common, but was cited. Physical discomfort obviously influences concentration, and the conditions mentioned could contribute to a negative picture of schools and teachers. Emphasis on emotional first aid and welfare activities may obscure the fact that the real problem can be coping with boring lessons and incompetent teachers. More surprising was a desire for careers help in the comments of some first years.

As a preliminary to staff development in the pastoral area it will be helpful to assess the needs of pupils and then debate the significance of the findings.

Fifth-year pupils show a strong tendency towards 'switched-off' attitudes and a critical and analytical view of teachers. Three trends are important:

1 School is seen as a process with an end product – a job.

2 This orientation to the future is coloured by awareness of unemployment and consequent anxiety.

3 They feel that personal help is intrusive.

Careers education was stressed as the proper aim of guidance. Pupils recognised the need for help with decision-making, interview skills and preparation for possible unemployment. The importance of life skills seemed to be accepted. Decision-making, coping with unemployment and DIY skills were endorsed as useful forms of guidance. Study skills seemed to be a legitimate form of guidance for many pupils. Examination techniques, revision strategies and coping with the tension between homework and revision were important. Endorsement of the need for more adequate and rapid marking of work again highlights what pupils see as important. Lack of co-ordination of demands was a source of stress. Pupils felt that the simultaneous pressure to complete projects in a number of different subjects should be prevented. There were some critical and derogatory comments about the quality of guidance with third-year subject choices.

Relationships with teachers were at the forefront of fifth-year pupils' needs. Tensions existed between rejection of school as irrelevant, accompanied by open criticism of teachers, and a desire for a more personal and adult type of interaction with teachers. Links were seen between 'the right teacher' and pupils' success. Pupils wanted responsibility – discipline seemed to colour reactions to the head of year or house. They were impatient with trivia, wanted to be treated as equals and with respect, were concerned about how teacher–pupil difficulties could be resolved. Pupils felt that teachers sometimes did not meet their expectations. For instance:

1 Teachers left their classes for a long time.

2 Teachers needed to appraise pupils' work more carefully.

3 Teachers behaved like 'repressive petty gossips'.

Opposition to uniform was sometimes mentioned, but more important was the demand for recognition of status through privileges, especially in the 11–16 schools.

The form tutor was considered of minor importance in problem-solving. Relatively few fifth years acknowledged the tutor as a significant figure, but there were exceptions where he was of great importance. Friends and their problems weighed fairly heavily with the fifth-year pupils, and they in turn relied on their friends. This interdependence raised questions about the adequacy of the advice they give one another.

The role of the form tutor as seen by fourth-year pupils
The evaluations in the fifty-five schools were based on the Mann-heimian principle that truth varies with position in a social struc-ture. Note that this is not a statement about the nature of truth, but about the individual's selectivity and interpretation. Fourth-year pupils would be influenced by their stereotypes, especially in their attitudes towards authority. Perceptions of the role of the teacher obviously influence assessment of tutors. Hence, caution is necess-ary in interpreting comments.

The following comments seem just. Wide variations were found. The strongest tendency was for the tutor's role to be seen in terms of checking and general administration. Some schools had achieved significantly more positive perspectives. Tutors were then seen as instrumental in creating a constructive climate in which personal relationships flourish. Within the general trend of a school there are indications that the personality of the tutor is crucial, pupils reacting to their differing interpretations of the role.

Tutors are mentioned as disciplinary agents in two ways.

1 Pupils have the feeling that tutors are informed about the misdeeds of the form and then checks. Certain schools stressed the 'praise and blame' functions of the tutors strongly.

2 'Letters home' and tutor contact with parents are seen by some pupils as negative.

Most striking is that tutors are seen as lacking in power and as functioning as agents of heads of house/year or others. Schools divide into those which have no clear duties for the tutor which pupils can see as constructive and significant, and those which have tutorial work and have created greater awareness in the pupils of the tutor's role. Vagueness in role specification could lead to pupils seeing the tutor as over-inquisitive, even prying, because no other more constructive role elements exist. There was evidence that pupils distinguished realistically between the ideal tutor role and the role as performed. There were cynical reactions and questions, e.g. 'Why does the tutor help?' which suggest that pupils are aware of more subtle forms of persuasion and control. Pupils expect the tutor to understand the tastes and viewpoints of pupils, to respect individuals, but also to be loyal to the form and act as a spokesman for them. This representative function of the tutor may have escaped attention as a means of making pastoral care more potent, although conflicts are inherent in it.

The implication of this section is that nothing is inevitable: some schools have established sound relationships and tutor work; whilst others have achieved little. Education of pupils about the tutor role and the purpose of tutorial work is as essential as it is for parents and teachers.

The role of head of house or year as perceived by
fourth-year pupils
There is no doubt that the disciplinary function takes precedence. The punitive role can prevent pupils taking problems to the year head or house head because pupils believe they see only those who are 'in trouble'. Frequent mentions of 'shouting' and 'uniform' alert one to the discrepancy between claims and reality. In another set of evaluations undertaken in a large county, there was evidence that those taking a 'trouble-shooter' role tended to locate themselves in the fourth and fifth years, and remain there. This phenomenon may be influencing the perceptions of pupils, although there is no evidence of it in the fifty-five reports.

The relative importance of head of year/house and tutors

There are two tendencies. The first, which is more frequent, is based largely on negative evaluation of the tutor. He is seen to be of low status, significance and power. The tutor may be seen as sympathetic and understanding, but is not valued because he has no power to effect change. Passivity accompanies the lack of power, and the tutor's tasks are accorded low status by both staff and pupils. The second trend sees the tutor as the primary source of guidance and help.

Pupils see the head of year/house as the representative of ultimate authority. Parents reinforce this view.

Tensions existed between head of house/year and tutors. Pupils noted them – perhaps exploited them. But, in any case, there were hints that the presence of negatively orientated 'policing' heads of year/house undermined the effectiveness of the tutor.

Negative perceptions and a limited concept of both roles appear fairly frequently. One could *speculate* that absence of team work and co-ordination underlie the reports of the fourth year. Perhaps the situation is well expressed by one comment: 'Form tutors would be surprised that pupils had views of what they should do.'

Tutors' perceptions of their role

Caution was necessary because different groups with distinct attitudes exist within a school. Complications derive from the social desirability inherent in the idea of 'caring', the impact of the current climate of stress and contraction of promotion, and ambivalence about the tutor role. Difficulty existed in distinguishing between statements of the ideal and the reality of performance in a few schools.

Generally, the strongest stress was on the administrative aspects of the role. Groups who see themselves as register markers exist in most schools. There were, however, clear indications that some schools were producing and supporting creative and committed tutors. Resistances rested on the following factors.

1 Lack of time and essential skills.
2 The sense of being over-stretched – too many demands were being made. Tutor activities could be shed most easily.
3 Perceptions of the role as *not* embodying real professional responsibilities, therefore not being worth while.
4 A feeling that initiative is *not* encouraged.

Those contemplating the introduction of in-school training could ask if some version of the following occurs in the school. Some tutors indicated that they feel blamed and are being taken to task unhelpfully when things go wrong in their tutor group. This leads them to:

1 Be reluctant to admit difficulties.

2 Perceive the head of year/house in terms of trouble or extra work.

3 Evade or reject suggested tutor group activities.

Despite the emphasis in the above paragraphs, there was evidence that many tutors held wider perceptions of their role than did pupils. The question, therefore, is how we can educate more pupils about the potentialities of the role (for some have very creative ideas about the tutor's function).

If stress exists for the tutor, it is imperative that the senior management work out a hierarchy of importance for tasks, allowing a rational approach to be adopted when pressures prevent full role performance. The situation often is one of compliance rather than active involvement – sometimes unwilling compliance based on pressure. Much stress stems from limited job specifications and the failure to undertake a skills analysis at both middle management and form tutor levels. It is insufficient to say *what* has to be done, we must specify *how* it is to be done.

The evaluations indicated ways in which the passivity of tutors could be modified.

1 The need for evaluation *during* the introduction of materials and implementation of programmes of tutor work. *Provision of early feed-back is therefore stressed as a prime consideration in development of effective pastoral work.* Bloom (1976) argues that early feed-back is one of the essentials of mastery learning – this is as true for the teacher developing skills as it is for the pupil.

2 The constructive impact of tutors feeling that 'they hold the reins in respect of their own group'. This demands a climate of trust and communication.

3 The presence of high, although reasonable expectations, of tutors. Middle management must bear in mind the existence of periods of pressure in the school year and phase tasks sensibly. Demands for administrative duties could be unreasonable in view of pressures emanating from such factors as 'falling rolls'.

4 Heads of year or house will benefit from relating innovation in tutor work to other areas of curriculum development. Greater legitimacy accorded to curricular activity is no guarantee that fears of change or irrational resistances will be absent. Trainers can *learn* much from observation of the tensions of change in subject areas.

The trainers must also explore the possibility that middle management may contribute to, if not create, difficulties. Some are confused or uncertain about their roles, yet tutors simultaneously regard them as experts. Distrust can be created by failure to overcome tutors' suspicions that the much vaunted communication is solely one-way, i.e. from tutor to head of year or house. Heads of schools have often attempted to delegate work to their deputies without real responsibility. Similarly, heads of year or house may have inadequately considered the issue of delegation. What is being delegated? Administrative minor duties or more professional tasks, such as supervision and implementation of a support programme for a pupil in difficulties? The key question must be: 'Is there a real sense of team interaction and sharing?' It is a curious situation where limited and imprecise definitions of the role of head of year/house are accompanied by demands for accommodation by tutors. To what do they accommodate? Many heads of pastoral work fail to see that they have as limited perceptions of their responsibilities and skills as the tutors of whom they complain. The fact that the administrative and disciplinary functions of pastoral work are easier to define and control may underlie current under-functioning because it invites evasion of responsibility.

The sixth form and pastoral care
It is illuminating to end this section by considering the views of the 16–19 age group. Doherty (1977) and Evans (1982) point out that pupils have limited perceptions of pastoral care. The former found that pupils see personal guidance as a threat to their autonomy. The issue of trust versus mistrust is a central pre-occupation for the sixth form as Hamblin (1983) demonstrates. It is therefore useful to see what was found in the fifty-five schools.

It was clear that this age group was given little personal guidance, nor did they want it. There were reservations about the helpfulness of personal guidance previously received. Much more guidance was requested on employment and educational matters. It appeared that the sixth-form student held unrealistic expectations of teachers' knowledge of the world of work and careers. Wankowski (1973) found that those in difficulty at university were in a state of drift – they had no clear career direction in mind. It seemed that many of the students in the sixth form needed help with life styles and planning.

More help was requested with choice of A-level subjects and explanation of the likely outcomes of different decisions. Mistrust of information was displayed, e.g. in the request that they be given the truth about their chances of success in certain subjects. Increased questioning of the relevance of subjects was also reported.

Trainers should examine the reasons for the negative conceptions of personal guidance. As the outcome of five years of pastoral work, it is reasonable to ask what contributed to it. As one school put it, the outcome of pastoral work is its dismissal and the weary resignation that 'nothing can be improved through pastoral work'.

The implications

1 The trainers need to assess points of agreement, disagreement and tension in the views of pastoral care held by heads of year/ house, form tutors, heads of academic department and pupils. The findings should be debated carefully.

2 A systematic search for self-defeating tendencies should be undertaken, e.g. negative tutor activity – nagging about uniform or breaches of school rules and passing on administrative instructions.

3 ATTEMPTS AT TRAINING WITHOUT CONSIDERATION OF THE FACTORS MENTIONED ARE LIKELY TO BE INEFFECTIVE. THEY MAY ACTUALLY HARDEN RESISTANCE.

Developing a strategy for innovation

Training is a form of innovation and cannot be undertaken blindly. After the initial evaluation, the next step is to formulate a training strategy.

Three types of objectives have to be examined. The *long run objectives* give a sense of direction and show how the pastoral system is contributing to the output of the secondary school. Part of this long-run output is the self-picture of the pupil, especially as a learner, and his sense either of being able to make an impact on a malleable world or of being a pawn. In a world of growing long-term structural unemployment, does a pupil take into the challenge of life a picture of himself as reliable, worth-while and competent or

10

does he carry with him a sense of inferiority, failure to meet expectations and inadequacy? Put simply, a pupil cannot have his reputation hammered daily into his head without something happening to his personality for good or bad. Training creates awareness of the processes of allocation of reputations, pre-categorisation of pupils' attitudes and likely response to discipline which reinforce, perhaps exacerbate, or even create problems.

Pastoral work in the long run is concerned with raising the level of performance of all pupils, eliminating self-defeating behaviours and tackling negative approaches to learning. Pastoral work does not remove anxiety – it teaches pupils to cope with it constructively, dealing with frustration and loss of face in mature ways. The importance of these issues to mixed-ability teaching is sometimes ignored by those responsible for guidance.

Social skills are closely related to learning competence. Pupils, whose energies are diverted into tensions with peers, and who erect defensive barriers between themselves and teachers because they cannot relate to authority figures, are unlikely to be using their ability fully.

Finally, tutor work is *part* of the school's planned endeavour to produce the morally educated person who has the skills of taking the standpoint of others, responding sensitively to differences, whilst maintaining self-respect, and who will have a sense of social responsibility, based on inner control and self-awareness rather than automatic adjustment to the expectations of others. What may be less obvious is that increased teacher job satisfaction in an age of contraction and teacher stress is part of the output of the pastoral system. Let there be no mistake – I am not advocating the situation cogently described by Best *et al* (1983) where procedural changes in pastoral care reflected administrative convenience rather than care for pupils. Tutor work should anticipate difficulties, providing pupils with coping skills and consequently reducing stress on teachers. My argument is that implementation of a tutorial programme dealing with the factors outlined is evidence of the teacher's professional status as one who has mastery of the processes of learning in social and emotional fields as well as in subject areas, building a sense of pride in teaching as a worthwhile career. Many teachers will need re-education because initial courses of training underplayed these elements or made them appear irrelevant to the task of instruction. We should beware of assuming either that if something helps the teacher it is necessarily not in the interests of the pupil, or that what serves the pupil does not serve the teacher.

Intermediate objectives indicate the steps that contribute to achieving long-run objectives. They state:

1 What the content of the tutor programme will be. What will be learned and the basis for selection of topics.

2 How what is done in each year relates to what has been done in the previous year and, where relevant, how it prepares for what is to come next year.

The principles are simple, yet vital. There must be a sense of progression, not only inherent in the material *but visible to the pupil.* This avoids the 'But we've done it before' complaint frequently met in schools where intermediate objectives are poorly articulated. Topics and materials must be significant to the pupils, stimulate intellectual activity and orientate them towards maturity and taking an adult standpoint. The latter is crucial for successful tutor work which overcomes resistances based on the 'mother hen' image or 'inferior welfare system' approach to pastoral care which is unacceptable to many teachers and pupils.

Intermediate objectives bring the pastoral team together. Rarely have heads of year or house examined intermediate objectives *as a team,* stressing continuity and development in tutorial activity. Structures as described in official documents can conceal fragmentation and compartmentalisation, which reduces efficiency because the relationship of the work undertaken in a particular year to the total scheme is not clearly understood. Intermediate objectives must be defined, refined and subjected to continuous scrutiny by heads of year/house and senior management. Feed-back from tutors and pupils will form the basis for their evaluation.

Immediate objectives answer the questions about methods. Intermediate objectives state what has to be done, immediate objectives are concerned with *how* it will be done. Teachers are better known by what they do in the classroom than by their subscription to long-term aims in education. Considerations of:

1 the relation between the methods required for productive tutor activity and those used by the teacher in his subject;

2 what works in teaching, and the nature of the relationship between teachers and pupils;

3 unquestioned assumptions held by the tutors of the nature and purpose of pastoral care;

will have to be included in training activity.

Sharpening of the first two types of objectives, coupled with identification of background factors which will make immediate objectives difficult to implement, is an essential step. Those responsible for training then set out to anticipate likely sources of failure. The history of previous attempts at innovation within the school provides clues, even if the activities were not concerned with the pastoral system. Clumsy attempts at innovation give rise to a defensive mythology which allows the unwilling to reject change – even the possibility of it – with a good conscience. The defensive attitudes are easily activated if we are not circumspect, avoiding unnecessary threat.

Gross *et al* (1971) state that the common explanation of failure in innovation is the inability of the change agents to overcome the initial resistance of teachers to change. Such explanations have a persuasive quality, probably based on common sense, but they can be over-simplifications because they ignore the following possibilities.

1 Teachers who were favourable to the innovation met impediments and frustration stemming from organisation and environment as they began to implement it. The senior management may not even recognise their existence, or if they do, fail to deal with them.

2 Negative attitudes may develop in those who were initially favourable, but these changes are either concealed or, if obvious, the reasons for them are not understood. (The reasons might include unanticipated resistances from pupils, recognition of ethical implications or problems involved in applying suggested activities, e.g. some activities concerned with judging others operate to reinforce stereotypes or prejudice.)

Blind imposition will draw the reaction that coercion deserves, but there could be undetected failures in communication:

1 Methods and ideas are interpreted differently from the way one intended. Some teachers have a gift for taking new ideas and ensuring they do not work, but this is often due to misunderstanding produced by lack of clarity in the objectives set.

2 Explanation may be offered, but it can be insufficiently related to the fears or anxieties stimulated by earlier attempts at innovation. Trainers have to bring the attitudes and predictions which were then created into their presentation of new ideas, inoculating colleagues against them. Such facts have to be brought into the open constructively, 'Perhaps you feel that . . .' Realism and trainer competence go hand in hand.

Implications

1 A gradual process of education is involved.
2 Piecemeal objectives (Davies, 1976) could be used. Limited objectives are presented, then a means/end dialogue begins. Short units are developed which allow for feed-back and evaluation at frequent intervals.
3 Note that this is not a haphazard process, but one involving negotiation, adaptation and organic growth, while protecting the trainers and preventing loss of credibility.

Trainers may be too anxious to get into practical training activities, ignoring the importance of paying attention to their own attitudes as well as those of others. Self-awareness is as important as techniques for the trainer. Examination of one's own leadership skills and management style is productive. A trainer could have knowledge and techniques, but fail to recognise an abrasiveness which alienated others. The reactors are then described as rigid or uncooperative! Some trainers are so relationship-orientated that they lose their sense of direction in their desire to accommodate to others.

We must avoid being hypnotised by an alleged need for consensus before we begin to innovate. He who waits for consensus in the secondary school will still be waiting at doomsday. Useful questions for discovering where innovations are needed could be:

1 Where do colleagues see a problem that needs tackling, to the benefit of pupils as well as teachers?

2 Are there particular problems in the school which have generated reactions which will affect attempts at development?

3 Who are relevant opinion leaders – not only the staffroom 'resident cynic', but those who will support the trainer's efforts?

4 Do groups exist within the school, perhaps originating from the original re-organisation or recent amalgamation, who will resent, automatically, new demands or changes? Will they need to be approached carefully?

5 Organisations contain latent factors which are not easily perceived, and which, although individuals seem unaware of them, limit what is possible and shape behaviours. It may be useful to ask:

i What is the ideal pupil model which underlies teachers' judgements? Are there different models for the sexes? (Girls still seem to be judged more by their demeanour than by their objective behaviour or by the nature of their misdemeanour.)

ii What strategies are used by the school to adjust to its intake? (Some schools, where the proportion of disadvantaged pupils is high, attempt to compensate by stressing effort rather than achievement.) Will these alleged adaptations influence trainers' attempts at developing achievement-orientated tutor work?

iii Are there powerful beliefs about the nature of ability, and what certain groups of pupils can or should learn? Will tutor work present a challenge to these views? How will colleagues tend to respond?

6 What image of teachers and the school is being created in the first two or three years which will influence the reactions of pupils in later years? By the fifth year pupils have sometimes learned negative things about the school and pastoral care.

7 What are the tendencies inherent in pupil/teacher interaction, control and disciplinary processes? Do they reinforce responsibility and self-control or reliance upon external checks and surveillance. The pastoral system can operate to reinforce passivity, dependence and denial of responsibility – a strange state of affairs!

8 What predictions about the success of pupils are incorporated into educational organisation and teaching methods? Is the importance of achievement in the social and developmental task fields given sufficient prominence?

9 At which points do pupils tend to dissociate from the aims and values of the school? What happens in the second year? How great is satisfaction with third-year subject choices in the fourth year?

10 Do certain individuals and classes acquire negative reputations? What measures are used to change the attitudes of classes who indulge in ritual performance, passive resistance, as well as active aggression, forcing even caring teachers to take up negative positions? How can the general underfunctioning in such classes be corrected? How effective are current measures?

11 If a pastoral curriculum is to be implemented, not only must there be purpose and real demands, but overlap with other

subjects, e.g. social education, must be avoided. Different aspects of a topic introduced elsewhere are legitimate, but care must be taken to avoid the situation illustrated by fifth-year pupils who complained, 'We're sick of sex, sir. We're having it in religious education, social education, biology – now we've got it in tutor time!'

Failure to discuss these issues will lead to training which will have little impact or be abortive. Within-school training is a form of staff development and system change. Mythologies of the kind which suggest that pastoral care has no intellect or is largely about punishment, vague encouragement and emotional first aid are validated by inappropriate training. Links with creative education and positive mental health are suppressed, and the contribution of pastoral work to autonomy in pupils and to job satisfaction of teachers never becomes reality. This preliminary work allows identification of those who are likely to co-operate, and of strengths of colleagues which can be employed.

Key points

1 Teacher confidence has to be boosted. Graduation of demands coupled with the strategy of 'one step at a time' is essential. Training is a process subject to modification and extension, therefore flexibility is essential. (This is not advocacy of drift.)
2 Anticipate doubts and anxieties – verbalise and explore criticisms rather than stifle them. Without communication there can be little trust. Without bringing issues into the open, there will be little co-operation.

Ask

1 How can the credibility of the trainers be established quickly?
2 How will colleagues relate the methods and ideas to their concern with control and order?
3 How will the methods relate to their beliefs about teaching? The grip of tradition is strong, teachers are the prisoners of their own professional socialisation and need to survive in conditions of pressure.
4 What demands can be made? Teachers are hard pressed – hence a common objection is, 'This is a ninth period.' (Obviously objections take appropriate forms, but we must not be intimidated by them or appear unrealistic.)

16

Discipline

Discussion has stressed that teachers' perceptions and judgements can act as cages which inhibit constructive innovation and impose uniformity unrealistically on widely differing situations. Nowhere is this more relevant than in the complex question of discipline and its place in pastoral care. Surprisingly little discussion at a professional level occurs about this central pre-occupation.

To function, and not merely survive, schools must look at discipline in depth. Ritual patterns of behaviour which perpetuate difficulties have to be discarded. Yet people are trapped and see no escape. A head of year, fundamentally caring, can say, 'I know it's no good hammering them, but I have to, or the other teachers will think I've gone soft!' Odd forces are at work. Teachers fear being seen as weak, but pupils resent those who cannot keep order. Pupils hate being talked down to or patronised, especially the older girl from a disadvantaged background. Yet, as Woods (1975) showed, many teachers adopt the strategy of 'showing them up'. Pupils then insulate themselves against the influence of the teachers, who lose credibility by their disciplinary approach. Discussions of discipline within the pastoral team must be realistic. On the one hand, we cannot assume that the child and his personality are the sole constituents of the problem: on the other, we must see that pupils provoke teachers into destructive confrontations or seduce them into self-defeating 'nagging', which they then use as a justification for ignoring the teacher's injunctions. Good discipline is based on respect, but this does not mean a blind belief in fostering self-esteem – some pupils are arrogant, falsely confident and have an ineffable sense of 'rightness' and omnipotence.

Salient issues for debate
Discipline is more than punishment. Positive emphasis on self-respect, striving for an ideal, and the control of impulsive behaviour are at least as important. Docking (1980) in a helpful survey defines discipline as the type of order fostered in a certain way for specific purposes. This draws attention to the match between disciplinary methods and the educational aims of the school. Discipline may habitually and strongly stress positional control, i.e. 'Do it because I'm your teacher', but the incongruence with the claim that the school attempts to inculcate responsibility is never debated. In a few schools, discipline is both custodial and determinedly anti-intellectual. Unjustified assumptions of determinism related to beliefs about early experience, familial influences on behaviour and the nature of personality operate, contributing to the cry, 'We've tried being hard. We've tried being soft. What now?' The relationship between personality, cultural factors and the mode of expression of authority has to be explored in a lively way. Many pastoral heads stress the need for consensus among staff, but fail to see that the presence of consensus is no guarantee of educational soundness.

Pastoral care is about the responsibility of the pupil, the creation of a constructive climate for learning and the nature of classroom interaction. The topics related to discipline include the following.

1 *The beliefs of teachers* about the nature of order, including fears of contagion and predictions about the development of nega-

tive behaviours into unmodifiable patterns of conduct. The stance of, 'They know where they can get away with it, and it's not with me,' probably creates as many difficulties as it solves. If it is accompanied by a primitive contagion theory, e.g. 'and they must not get away with it, or the rot will spread', then it is unlikely that the teacher will be reinforcing moral growth and self-responsibility. They are more likely to strengthen pupils' tendencies to classify teachers into 'strong' or 'weak', implicitly encouraging them to exploit the more civilised teacher who expresses concern and is caring.

Let there be no mistake: what I have said does not deny the importance of effective classroom management. Nor does it disregard the need to adapt to the fact that, as Sumner and Warburton (1972) point out, some pupils believe that, 'The teachers ought to make us work, and if they don't, they are soft!'

2 *The creation of identities* is involved in discipline. Behind classroom interaction is the creation and assignment of identities, some of which are negative, which increases and sometimes creates problems.

3 *Classroom climates* will have to be studied as the emotional and value-laden elements which facilitate or inhibit performance and identification with the school. The hidden curriculum is concerned with the unintended aspects and outcomes of classroom interaction. Judging from the evaluations given early in the chapter it is likely that it will involve coping with boredom, maintaining status with peers, surviving in an insecure situation where the teacher is inadequate or dealing with assaults on dignity.

Good discipline, which builds up the desire to achieve and respect for self and others, depends on providing pupils with the skills of dealing constructively with:
  – loss of face;
  – frustration in learning and social relationships;
  – negative predictions and comparisons;
  – peer pressures and emotional blackmail.

A framework for investigation

Step 1
  1 What should or could certain pupils learn? Are low expectations being communicated to the pupils?
  2 What beliefs are held about the nature of rule-breakers and the

19

motives for rule-breaking? Phrases such as 'those young delinquents' may be more meaningful than appear at first sight. If some pupils who break rules are seen as the equivalent of adult criminals in the larger society, they may become the focus for negative expectations which they proceed to fulfil. Perceptions and labels of this type can function to justify under-teaching or to prevent a search for more effective curricular content and teaching methods.

Step 2

1 Examination of the conditions which enhance or erode self-respect. Lickona (Ed.) (1976) and Ward (1982) indicate that conscience and moral development are tied to self-respect. (The relationship is inter-dependent rather than unilateral.) This will mean looking for practices which humiliate pupils and create chronic resentment, and striving to eliminate them, e.g. talking about pupils as if they were not present; imposing unnecessary permission-seeking rules; or keeping pupils waiting unnecessarily for attention.

2 The sanctions operated by teachers are crucial. Teacher stress or insecurity may be accompanied by increased use of sarcasm or humiliation, which create a climate of threat for pupils.

3 The social climate of classrooms can either be one where pupils feel encouraged to learn and extend ideas, or one where they fear loss of face if they do not produce the right answer. The latter restricts learning and constructive exploratory behaviour. By asking teachers what is habitually rewarded or what they pay attention to, change can be initiated.

4 Pressures towards deviance exist, as Hargreaves *et al* (1975) demonstrate. They claim that, among other things, the teacher who provokes deviance:
   – puts the responsibility for change *solely* on the pupil, ignoring the possibility that change of methods and interaction will yield benefits;
   – predicts change will not occur, or if it does, it will be only temporary;
   – automatically attributes negative intent to pupils;
   – blames the family background.

This approach gets to the causes, rather than tackling surface manifestations only. It is essentially positive, giving heads of year or house the real responsibility of stimulating analysis at a professional level.

Step 3

This involves a questioning of beliefs and assumptions about the functions of discipline. Should it modify behaviour, be a form of retribution involving a tariff approach, or help the pupil acquire positive attitudes to school? Discipline formerly rested on pupils' perceptions and acceptance of the relevance of what school offered, and of school as necessary for the achievement of a career. The rewards stemming from being a good pupil had incentive value. Today, the school has to some extent lost this function, making the rationale for discipline less compelling. Not only has the teacher lost status, but the authority of the teacher has lost its legitimacy.

The discussions of discipline can be based profitably on the understanding that it is not so much *which* punishment will be effective, but *under what conditions* it will be effective, and *how* it has particular effects. Group affiliations of pupils, their concept of toughness and maturity, and their views of the motives of the teachers will be taken into account.

A constructive approach is crucial. Discipline is not merely the control of impulsive behaviour, it is stimulation of the ability and resolve to focus energy and personal resources on the active pursuit of a goal. It involves the capacity to act on a standard of excellence without reliance on external surveillance. Discipline, unlike punishment, does not inhibit but seeks actively to extend standards. It is not easy, but there is welcome evidence from Rutter *et al* (1979) that concerted effort results in a productive climate. We may deal with superficials, failing to see that educational methods attack self-respect. Overt streaming has declined, yet the factors touched on above cause some pupils to be groomed as assiduously for failure as others are for success. The responses from the fifty-five schools highlight the need to ask:

1 Are pupils offered clear ideals?

2 Have we recognised the need to provide pupils with clear, short-term targets which give frequent boosts to the individual's sense of success?

3 Do we present pupils with models of enthusiasm and competence?

Good discipline implies adaptation. This is not permissiveness or weakness. Instead of the automatic penalty or 'tariff', we ask what will be productive for the individual. Automatic punishment can hurt the innocent: in cases where bullying has developed into a campaign against the individual, punishment of the aggressor increases the repercussions on the victim because other pupils become hostile, and the victim's sense of isolation and helplessness is increased.

Good discipline is founded in choice and responsibility. It does not humiliate or reject the pupil as a person or convey the message that he is incapable of change. We must express the belief that he can act responsibly and is capable of change. His involvement is crucial in eliminating undesired behaviours and acquiring new ones. The role of verbalisation is often underestimated. Pupils have to be helped to evaluate their actions, relating them to a positive picture of self. We help them examine our reasons for judging the act to be wrong, comparing them with their own, assessing the effect of the act on others, anticipating future occasions so that they do not behave similarly. Briefly, we encourage them to:

1 take the standpoints of others;
2 examine what triggers off the behaviour;
3 look critically at the way they justify their actions;
4 work out carefully a different way of behaving.

Our aim is to help the pupil understand a chain of events, and assess his own contribution to it. Ways of making restitution and repairing damaged relationships should be sought. This does not mean coercing individuals into false apologies or unwilling action. No moral development is inherent in this type of unreal recompense which fosters hypocrisy. Undoubtedly this approach is more time consuming in the short run, but in the long run it is economical, especially if it is applied by the year head to those with whom he works directly. Simpler methods of reassurance, warning, praise and punishment can be applied by the form tutor. We may feel we have insufficient time, when the relevent question is, 'Are we using the time we have efficiently?'

Punishment
Punishment is widely used, but why is it so ineffective? The pastoral team should begin a discussion based on straightforward questions.

1 Is punishment justified as a practice within schools?
2 Is it justified as part of pastoral care?
3 Is punishment a deterrent which, however, has little positive educative value?
4 Does punishment produce order, or are teachers' skills of classroom management and their ability to relate to pupils more important?

These questions lead us to think about the arrangements for early detection and the way in which the first incident of aggression or illegitimate absence is dealt with. The Home Office (1976) in *Crime as Opportunity* suggested that we could pay too much attention to the personality of miscreants and undervalue the contribution of the environment. The pastoral team should look at the physical environment, assessing the opportunities given for misbehaviour, and the way it creates frustration. Discussion of disciplinary problems which omits assessment of these factors is in danger of being misleading. Parental contacts must also be assessed. Our communications with the home may puzzle, irritate, confuse or alienate many parents. Their reactions then encourage pupils to misbehave.

Reynolds & Murgatroyd (1980) suggest that the involvement of each age level in the authority structure of the school reduces difficulties. The sixth form can support the prefects in each year, creating the climate for affiliation in the school.

Finally – perhaps waywardly – I would ask why heads of year or house avoid this wider analysis. Do they need their punishment function as it currently exists because it provides evidence of status, or have they no idea of more constructive approaches?

Integrating the pastoral and the curricular falls into place when such issues are explored. Teacher decision-making is closely related to discipline. A relevant discussion can be found in Eggleston (Ed.) (1979). Awareness of the restraints on teacher decision-making stemming from organisational factors is pertinent. Most of the teacher's behaviour is not directly related to teaching, but springs from allocation of resources and anticipated evaluation by others. Teachers are forced by the dual pressures of their professional standards and the constraints of reality to develop survival techniques which insulate them from pressures. But these techniques may reinforce problems, or perhaps create them.

Behind role stress which may be associated with poor discipline lie conflicts about scarce resources – especially time, the needs of family, energy, and teaching versus pastoral functions. Passive acceptance of the expectations of others can complicate. Conflict, however, centres on which expectations are legitimate and the hierarchy of obligations – which are to be honoured first? The discussion in Eggleston (1979) raises issues which heads of year or house should explore with tutors. Decision-making in the classroom involves elements of which greater awareness would be profitable, e.g.

– recognition and definition of a problem;

– prediction of the likely course of events;

– prediction of the probable effects of treatment of or reactions to the problem;

– selection of a reaction or treatment.

Exploration of issues such as under-functioning, insolence or anxiety, using the steps above, could be beneficial. It is important, too, to examine the complications posed by decisions about acceptable noise levels or the timing of sections of the lesson.

Most helpful is the insistence on the need to explore the growth of 'policing' in some schools. Serious attention must be given to this because with the less able or the disadvantaged the moral features of classroom life take precedence over the intellectual. There is a strong moral element which causes control to pass for teaching. The survival of the teacher comes to the forefront. Rigorous control over pupil talk and movement creates confrontations. The superiority and authority of the teacher then become the focal point of an unending struggle. Heads of year or house must create awareness of these factors, modifying gradually the assumptions about the needs and intent of disadvantaged pupils who create disciplinary problems.

Final points

1 These issues must be examined by senior management and heads of year/house initially. Discussions of them will lead to more relevant training strategies which have a greater probability of success.

2 Once a grasp of them has been achieved, they can be introduced into the training of tutors influencing classroom procedures.

3 Careful phasing of introduction of issues and arrangements for returning to them are essential. The trainers should think of a period of 4 to 6 years rather than a relatively short 'once-for-all' activity. The objective is positive system development.

Summary

1 Work from schools is cited which shows that pupils have expectations of teachers which are not always met. The general tenor of the findings is that a wide range of attitudes and methods exist, especially in relation to the form tutor. In some schools, the role is seen by both pupils and teachers as being of little consequence, whilst in others it seems that the

tutor has a positive impact on the development of pupils and their school performance.

2 The need for planned examination and the development of a whole school policy on discipline is stressed. Problems of control and order preoccupy the staff, particularly pastoral heads, yet there is little evidence of systematic evaluation over a period of time and the development of a consistent policy which fosters self-control and self-respect in pupils.

3 Evaluation of processes and factors which create the value climate of the school is described. The initiation of training without such preliminary assessment is likely to be ineffective, if not counter-productive.

2: Developing the professional caring skills of head of year or house

General considerations

The professional development of the heads of year or house should be facilitated and co-ordinated primarily by the deputy head responsible for pastoral care. Other deputies should be involved to prevent the separation of the pastoral and curricular being crystallised at senior management level. The basic assumptions behind within-school training are:

1 The head of house/year can make worth-while contributions to the achievement of the school's educational objectives.

2 There are specialist skills attached to the role which are *complementary* to those of the head of an academic department.

3 Trivialisation of activities *can* be avoided. The lack of training facilities has created a situation in which, despite commitment and lavish expenditure of energy, heads of year/house engage in routine trivial tasks which would be unnecessary if the pastoral system operated efficiently.

4 The efficient system is one that balances preventative work against remedial or 'after the event' action.

Trainers will find it profitable to keep consideration of the following at the forefront.

1 Certain managerial skills are often neglected. Whilst the head of year/house has to become aware of his managerial style, the normative fallacy has to be avoided, i.e. the belief that there is one 'right way'. The blend of task orientation and relationship orientation will vary with circumstances, and with the personality of the individual. Rigidity and over-emphasis on one element creates, or reinforces, inefficiency. Therefore:

26

a Too strong a task orientation produces resistance because there is little negotiation, and insufficient attention is paid to tutors' feelings and their views are ignored.

b Too much emphasis on relationship orientation produces a state of drift, evasion of difficult issues and productive confrontation. Energy is dissipated in a fore-doomed attempt to please everyone.

The four basic management skills are set out below.

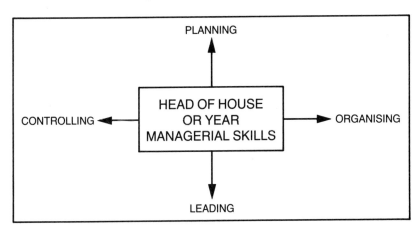

Discussion of these four skills makes a good introduction to the training sessions.

Planning

This includes the following:

a Constructing units for a pastoral programme which are relevant to the needs of the age group and perceived by both pupils and teachers as such.

b Incorporating into the programme activities, e.g. decision-making exercises, simple games and questionnaires which have clear objectives and which can be used by the tutor without a great deal of preparation.

c Testing out the materials, indicating the approximate time that will be needed for
  i the introduction
  ii the activity itself
  iii the follow-up part of the tutor period, in which the tutor shows his form the application of what they have learned.

Organising

Organising is the logical outcome of planning, yet the detailed organisation is often inadequate. Behind organisation lie:

a Anticipation of snags and unwanted outcomes from the activity.

b Precision about the phasing of tasks and availability of materials.

c Measures for dealing with crises and problems e.g. tutor absence or unexpected delays in duplicating.

Leading

This includes more than the efficient collection, construction of material and organisation. It means that one has to develop skill in:

a Taking a social-emotional leadership role, where tensions are reduced without creating unproductive confrontations.

b Involving teachers in the planning stage and in the production of materials.

Controlling

This implies the need for monitoring and evaluating what is taking place in pastoral periods – the discrepancies between objectives and outcomes and also between what we claim we do and what actually occurs. Evaluation will be discussed more fully in a later chapter.

Follow-up sessions on exploration of style of management

First – scrutinise the trends in interaction with tutors which may influence your credibility and success. This leads to a sense of control.

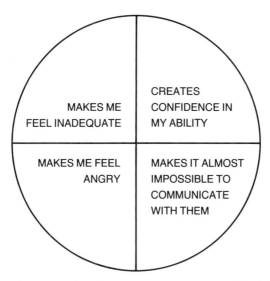

To understand your style of management you may find it helpful to fill in the sectors of the circle. Be as concrete as possible. Then try to work out the implications of what you have written for your success in the post of head of year.

Next – we need to examine the *discrepancy* between our *formal statements* and what we say we do and *ideas in action* or what we actually do. Some idea of the underlying assumptions which shape our managerial behaviours can be obtained by the following well-known exercise.

Take a recent situation which involved you in challenging inter-action with a colleague, and where pastoral care, tutorial groups or the behaviour of a pupil was the subject of the discussion. Please do not assume that challenging interaction is necessarily negative interaction. Please state your beliefs about how people *should* behave in this kind of situation.

First

Beliefs about how people should behave in this situation.

Then

State your objectives. Give details of what you hoped would occur, the difficulties you may have expected and your idea of how this could be achieved.

Now – write out as exactly as possible what you both said and did. Do this as if it were the script of a play. We are all aware that our external responses conceal different feelings and ideas within us. To look at the significance of internal events and relate them to what happens is to give us added control.

Put each statement and action on the left-hand side of the page and then go immediately to the right-hand side and state what you were thinking and feeling at *that* moment in time.

The pattern is like this:

What we both said and did	What was in my mind
1a He said, 'I want to be helpful, but I am sure you know how great my work load is.'	1b Here we go! The usual preliminary to an evasion. Why can't he be honest?
2a I replied, 'Yes, I do appreciate this but perhaps we can do something about it.'	2b Am I being weak again? Will he exploit my hesitancy to push?

Finally – after writing your script, examine it carefully. Look for:

  a Contradictions between the outer and inner behaviours and ideas – asking yourself why the difference exists. What purposes does the discrepancy serve?

  b Ways in which you could improve your control positively.

  c How you could increase co-operation and avoid confrontation, situations of stalemate and frustration, etc.

  d Anything else you have learned.

The next steps

Examination of the significance of job specifications stimulates awareness. The evaluations from the fifty-five schools suggested that, in practice, discipline and minor administrative duties took precedence over the duties more pertinent to the conception of pastoral care. Trainers will find the work of Blackburn (1983) useful as background reading which provides many practical and worth-while ideas. The following list of duties should be presented:

Duties of head of year/house

1 Diagnostic skills, positive discipline and working with difficult pupils in depth.
2 Leading and training a team of tutors – including developing the skills of guidance and counselling in the tutor.
3 Developing and providing materials for a pastoral curriculum – involving tutors in the processes.
4 Evaluating and developing constructive links with the outside agencies.
5 Group counselling activities with certain pupils, e.g. disruptive, withdrawn or socially inept and underfunctioning pupils. This group work is an extension of what is happening in tutor periods.
6 The development of expertise in areas helpful to colleagues, e.g. one-parent families, underfunctioning, sexual difficulties or aggressive behaviours.

Trainers will have to deal with the almost inevitable 'theory of the impossible task'. The rejoinder must be that training allows more effective use of time. Equally important is helping the heads of year/house realise that pastoral development is concerned with the art of the possible – that, if we are effective in what is possible this year, further steps forward can be taken next year. Training is not a once-for-all event, but a process extending into the future. The skilled trainer builds on the strengths of the middle-management team, providing a structure with achievable objectives, refusing to reinforce either negativism or blind optimism and keeping the way open for further innovation. No easy task! But the hard truth is that pastoral care is developing. We are moving away from the 'inferior welfare system' to a model which incorporates teacher job satisfaction and pupil success, recognising there can be no final form of pastoral care. As society, schools, the curriculum and teaching methods change, so must pastoral care adapt. This does not mean passive reaction, but reciprocity – the pastoral system in responding to curricular development can, by that response, initiate further change.

The role of head of year or house
The role contains two major elements: the caring element, which is after the event and therapeutic in intention; leading a team of tutors who are working on tutorial activity which is developmental and

aimed at preventing difficulties. Caring and welfare have been stressed, therefore it is astonishing to find that this is the area where, in practice, heads of year and house are weakest. Counselling skills are often conspicuous by their absence, yet, without them, caring cannot be expressed constructively.

The caring functions of head of year or house

First we must ask with whom the head of year/house will work directly. Note that 'directly' does not necessarily mean individually – work with groups should be given more prominence in the head of year's job specification, allowing him to use his experience and teaching skill to the full. Economical use of time and the fact that what is learned in the company of peers is more likely to transfer to other settings strengthen the desirability of the group approach. Note that it also gives the tutors greater professional responsibility. Certain schools in the evaluations cited earlier had achieved the position where tutors were highly significant figures in the school lives of pupils. Again, let us rid ourselves of the theory of the impossible task.

The head of year or house will deal directly with those who show signs of maladjustment. The Underwood Report (1955) suggests that the maladjusted pupil is developing in a way which has a bad effect upon himself and others. He or she does not respond to simple measures of love, reassurance and comfort. The usual disciplinary measures do not achieve a permanent improvement in behaviour, indeed, they may exacerbate the difficulties. Caring may be best expressed by group work which gives help with coping with the daily problems of living, e.g. frustration, peer pressures. Maladjustment can be usefully conceptualised as self-defeating, disordered and ineffective patterns of living. The head of year's group work is a process of re-education aimed at providing essential skills, rectifying deficits and replacing maladaptive behaviours by more productive ones.

This may sound cold, but we have to see that effective counselling has to be conducted in an atmosphere of warmth and acceptance. Focus on behaviour and skills learning does not modify this. It is more likely to create the conditions in which warmth can be expressed by the teacher in a credible way. Definitions of maladjustment seem to condense to:

1 Impairment of the ability to make relationships.
2 A condition of insecurity and unhappiness to which adolescents respond by defensive measures of fight or flight.

3 A state of disequilibrium between the individual and his environment, coupled with social incompetence and/or costly ways of coping.

4 Distortion or retardation in development marked by grossly age-inappropriate symptoms, e.g. bed-wetting, thumb-sucking or temper tantrums at ages when they have usually disappeared.

The deputy head(s) or others responsible for training should encourage discussion of the fact that maladjustment has many causes and is revealed in many ways. The search for a single cause is unhelpful and distracts one from helping. I am not advocating an anti-intellectual stance but realism. Discussion should lead to the clarification of criteria for referral for specialist help. Valuable insights into such problems will be provided by educational psychologists, if they are involved in the training. Heads of year/house should be encouraged to submit their implicit personality theories or naïve psychology of behaviour and motivation to mutual critical scrutiny. Caring activities are often shaped, unnoticed, by determinism, limited notions of causality or over-simple assumptions about the universality of reasons for stealing, sexual misdemeanour or aggression. Many influences lead us to divert blame from the school and its organisation to the individual by giving pseudo social-work, psychological or psychiatric labels to the pupil. In talking to caring teachers, I often hear echoes of medical paradigms based on 'sickness' or of a world view which encapsulates a determinism often related to early childhood, ignoring the complexity of causality, developmental processes and learning. Superficial explanations bereft of the discipline of theory and research have often contributed to the poverty of caring in the secondary school. If we subscribe to self-fulfilment theories of personality – as I do – then we must check that our arguments do not contain a circularity that makes them of doubtful validity. I may look at a pupil's observable behaviour as a measure of potentialities, but at the same time I say that potentialities determine behaviour. Therefore, I have defined what is to be explained in terms of what has to do the explaining. If I realise that the environment contributes significantly to development, rather than solely concentrating on personality, do I then slip into a view of the pupil as passively reacting to environmental forces, rather than interpreting the reactions? Meaning emanates from the individual – what is threat or reward varies from person to person. I should question the adequacy of my views of causality. Because I feel that the self-image of the pupil is taken for granted and that personality is ignored or treated in stereotypes, do I stress one side of a problem, e.g. arguing that he is having reading difficulties because of personality factors such as anxiety, leaving out the possibility that those personality factors are partially produced by failure in a socially important task?

Continuous debate on such issues is essential. Training must foster it. Caring does not mean evasion of responsibilities to society, but neither does it mean we substitute a more subtle form of conditioning for current punitive approaches. We could operate a system of tension management which mitigates against curriculum reform. Counselling which enhances the responsibility of the individual, building up autonomy and the mastery of *meaningful* tasks will be the way in which caring is best expressed by head of year or house. (The word 'meaningful' highlights the relationship with the curriculum.)

A profitable exercise is for heads of year/house to examine the following, looking at the implications and assessing preventative measures. The judgements and assessments merit close attention.

Francis: A case history

Notes
The following are statements from this boy's school records and show what happened to him from entry to the infant school until the age of fifteen. No additions or deletions have been made. The only alteration is the substitution of a fictitious Christian name for his full name and a small change in the date of birth.

Primary school reports: Francis (16.11.67)

Age 6   A quiet, friendly boy. Keen on toys and puzzles and likes to read. Finds concentration hard in number.

Age 8   A quiet boy who gets on well with other children. He has ability but seldom does as well as he could. He appears to be lazy and not really interested in any written work. He reads well and is very willing to help the slower reader.

Age 9   Unco-operative. At times sullenly resentful. Has a chip on his shoulder which advertises itself in his attitude to teachers and to any kind of authority (thus, must have root cause in home and parental contact). In trouble with school and society. Needs psychiatric treatment. Very intelligent and knowledgeable but gives no sign of wanting to use his abilities.

Age 10   Very quiet, rather devious, one feels. Francis has intelligence but as yet is not sufficiently interested in work to make much progress. He has a few friends but does not contribute much to the class scene. Needs encouragement and as much sympathy as one can give. Reads very well. Has little idea of number.

Age 11   A quiet and withdrawn boy, not an easy child to make contact with. Must be carefully watched as he could become a nuisance. Can be rude if he mixes with wrong boys. As he keeps very much to himself this could easily happen, as he has few friends who are really close. Not easy to see at once whether or not Francis can be a nuisance as he is the quiet, thinking type and often leaves his friends to carry out the 'stupid' actions.

Secondary school
Entry form filled in at school.

Family   Francis is the eldest with 1 brother and 2 sisters, Mother and Father. Father permanently at home – illness? Will be OK but very little help from Mother. Will need clothing and dinner allowance. A Social Welfare Worker main stabilising factor in home. Francis likes English and reading best but does not belong to public library. Says cooking is his hobby. Mother attended interview. (*Note that this boy, was, in fact, the youngest*).
(*For trainers only*: This is merely one example of the fact that school records often contain uncorrected errors.)

Educational Welfare Officer's report   Very bad home background. Father will 'lam out' at all the children when he is drunk. Mother was seriously ill last year, family disrupted and Francis stayed out till midnight.

35

May 1980	Father dies. Headmaster passes a note: 'Francis is extremely upset and should be treated with care'.
Age 11	Francis is very quiet in tutor group and very reliable. He must try to put more effort into his work.
Age 12	Francis is very quiet and withdrawn though usually willing to help if asked. His absence rate needs to be curtailed if he is to do well. (Absences may result in official action.)
Age 13	Absence rate is unbelievably high – rarely at school. Letter from child guidance clinic asking if he could:

a transfer to school of his first choice so that he could go home to dinner;

b or be taken to court for Fit Person Order followed by boarding school;

c or have pills to 'help him to feel more confident when he makes an attempt to attend school again.'

Transfer arranged

Summer report	Francis (and his sister who attends another school) has a long history of truancy. His attendance, punctuality and behaviour have become progressively worse. His case would certainly have been the subject of court action if it had not been for the intervention of the Children's Department on mother's behalf. She is most inadequate and has abdicated all responsibility for the children. It is unlikely that Francis will stay out of trouble for long. Undoubtedly his own lack of self control will prolong the situation.
Autumn	Francis committed an offence (theft) and appeared before Juvenile Court in summer. Put under supervision to probation for 2 years. Still not attending school. Second court appearance in December (stole a bottle of whisky). Fined £2.

Age 14   Mother says she cannot cope with him.
               Case re-opened at CGC. Recommended transfer to
               day school for maladjusted pupils.

Age 15   Again in court for burglary. Court agreed to Francis
               going to live with the man Mother intends to marry.

Counselling skills for the head of year or house
Stott (1966), in a study of troublesome children, brings to our
notice the concept of vulnerability based on congenital factors,
i.e. present before or at birth. This does not exclude environmental
factors for, once the individual's stress threshold has been over-
stepped, the form of the reaction will be determined not only by the
somatic and psychological weaknesses to which the individual is
subject but by the possibilities inherent in the environment. This
view is very useful for those attempting counselling. Those children
who come from under-privileged environments may well show
stresses related to physical factors – toughness, deviation from
sharply defined sex role behaviours or peer pressures. Problems of
learning, achievement and parental expectations may loom larger in
the difficulties of those coming from middle-class backgrounds.
The point of departure in counselling is often these habitual
reactions to stress situations – responses which themselves cause
difficulties.

Themes which appear in different contexts and with varying
content are:

1 Loss of face
2 Coping with frustration
3 Social anxieties
4 Peer pressures
5 Learning difficulties

Individual or group counselling tackling variants of these situations
will be helpful developmentally, provided the head of year/house
conducts it within a structure stimulating a sense of potency in the
pupil (see below).

A simple structure for constructive counselling

1 Preliminary   What are my objectives?
   questions   What information do I have?
                      How valid is it?

37

	What are the likely reactions of the pupil? Will he see my intervention as legitimate or punitive, or will he misinterpret the purpose of counselling? How shall I work with him? In a group or individually – what methods seem appropriate?	
2 Exploration and diagnosis	What does the situation mean to him? What strengths has he? Who can give support? What skills does he need to acquire? How will other people react to his efforts to change?	What does he predict? What is his view of the world, e.g. all a matter of luck? How do my emphases fit his picture of himself?
3 Taking action	Surveying the possibilities. Selecting one. Working out the steps that will have to be taken. Working on the first step.	

This structure is based on certain assumptions. First, the head of year/house must adapt his methods to meet the needs of the pupil. There is no one 'right' role but many roles which change with different pupils and also during the course of individual counselling. We also change as the pupil progresses – in later sessions he is able to accept, perhaps welcome, challenges. Many behaviours can be included. Advice-giving, listening, elaboration, skills-teaching, reassurance, constructive confrontation and limit-setting all play a part. The criteria for inclusion is their relevance to the needs of the particular pupil at a particular time. (For a full discussion consult Hamblin (1974).) Intellectual integrity and flexibility is essential. A healthy respect for the evidence, and the ability to build up hypotheses is required. Intuition is refined by clear thinking.

There is little point in repeating what I have written elsewhere in 1974 and 1983. Let me simply say that from the beginning we set out to reinforce the positive in the pupil and emphasise our positive expectations. Those taking a counselling stance have to see that respect for the pupil means that we have to explain what we are doing. We cannot complain if the pupil objects, becomes unco-operative or imputes negative intention to us. Failure in these elementary matters probably accounts for pupils' rejection of personal guidance, and their reservations about our helpfulness. The process of clarification of a problem involves creating a climate of safety and warmth, through open questions and the techniques of reflecting back, that is, *not* asking questions which suggest the answers we would like to have or which require merely a 'yes' or 'no' answer, but looking for feelings and then repeating the phrase used by the pupil. For example, the pupil may say, 'When I attempt to improve my work it's never any use.' We might respond, 'Never any use, Jim?' The pupil then elaborates and we learn much more, which allows us to give valid guidance. Open questions are often such more by the tone of voice and questioning look than by their literal content, e.g. 'Then you went to bits?' We have to establish the meaning of the problem. This is more economical than imposing our definition of what the problem *ought* to be, based on our inaccurate assumptions. We learn to check ourselves when we begin to say, 'What you mean is . . .' Agreement often only reflects the well-learned tendency of the pupil to acquiesce as a way of coping.

Respect is communicated by the way we greet the pupil. An initial statement which conveys liking and acceptance is essential – especially at a disciplinary interview. Docking (1980) shows that discipline, to be effective, must be administered in an atmosphere of liking, respect and consideration. Position is part of respect. Choice can be given about where the pupil sits. Excessive distance, unnecessary barriers (such as a desk) or threatening proximity have to be avoided. Heads of year/house know that for many pupils the interview is associated with trouble, and that features such as a desk with a chair in front trigger off reactions of 'us against them', yet some fail to anticipate feelings and response which negate their declared objectives. Fewer still detect reservations and bring them out into the open. Defensive attitudes or false assumptions could lead to a productive part of the counselling, e.g. 'You could be feeling I'm asking questions I've no right to ask. If you are, let's see why that is.' Explanation of our purpose enhances rather than diminishes our status in the eyes of pupils and creates greater probability of co-operation.

The following diagram forms a useful guide to trainers. Each step forms the basis for a training session.

Counselling skills for head of year/house

1 Principles

A climate of safety – eliminating unnecessary threat.

Fostering an atmosphere of trust and warmth.

Accepting pupil's feelings.

Having clear objectives which are shared with the pupil.

2 Mechanics

Personal greeting.

Providing explanation.

Adjusting physical setting.

Adapting style of working to the pupil.

Setting target, 'step-by-step'.

Positive ending.

3 Skills and techniques

Listening.

Appropriate use of eye contact.

Realistic adaption, e.g. to anxious or inarticulate pupils.

Using open questions.

Encouraging elaboration and expansion.

Giving pupil undivided attention.

Ability to accept challenges or hostility without defensive or punitive reactions

Using active methods, e.g. diagrams, drawings, role play.

Points which can be developed by trainers include:

1 The need to set targets for pupils, not only in a step-by-step way but in anticipating difficulties, e.g. 'What will your friends say?' 'How will you cope with it?' We must anticipate and inoculate pupils against stresses and counter influence. Failure to include this often means we waste our time.

2 It is the responsibility of the mature professional to adapt to the needs of the client. We are often unable to let pupils bring out negative feelings, not realising that this is a necessary step in building a more positive relationship. Equally, we must learn not to respond to challenges, such as 'You're not going to change my mind, you know.' If I try to justify myself, the

interaction is taken off course. My response of 'Sure' or 'Of course' registers reception of the comment, but does not allow it to become a diversion.

3 If change is to occur, then the pupil has to feel that success is possible. We use the principle of graduation – arranging problems or the steps to be taken in order of difficulty. This creates for the pupil the sense of being in control and gets away from the 'impossible task'.

4 We may neglect the need of the pupil to talk about ways of solving the problem. To talk over-much ourselves is to ignore the principles of learning. It is useful to take a problem similar to the pupil's and to ask how it could be tackled. I then note the positive comments and use them as a basis for dealing with the pupil's own problem. This indirect approach yields results.

Training activities

A caution

No attempt will be made to provide a package of activities alleged to provide a basic training – this would be fraudulent. Training has to be adapted to the current state of the school and negotiated with the trainees. The ideas given are illustrative and not exhaustive. They should, however, allow trainers to develop useful units for use in their school.

Training unit 1: Basic orientation

Diagnostic skills

Session 1

1 These are practical skills because they allow us to assess the situation. Begin by asking trainees to develop a list of questions which they feel it is important to answer about a pupil with whom they work directly. Partner work or work in triads is productive – larger groups tend to become the equivalent of a committee, i.e. a recipe for inaction. The aim is to produce a developmental check-list and create awareness of the dimensions of assessment.

2 Supportive stimulation is provided by the following suggestions. What do we need to know to help us deal with pupils constructively?

e.g. – What makes him frustrated?
   – How does he react to that frustration?
   – What roles does he take up in relation to other pupils, e.g. a bully, a know-all?
   – What has he learned at home which impinges directly on performance at school, e.g. prediction of failure.

3 After activity and discussion the trainer could take the ideas away and produce the check-list, which is then subjected to further refinement in the next session. Final discussion might be sharpened by the presentation of a framework for assessment such as this.

Positive developmental needs

Underlying assumptions

1 Guidance is not restricted to problems in a limited way, therefore the 'sickness' paradigm implicit in many approaches is rejected.
2 Guidance is concerned with the development of positive functioning and with helping the individual discard disordered and ineffective styles of living.
3 Guidance is preventative and educational rather than remedial.

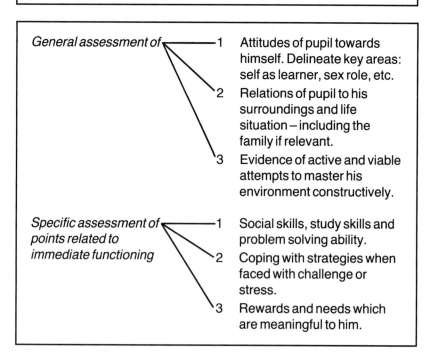

General assessment of

1 Attitudes of pupil towards himself. Delineate key areas: self as learner, sex role, etc.

2 Relations of pupil to his surroundings and life situation – including the family if relevant.

3 Evidence of active and viable attempts to master his environment constructively.

Specific assessment of points related to immediate functioning

1 Social skills, study skills and problem solving ability.

2 Coping with strategies when faced with challenge or stress.

3 Rewards and needs which are meaningful to him.

Session 2

Objectives To develop and use simple diagnostic approaches to counselling.

Training material Diagnosis replaces blind encouragement, sympathy and coercion. We must also recognise that the situations in which behaviour occurs are probably as important as personality. A simple diagnostic approach is:

In what situations does he show this behaviour?

In what situations is this behaviour absent?

Are there significant differences between them, which could account for the behaviour?

How does he show the behaviour – directly, indirectly, passively, etc?

What pay-off does he get?

What part do his peers play in maintaining the behaviour?

What seems to trigger off his behaviour?

The last question is crucial. The competent teacher with good classroom control is the one who has learned to 'get in early and positively'. The point of initiation is where behaviour can be changed economically. We will probably have to ask if the classroom situation has to be modified. The pupil may have taken up a role, e.g. clown or creep, which is linked with the behaviour of others who now expect him to behave in this way. Change in his behaviour forces change on them, e.g. the clown functions to test out the teacher; the troublemaker reads the cues and decides the likelihood of success.

We must then ask:

What behaviours must he acquire or strengthen?

What behaviours must be weakened or dropped?

Activity
Heads of year/house select a pupil whose attitudes and behaviours have given cause for concern.

1 Work out what *functions* his/her behaviour seem to have.

2 What basic picture of self he/she is trying to present?

3 What role does he/she tend to adopt with a group of peers? (Ask how this agrees or contrasts with the picture he/she present to adults, especially teachers.)

4 Speculate on the motivation that underlies the behaviour you have described. Ask how you would check your speculations and judgements.

5 Suggest ways in which the pupil could change with benefit to himself and others. Identify factors which could prevent or restrict change and sources of support.

6 Work out a strategy for change as precisely as possible, showing the steps he/she would have to take.

7 How would you initiate it with the pupil?

The last point draws attention to the need to explain and involve the pupil.

Follow-up
Participants could check their analysis by further observation and report back. This will lead to the salient issue of accuracy of judgement.

Session 3

Objective To create some awareness of the complexity and subjectivity of apparently rational judgements. We should note that the introduction of profiles heightens the need to look at the basis of our judgements.

Points for trainers to make on person perception and judgements.

1 These brief notes only touch on certain aspects of the topic and certainly do not give a complete treatment of the selected areas.

2 *Basics*
    a The first simple, and yet profound, element is given below.

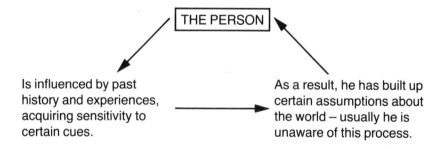

This means that perception is a function of assumptions. *As the person assumes, so he perceives.*

44

The significance of this is that different people have different sets of assumptions and, hence, different perceptions. We therefore 'see' the same situation very differently because of our network of assumptions, which interprets, perhaps actually creates, our social reality.

Perception is therefore a process of attribution and inference which is not random but purposive – it furthers our needs and intentions.

b This in turn leads us to a recognition of the possibility of a central directive state which determines our perceptions and judgements. Perceptions and judgements are imbedded into and interact with our psychological needs.

This implies that interpersonal perception is directed towards the satisfaction of our needs in either a positive or a defensive way.

c Basic processes lie behind this.

 i The built-in tendency to assume cause-and-effect relationships, which has been observed, even in people watching the random movements of shapes projected on a screen.

 ii *Perception is largely inference, therefore we should submit these inferences to rational evaluation.*

Points which those working with others in a developmental way should consider are:

a Perception is selective. Why do we focus on some things and ignore others?

b Inferences take place on the basis of minimal cues, giving us freedom in our judgements, but also creating the possibility of distortion.

Although we are apparently responding to a total situation or person, we are selecting certain features of instrumental importance and focusing on attributes of the person which are salient to us.

Hence:

 i we ignore detail, but also fail to perceive much that is unique and specific to a person or event;

 ii identification of one salient characteristic triggers off an automatic sequence of judgements and responses which are never checked. If such minimal cues form the basis of our inferences, surely we need to examine them and teach our pupils to do the same?

c *We should also consider the following sources of error in our perceptions.*

 i Do we judge people on the basis of *real* or *assumed*

similarity? Do we too readily assume a likeness to us which is unjustified or differences which are not present?

ii Are our judgements distorted because of a halo effect, stemming from a dominant attribute in the situation or person? This means we assume that a number of other characteristics are possessed by the individual without any evidence.

iii Do we unthinkingly apply a framework of judgement which may or may not be appropriate? We still judge girls on different criteria from those applied to boys.

iv Have we a tendency towards either extreme or central judgements which may be more influential than the situation or the person in shaping our reactions? This even influences marking.

v Does it often boil down to the fact that we see:
  – people whom we like as similar to us;
  – those whom we dislike as more dissimilar to us than they really are?

The importance of different perspectives

1 Laing *et al* (1966) suggest – as do other writers – that the person's self-concept is crucial in perceptions and judgements of others. The discrepancies between

my view of myself

and

my view of your view of me

bedevil and confuse interpersonal judgements and perception.

2 This can be presented as:

teacher's view of himself	pupil's view of himself

(Does each understand how the other sees himself?)

Next we have:

teacher's view of pupil's view of the teacher	pupil's view of teacher's view of the pupil

(Note the many opportunities for error and misunderstanding which are evident in the above.)

This can be taken further:

teacher's view of the pupil's view of the teacher's view of the pupil	pupil's view of the teacher's view of the pupil's view of the teacher

(Most of the difficulties in communication stem from this level of analysis.)

3 This way of looking at perception urges us towards self-knowledge and constant evaluation of the basis of our judgements. It may be tempting to say that what is simple is being made unnecessarily complicated, but this is not true. The simplicity is delusory and leads to sterile and self-defeating interaction between pupil and teacher. Understanding puts us in charge of interactional processes in a truly educative way.

Activities

1 Discuss the values which might shape your judgements in this situation.

'The mother of a girl visits you to complain about the sex education in the school. The parents are staunchly, perhaps rigidly, religious, therefore both parents feel that you have a special concern with the moral development of your pupils – surely that is what pastoral care means? She insists that Diane is a 'good' girl and that such sex education will contaminate even the best of girls. She is particularly annoyed that contraception was discussed because she regards this as collusion with 'the lowest in people'. You know your pupils well and you are aware that the girl is very different from her mother's perception of her. Yet you are sure that the mother is sincere. Your private view is that information about contraceptive devices (which she has probably already obtained elsewhere, because you believe her to be on the Pill) is absolutely essential.'

2 Identify the less obvious sources of distortion in this situation.

'Your son has been a source of anxiety to you. His interest in pop music is great, but his talent as a pop musician is not. He could have done well academically but opted out. Your relations with him are ambivalent – you care, but his lack of consideration, his refusal to think prudentially and his arrogance reduce you to impotent anger. Mrs Whittle, who is a teacher in a neighbouring public day school for girls, arrives distressed. Her son, who is in the fifth year and who is very bright, is refusing to go into the sixth form. He has been offered a post as trainee manager in a large department chain. She says she trusts you, knows that you have a good relationship with him. Will you please investigate and try to persuade him to go into the sixth form as a prelude to university?'

3 *Follow-up.*

Identification of situations where judgements are distorted by expectations, e.g. experience of older brothers or sisters.

Objectives To help heads of year examine the way inferences are made, and to look at different strategies for dealing with situations. Often they have not looked at possibilities and hold very limited conceptions of what can be done. Trainers should reinforce the theme of there being no 'right way', but professionalism demands flexibility and regard for the pupils' best interests.

A case history: Larry

Instructions

1 We shall use this case history both for individual exercises and as a basis for group discussion. To prevent identification it has been necessary to change the name of the child and certain other details.

2 Please do not turn over the sheet or scan the whole history, otherwise much of the point of the exercise will be lost.

3 Once you have read each section, please answer the questions set and then proceed to the next section. Do not add anything to a section once you have finished your answer.

4 Imagine you are the head of year/house who is helping Larry.

Page 1 (The page number indicates what would be on each page when the exercise is duplicated for use in the school.)

Larry is a fifth form boy of average attainment or below in most subjects, except in physics and mathematics, where his work is excellent. Most of his teachers like him, but they are puzzled by him. They are also convinced he is working below his ability.

The head of physics, with whom he has an excellent relationship, has referred him to the head of year as he feels there is something wrong. Enquiries made by the head of year of his teachers and tutor yield the following information.

1 Larry tends to make spontaneous, inappropriate remarks in classes.

2 He can never walk anywhere, but runs.

3 He seems to be unable to get along with other pupils, although he does not provoke fights. He gets on better with girls than with boys.

4 Sometimes in class he seems to withdraw into day-dreaming.

5 He often offers to help teachers and is obviously pleased when the offer is accepted.

6 He seeks adult attention at the most awkward times, not seeming to realise it.

What do you think this information is saying about Larry? Does it seem to suggest directions for investigation or give clues about the nature and source of his problem? Make brief comments below:

Page 2

You have interviewed Larry, who was very eager to talk to you and anxious to co-operate. You feel from your experience with him that he is seeking attention and recognition in an almost desperate way. After seeing him on three occasions you find out that he is anxious before he comes to see you, complaining of feeling sick. He has also started hanging around after school and has to be told to go home.

What, if anything, does this add to your ideas about his difficulties? Comment below.

At the meeting today you learned that he has to get up and make his own breakfast, and get his seven year-old brother ready for school. His mother stays in bed until both children have left the house.

Now make a careful statement about what his problem is before turning over the page. Give yourself enough time to write it out fully.

Page 3

Larry has seen you on four occasions now, but you don't seem to be getting very far. He talks fluently, but often when he begins to talk about home and family he suddenly changes the subject. When you ask him a question, or try to get him to elaborate, he becomes evasive, bursting into a torment of nervous remarks which have little to do with your question.

Please put a ring around the answers you think might be correct below:

1 Larry is well aware what drives him to the attention-seeking behaviour.

    YES   NO

2 He wants to talk about it, but cannot bring himself to do so.

    YES   NO

3 It is essential that you try to bring it out into the open.

    YES   NO

Page 4

The head of year felt that, to help Larry, the problem had to be
brought into the open, so that they could face it together, involving
the head of physics if Larry agreed. He also said that Larry was
hurting himself by his behaviour and that he seemed to want to say
something, but couldn't manage it. He carefully suggested that the
boy must make his own decision and not feel pushed. He should go
away and think it over, knowing that his decision would be
accepted.

What do you think of this technique? How would you approach the
problem area?

The boy cried violently at this – he wanted to tell the head, but was
not sure if he should – anyway he might think Larry was being
stupid. The year head accepted this and reassured him that he
would not think anything that caused such tension was stupid. It
was again made clear that the boy would not be pressured. Larry
would be left alone, undisturbed, for five minutes to think about it.
It might help if Larry wrote down his thoughts, using the paper and
pens which were always on the table.

What, if anything, was behind the techniques of

- going out of the room;
- ensuring Larry was not disturbed;
- making it possible for him to write down his thoughts?

In what way would you have acted differently? Why?

Page 5

Larry revealed that he was afraid that his family did not want him and he was particularly clear that his mother rejected him. She is inconsistent and physically punishes the boy despite his age. The father stays out at night, avoids her as much as possible, and shows no interest in the children. The mother is harsh and violent, tearing up books, destroying models and other possessions. She tries to set the younger brother against Larry and makes fun of his appearance, aspirations and achievements.

You are now in possession of the crucial facts. Imagine that you are the head of year, thinking about the situation.
Answer these questions.
   Would you continue or call in the outside agencies?
   If you go on helping Larry, how will you set about it?
   What complications can you envisage?

For trainers only

Discussion can be productive. Bring out the limits to the task of the head of year/house. Sharpen the criteria for referral. What role will the parents play?

Training Unit 2: Basic communication and counselling skills

Session 1: Listening
Objectives To create awareness of skills involved in listening, and to help participants evaluate their strengths and weaknesses.

Activities
   1 Present the following list of skills involved in listening.
      Not interrupting.
      Encouraging the pupil by smiling.
      Nodding to show you are attending.
      Giving help when he seems to be stumbling over what he wants to say.
      Keeping eye contact.
      Asking a positive question when he stops.
      Adopting a relaxed position.
      Not criticising.

a Teachers briefly discuss them with partners. Then trainers ask teachers to rank them in order of importance.

b Then work in twos playing roles as set out. One is the head of year, the other the pupil. The pupil is worried about staying on at school. He wants to, but his father wants him to take a job in the office of the firm where he is a supervisor. Father feels that it is too risky to stay on into the sixth form. The pupil would like to take A-levels, although uncertain about higher education. He/she has no clear career direction. (The role player can add other ideas as wished).

The interview is simulated. Then the 'pupil' evaluates the listening skills of the 'head of year' in as helpful a way as possible.

3 Trainers then raise the following points.

a Have we considered the impact of tone and volume of voice as part of active listening? We may encourage pupils to go on talking, but we can do it in a self-defeating way because our voice lacks warmth.

b How did the hierarchy of importance match what was displayed in the role play?

4 Trainers should anticipate the usual disclaimers of 'I'm different in real life', 'It's an artificial situation' or 'I felt I was being watched.' Experience over many years has shown me that people bring into simple role play the habits and techniques they use in real life.

5 Role reversal is important. Therefore, in the next session the 'pupil' should become the 'head of year'. Reality is increased by asking that the 'pupil' be played on the basis of a problem recently encountered by that head of house/year.

Session 2

1 *Objective* To create greater awareness of participant's tendencies or style of communication.

2 *Situation* Divide the training group into two. Set a topic for discussion relevant to their interests, e.g. ways of developing our effectiveness in pastoral care with this school.

a Half the group sit in a circle and discuss the topic. Each member of this group has a partner who sits opposite in an outer circle in order to observe.

b After 15 minutes' discussion the observers take their partners away, reporting on what they have noted and making constructive suggestions for improvement.

c The discussion and observation is resumed. After 15–20 minutes the observers again report back to their partners, trying to be as helpful as possible.

3 *Follow-up* Trainers lead discussion related to improving communication.

Session 3

1 *Objective* To focus on key elements of communication and consider them in depth.

2 *Activity*

a As in Session 2 but with a new topic. Selection of the topic is by the group. Roles are reversed, observers becoming members of the inner circle. Observation focuses on the tendency to:
- support other people
- build on their ideas, taking them further
- disagree
- attack others' viewpoints
- defend one's own viewpoint
- give others information
- ask for information
- admit when one doesn't know
- exclude others from the discussion
- try to dominate or take over.

b Discussion should last 20–35 minutes. Feed-back is again given by the partner and not in the total group.

3 *Follow-up* Participants build a check-list of communication skills associated with effective counselling. Trainers then ask teachers to consider how they would create greater awareness in form tutors.

Session 4

1 *Objective* To look at the importance of sending signals of acceptance, and the ease with which pastoral interaction can become negative.

2 *Activity*

a Participants examine the diagram on p. 54, based on a situation where a pupil comes to complain that someone is bullying him, i.e. 'keeps starting on me' or 'picking on me.'

b Trainers point out that an accepting response is necessary for efficiency. Without it, the pupil feels rejected, or that the head of year does not understand or is punitive when someone is in trouble. Absence of an initial accepting

Style of guidance

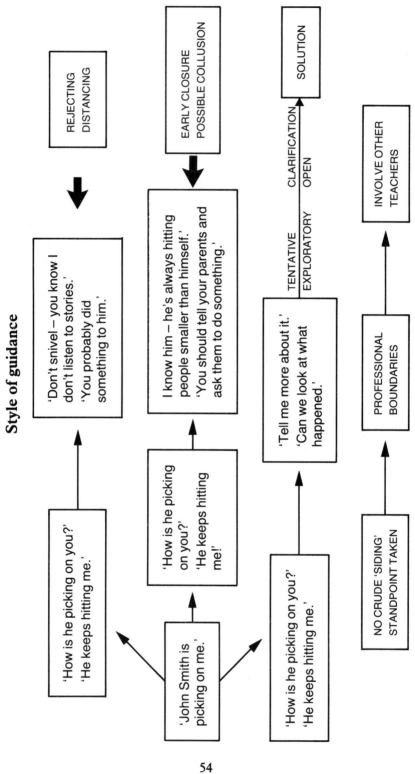

REJECTING
DISTANCING

'Don't snivel – you know I don't listen to stories.'
'You probably did something to him.'

'How is he picking on you?'
'He keeps hitting me.'

EARLY CLOSURE
POSSIBLE COLLUSION

I know him – he's always hitting people smaller than himself.'
'You should tell your parents and ask them to do something.'

'How is he picking on you?'
'He keeps hitting me!'

'John Smith is picking on me.'

CLARIFICATION   SOLUTION

TENTATIVE   OPEN
EXPLORATORY

'Tell me more about it.'
'Can we look at what happened.'

'How is he picking on you?'
'He keeps hitting me.'

INVOLVE OTHER TEACHERS

PROFESSIONAL BOUNDARIES

NO CRUDE 'SIDING' STANDPOINT TAKEN

54

response can create interaction where existing negative attitudes are strengthened and opinions polarised.

    c Participants discuss what would be effective accepting responses in these situations:

       i A pupil has been sent by the tutor because he has been bullying.

      ii Someone has failed to do as well as they and you expected in an examination.

    iii A pupil claims that a teacher is 'picking on me.'

    iv A third-year pupil wants to take a subject in which his success is unlikely.

3 *Follow-up* Careful discussion of the difference between signalling acceptance and blindly endorsing undesirable behaviours should follow. Pitfalls as well as benefits should be considered.

Session 5

1 *Objectives* To help heads of year or house assess their performance as counsellors.

2 *Activity* The participants are given the following list of attributes and asked to discuss them for 10–15 minutes with a partner.

  1 How supportive am I?

  2 Do I tend to interrupt a pupil and not let him finish?

  3 Can I admit that I don't understand?

  4 Do I set out to reinforce the positive things said by the pupil?

  5 How do I show I respect the pupil and his problem?

  6 Do I create an atmosphere of warmth or one of threat?

The trainers allow general discussion and then move to sources of distortion.

The following issues are explored:

1 When do I tend to say to a pupil, 'What you really mean is . . .'? This anticipation is unhelpful, but we may be doing it without realising.

2 When do I try to reassure pupils rather than deal with the problem?

3 Do I find myself saying, 'If I were you' or 'When I was your age'? What is the pupil's inner response likely to be?

Session 6

1 *Objective* To extend the work on distortion by looking more

closely at the emotional factors involved for both teachers and pupils.

2 *Activity*

Step 1 Participants are asked to list the characteristics of the type of pupil they dislike and those of the type with whom they get on well. Group discussion of the significance of this for 'helping' activities then follows. The danger of putting on a phoney front is discussed.

Step 2 The following taped dialogue is presented.

Head of Year/House	'Well, Sue, I wonder how you are getting on at home these days?'
Sue	'It's nothing to do with you – you're a teacher, and your job is to teach me!'

This opens up the question of pupils' perceptions of the legitimacy of pastoral care. Has the teacher any right to intervene? Trainers should help heads of year/house to clarify their reaction to the intuition that the pupil, although submissive, feels the teacher has no right to interfere. Will they gloss it over? Is it better to bring it out in the open by saying, 'You could be feeling I'm an interfering old nosy parker'?

Pupils misinterpret as well as resent. I may feel that a boy has potential, but he sees me as either putting him down or labelling him as a nutcase. We have to be sensitive to those possibilities, using a tentative approach. 'Well, Jim, I sometimes get the feeling that you think I'm seeing you as different from the others.' Tact is necessary, but it would be foolish to try to help a pupil without bringing these issues to the surface. (For a fuller discussion see Hamblin (1974).)

Step 3 Partner work on detecting and dealing with such misinterpretations.

Step 4 Group discussion on ways in which pupils can be taught about the positive nature of the helping activities of head of year/house. Pupils have to be alerted to their pre-categorisations and negative assumptions as much as teachers.

For trainers only

The failure to recognise and deal constructively with pupils' resistances and doubts is one source of ineffective pastoral care. Pupils must be educated about the functions of head of year/house and tutor on entry to the school.

Session 7

    1 *Objective* To create awareness of unwitting, self-defeating remarks which undo efforts at caring.

    Introductory ideas

        Simple, perhaps stark, presentation of the notion of double-bind allows application to real life. Briefly, double-bind involves

- the situation where a second message follows the first immediately
- that second message contradicting the first, or qualifying it in some negative way, i.e. 'a sting in the tail'.
- an important situation which is important for the pupil or has strong emotive connotations and therefore cannot be ignored.

The following examples are mainly concerned with the folly of reassurance as a substitute for dealing with the problem constructively.

- 'I know you will be able to deal with it now, Jim, but remember I'm around to give you support.'
- 'I'm sure you're going to do well in those O-levels, but don't worry anyway, there's always another chance in November.'
- 'Yes, but . . .'

The reassurance often 'boomerangs'. The pupil responds to the sting in the tail, feeling more helpless. We may not recognise this has occurred, and perceive them as anxious people who are not responding to our support. Through such unrecognised mechanisms, pastoral care allocates to some children identities as problem pupils. The last example takes double-bind into the discrepancy between offering acceptance and then apparently rejecting by our verbal responses. 'Yes, but . . .' is not a just figure of speech. The pupil feels we are contradicting or rejecting his statements.

    2 *Activity* This is based on specification of situations in pastoral work where the head of year

- feels insecure and not able to cope
- embarrassed (Certain sexual problems may produce this reaction.)
- dislikes that type of pupil.

The link between insecurity, anxiety and the appearance of double-bind should be appreciated in the discussion.

Sessions 8 to 11

    1 *Objectives* These four sessions will be concerned with refining a

model of decision-making for the head of year or house. Case studies and situations will then be discussed.

Trainers introduce and discuss the following model of decision-making for the head of year or house.

Decision-making: A framework for pastoral care

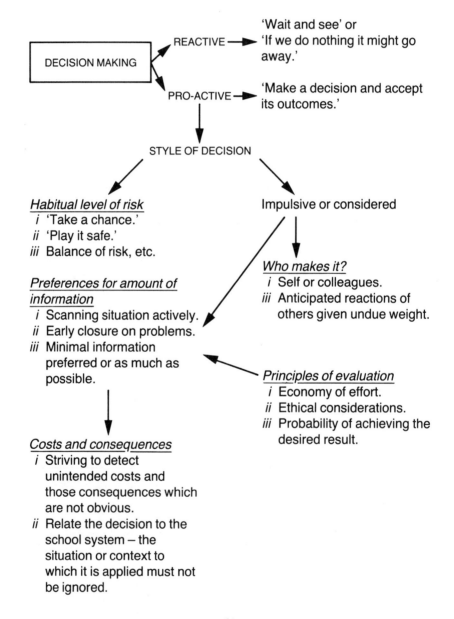

Our aim is to create some awareness of the complexity of the decision-making process involved in the management and co-ordination of the pastoral system. For the moment, however, trainers should relate the model to work with individuals. *It is not intended to be a complete model of the process. It is suggestive rather than exhaustive.*

Each underlined section should be discussed at some point in the four sessions. In the first session they should be related to the following situations. Trainers can split the group into pairs which deal with one situation in depth, later reporting back to the total group. The whole group can discuss each situation, ending with a summary discussion.

Situation 1

A girl of 14 has been wearing a gold ring to school, even though the school rules forbid the wearing of jewellery. Although she was sent home, she obstinately continued to wear it. As her head of year, you have built up a good relationship with her. You gently suggested that she should leave the ring at home. To your surprise, this usually stable and co-operative girl burst into tears and ran out of school. She was absent for a fortnight. The mother refused to discuss the situation with the Educational Welfare Officer. The mother and girl have now arrived to discuss the matter with you. The mother, who is deeply resentful and antagonistic, says that the ring was given to the girl by her grandmother who brought her up as a baby. (The mother was in the tropics with her husband, who was in the army.) The grandmother and girl were deeply attached. The grandmother had died three months ago. The girl refuses to take off the ring at home. The mother considers the school rule unreasonable and inhuman in the circumstances.

How do you, as a year head, deal with this?

Situation 2

You have been seeing John intermittently during the last year. He is a very conscientious boy of fourteen, who is of good ability and attainment. Yet he is constantly expressing anxiety about his academic work.

During the terminal examinations – just ten minutes before he is due to take an English examination (a subject which worries him) –

he appears at your door. His voice is strangled, and, to your surprise, he appears on the verge of tears. He asks, 'Can I talk to you now?'

Indicate

1 Your specific response to the situation.

2 Your thoughts about it, particularly anything that you would find especially disturbing.

For trainers only

Note that question 2 *could* bring questions about over-dependence or what has been reinforced.

Situation 3

Earlier today you saw David, who is beginning his second year in the sixth form. His eight O-levels were excellent, but his work deteriorated badly last year and he is now behind with his essays and assignments. He felt you could provide him with a solution, but he now realises it isn't so easy.

At 4.15 p.m. David's father comes to your room. His son telephoned him, telling him of the situation. His father had not known things were so bad, and he was especially worried by David's statement that he wanted to leave school. (David had made no mention of this to you.) His father bluntly asks you if it would be best for him to leave school.

1 How would you reply? What considerations would you have in mind?

2 What values shape your reply? How does this situation activate them?

Mair: A case history

Mair is a 15-year-old girl referred for being disruptive and obstinate in class. She is tall, slim, with neat dark hair and large attractive eyes. Always well-groomed, she is often in a brown leather coat which she wears well.

By herself, once her confidence is gained, Mair is likable and interesting. She says, 'I am good at most things I want to be. I like making friends, cooking, looking smart, saving, being kind to my family. I am kind to animals and they are kind to me.'

Boyfriends
She talked about her boyfriend, with whom she had an argument last Wednesday. She had decided not to go with him to a wedding party – 'he plays around with the girls' – so now she feels lonely. He gave her a jewellery box for Christmas; she gave him an LP which she's had back, but not the pullover – it would be too big for her! He was her first real boy-friend, and they had been friends for 17 months.

In October her parents asked the school for assistance. Mair had several times come in late after she had been drinking, and twice had had bruises on her face. The parents thought the boyfriend was to blame, but Mair gave them little information. The Senior Mistress talked to her about contraception and reported that Mair had responded well and responsibly.

Parents
Mair's father is tall, broad-shouldered and handsome. He is proud of his academic achievements and his present job as a chemical engineer. He is strict and authoritarian in his demands on the whole family. His wife is less authoritarian, a warm, understanding woman, who takes great pride in her domestic responsibilities. Mair's father leaves for his evening shift after Mair has come in at 9.30 p.m., and it aggravates her to have to be in so early. He goes to chapel regularly, he says, 'to set the example'. Perhaps Mair believes there is little other reason, and if she goes, it is with reluctance.

Brother
Mair feels her younger brother Llewellyn is treated with unfair indulgence. He is good at sport, but slow at school work. Rather than show his impatience and disappointment with Llewellyn, the father seems to give him more freedom and accept whatever standard the boy offers, whereas Mair feels she can never please her parents. 'They always ask for a higher standard than I've given.'

School work
Mair's needlework has been outstanding, and she has responded well to the suggestion that she change from commercial subjects to Home Economics. Her behaviour in the new classes and her attention to homework pleases both her teachers and her parents, and she is more confident in her own future.

Questions and feelings
Mair's father asks, 'Where have we gone wrong?' When it is suggested that Mair be allowed to *earn* her pocket money and take

increasing responsibility for her own decisions, he says, 'What decisions has a fifteen-year-old girl to make for herself? I decide that she goes to school, and what sort of job we want her to have . . .'

Mair stopped seeing her ex-boyfriend over a month ago. Now she has two love-bites on her neck, and said her parents hadn't noticed.

1 What response would you make to father's query?
2 How could you help Mair cope maturely when her father takes the viewpoint above?
3 Have you any right to intervene because of the love-bites?

Case study: Charles – aged 17

Referral
Charles was referred by his sixth-form tutor because of social isolation. He had no friends and would not stay in the sixth form unit during break, lunch-times or free periods. He would go to the school's general office and help the secretaries by performing errands. This he had been allowed to do for several years. During interaction with his peers he showed high levels of social anxiety.

School background
Charles was studying five CSE subjects and one O-level and was very conscientious and meticulous. Towards the staff he was very friendly and cooperative, observing school rules and instructions punctiliously. During his school career he has been involved in some incidents of violence, when he had fiercely attacked another pupil after enduring prolonged teasing. This had earned him a reputation for being unpredictably aggressive.

Home background
Although 17 years old, Charles invariably stayed at home each evening, doing his homework, watching television and amusing himself with his hobbies. He went out only when accompanied by his parents and older brother. He was not allowed to join clubs or societies, or to have any social life outside the confines of his home. Charles was the scapegoat of the family, the focus of the mother's aggression. If he disobeyed or showed any tendency to remonstrate with her, she would lose her temper and send him upstairs to his bedroom. Any prevarication on his part would be countered by blows from his brother and father. He was regarded as odd by the family and was unfavourably compared with his brother and sometimes with his peers.

The problem

Charles had a strong sense of being the 'odd-man out' which was continuously reinforced by the family communication system and by his gauche attempts at social interaction with his peers. He was hyper-sensitive to normal teasing and often perceived his class-mates' banter as deliberately provocative. His only social contacts were with older people – parents and staff. Charles regarded himself as being at times uncontrollably violent and as an object of ridicule to his peers. This made him adopt elaborate strategies to avoid close interaction with them: yet he was desperately lonely and desired a close friend. He had very rigid views about swearing, salacious jokes, drinking and being a good boy, associating long hair and the wearing of denims with hooliganism. In school, unlike his peers, he was always dressed in school uniform.

Questions

1 How far did the pastoral team reinforce his sense of deviant identity by accepting the situation, by labelling him as violent, and by covertly encouraging him to avoid social contact by going to the general office? Was this unwitting collusion the result of the fear of further violent outbursts?

2 Charles had been isolated throughout his school career. Why were his problems overlooked for six years?

3 How far did his conforming behaviour towards school rules, his deference and friendliness to staff contribute to the delay in instigating positive strategies to help him?

4 The pastoral team regarded Charles's home as excellent and the parents as keen and cooperative. Their interpretation of the situation was superficial, based on loose comments by staff and two or three formal contacts with parents. What measures could be adopted to ensure more accurate information about the home, instead of glibly accepting unsubstantiated opinion?

5 What is the school's role in helping the parents to understand their pattern of interaction and its consequences for Charles's self-image? Is intervention in such matters justifiable?

6 What measures could have been taken to increase Charles's social skills, especially in peer interaction?

A brief decision-making exercise

Situation 1

Ms Bette Jones (a history specialist noted for her intolerance and inability to communicate with pupils) has pushed John Williams into your room. She says she will not have him in her class again, although he is taking his O-level in history next term. John was fighting as she entered the classroom and, when she intervened, he told her to 'get lost'. He is bright, usually cooperative, and school is a haven for him, as his widower father has little time for him. John is trying to control himself but is obviously angry. Ms Jones's parting remark is, 'I will leave rather than put up with him again.'

1 How will you deal with John now?

2 What will you do about Ms Jones?

Situation 2

An intelligent, pleasant, well-dressed boy, who has recently come to the school, has seen you on several occasions. The alleged problem has been the change in school work and difficulty in settling down. You feel you have got nowhere. Today he tells you he is having sexual intercourse with a girl of his own age, fifteen, and that his friend next door, who is a year older, is similarly involved with this girl, who is a pupil of the school. The friend attends a youth club where you work two evenings a week. This friend left school last term.

1 How would you deal with the revelation?

2 What, if any, further action would you take?

Situation 3

The head is away, and the senior deputy has gone to a course at the teacher's centre. School has just finished. The second deputy is not the strongest or most energetic of characters. He appears at the door with the parents of a boy in your year. He rushes away. The parents claim that their son was badly beaten up at lunch time by other boys in his class. They say that not only will they go to the police, but they will go to local and national papers and expose this sort of thing, which has happened before. You know there is a grain of truth in this last statement, as concern about episodes of bullying was aired at the last staff meeting. You resent the 'passing the buck' of the deputy head, but you can see that the situation is potentially dangerous for the school, especially as father is just saying that the boy was waylaid, his trousers were removed and that sexual interference occurred.

1 What *can* you do?

2 How much *should* you try to do?

Situation 4

A boy has asked to see you. You don't know much about him as he presents no difficulties. For the first time you are aware that he has a slight speech impediment – a lisp. He is very agitated, saying he enjoys his school work but the boys in his year call him 'girlie' and make remarks about his slight build. He says that the men teachers know about this, and one PE master overtly encourages them in the gym and on the field.

1 What line will you take?

2 What complications will need special care?

Interview techniques and working with the less able or inarticulate pupil

Trainers should consult Chapters 3, 4 and 5 of *The Teacher and Counselling* for essential background knowledge and techniques. The following notes will be useful as the basis for initial training sessions with the heads of year/house.

Basic considerations

1 Those who interview must be aware of the negative connotations of the interview. For many pupils, especially those with restricted language skills, it is associated with 'trouble'.

2 Pupils who are sensitive to authority and influenced by the context and physical surroundings in which the interview takes place are liable to resort to superficial agreement and conformity.

Preliminary factors

1 The interviewer should clarify his *objectives* before the interview, specifying what he hopes to achieve. Changes in attitude, behaviour, interaction with teacher or peers may be the target areas, but the interviewer needs to define the intended outcomes as precisely as possible.

2 Next the input should be assessed.

   i What information is possessed about the pupil and relevant factors? How credible are the sources? How valid is the information? Hearsay and second-hand information needs to be scrutinised carefully.

   ii Then specify the information that needs to come from the pupil. The barriers to obtaining it need to be recognised, e.g. friends labelling as a 'splitter'.

   iii Assess the perceptions the pupil is likely to hold of the purpose of the interview and the intent of the interviewer.

3 Assess the way in which you will create *rapport*. Even in disciplinary interviews the creation of antagonism is counter-productive. Pay special attention to your first few remarks to the pupil. They should convey respect for the individual and concern. Recall that an interview is more than the verbal messages. Latent content exists.

4 The interview has two main components.
   a The *diagnostic* element, where we identify the nature of the problem and its causes. The former is the area in which skill is essential. The presenting problem may not be the real one.
   b The *action* element, in which decisions are made about actions to be taken. Pupils should be helped to see the steps that they can take to resolve the situation. Actions must be clearly specified so that they know what to do. They should know that others are assessing them. Vague encouragement and global prescriptions offer little that contributes to change.

5 Points to watch
   a A frequent source of difficulty is the tendency to ask a question and follow it up by another before the pupil has time to answer the first one. The pupil may make an affirmative response, but the interviewer does not know if he agrees with one or both.
   b Interruptions are sources of distortion. By interrupting the interviewer cuts the pupil off, and redirects his flow of thought.
   c Assumptive statements are used too frequently by the poor interviewer. This means the interviewer anticipates what the pupil says, or tells him what he thinks he will say.
   d Certain pupil behaviours must not be tolerated. In this case, pleasant but firm interruption is essential. It will often be important to discuss the significance of this behaviour. Examples are:
      i The constant resort to 'Don't know'.
      ii Long monologues by the pupil.
      iii Non-verbal signals of boredom or indifference.
   e The good pastoral interviewer always notes hesitations and change of topic by a pupil. The skill of recognising less obvious signs of anxiety and tension is crucial, e.g. foot-tapping.

Sources of threat for the interviewer
 1 Objectivity can be lost when:
   a The problem is one experienced by the interviewer in childhood. This may stimulate the 'If I were you' approach, which alienates pupils.
   b The situation is one which the interviewer has not resolved successfully with his own children.
 2 The expectations of others can impinge negatively on the interviewer's treatment of the problem. This has to be faced honestly.

Closing the interview
 1 This is the weak point in many interviews. The good which has been achieved can be destroyed by a weak or negative ending.
 2 End with a clear summary making sure that the pupil feels something has been achieved or learned. Even in disciplinary interviews the positive ending is crucial. Firmness can be given positive expression.
 3 The final signals should reinforce the pupil's self-respect. Diminished self-respect lessens the likelihood of responsible behaviour

Session 12
Objective To help heads of year/house understand some of the latent processes and communication difficulties in an interview.

Step 1
Trainers present the following: *Confusions in communication in the interview.*

 1 Misunderstandings often occur because the interviewer does not understand what is happening. Consider the following *thoughts* of participants in an interview.

Pupil	*Head of year/house*
1 I am really worried about this. He doesn't seem to care.	He seems to be upset. If I listen to him it may help me to understand.
2 He keeps saying he cares, but he doesn't show much sign of it. He must have noticed how I feel.	I wonder what's bothering him. Fools rush in, so I'll wait.

67

Pupil	Head of year/house
3 I can't stand him sitting there silent – it gets on my nerves. What is he thinking about me?	He seems very restless and irritable. Should I try to reassure him?
4 He's getting at me. I think he's really enjoying this. I'll never come to him again.	I wish he could see I'm only trying to help him.

Trainers should ask participants to examine these situations of *impasse*. If they experienced them, how would they constructively resolve them? Then they are asked to find examples of such breakdowns in communication and discuss them with a partner.

Step 2
Berne's (1966) well-known concept of games is introduced. The intent is not to discuss the theory but to help participants assess the dangers of:

– I'm different from all the rest.
– Only I understand you.
– I'm only trying to help.
– Do it, and you'll please me.

Heads of year are required to think deeply about their skills. Understanding of the mechanisms involved in interviews has to be acquired. Many have interviewed pupils for years without comprehending the importance of these factors to their effectiveness. A final group discussion could look at the way in which we can

– make the pupil/tutor feel guilty unproductively.
– set up a smoke-screen for self-protection.
– indulge in overt or implicit bargaining without questioning its effect.
– issue implicit threats under the guise of benevolence.

Session 13
Objective To help participants take a wider view of the interview.

Step 1
Trainers remind participants that the interview does not happen in a vacuum. Transactions across the boundary of the interview occur with the tutor, other teachers, parents and the pupil's classmates. Wider issues are involved as the check-list of key questions suggests.

The wider implications of pastoral interviews

1 How do I try to involve the tutor in my work with a pupil? Is there a partnership or do I tend to work in isolation?

2 Do I raise relevant questions about pupils with other teachers? If so, am I aware of the way in which they interpret those questions?

3 How do I assess the validity of the information I get? Do I take its accuracy for granted?

4 Does my interaction with colleagues stimulate labelling of pupils because I give the impression that my role as head of year/house is almost solely concerned with deviance or 'trouble'.

5 Have I considered more flexible ways of working, involving friends of the pupil as helpers?

Less able and inarticulate pupils
Heads of year/house are well aware that many pupils have a preference for the visual and active in the field of learning. This is used in interviewing and counselling activities. Hamblin (1974) writes about the use of drawing, diagrams and simple activities as part of counselling. They take the threat away, reduce the sense of interrogation and get the pupil to contribute actively. Simple life-space diagrams are useful, e.g. the pupil is asked to look at his life space in a way which frees him momentarily from his subjective reactions. A simple example is given overleaf.

Friends

1 Laugh at me.
2 Get me to do things I don't want to.
3 Let me down.

Mother

1 Cooks good meals.
2 Nags me about being untidy.
3 Won't let me out on my bike after tea.

John

1 He always gets into trouble, but doesn't want to.
2 Not very tidy.
3 Would like to do well in school.

Father

1 Works late.
2 I like helping him clean the car.
3 Has a joke with me.

Teachers

1 Tell me off.
2 Won't let me help them.
3 All right, especially Mr Smith, Metalwork.
4 Shout too much.

The simple life-space diagram helps the less able to think about the problem without feeling attacked. Writing disability is no handicap; we can fill it in as he instructs us. Role reversal of this type is therapeutic.

Another device is illustrated below.

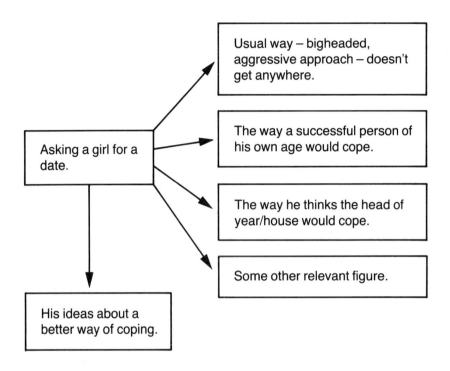

The boy obviously is failing in a key area. He needs to extend his repertoire of behaviours but has limited ideas. A direct approach will bring the response, 'Don't know' or 'It won't work.' Therefore, we get him to look at it indirectly, beginning with someone of his own age. His ideas begin to take shape. We might then ask him to look at the standpoint of the girl and try to understand why she rejected him. Note that this apparent illogical order of events is practical. Barriers would be erected and his appraisal would be defensive if we tackled the problem directly.

Nothing esoteric is required – we merely apply sensible approaches to learning. A first step can be that of asking the pupil to go away and observe himself for two days, noting where he experiences difficulty and how he reacts to the situation. To observe is often to initiate change. Next, the less able often feel, 'They tell me to change, but not how.' This often means we have been insufficiently concrete. The principles are:

– one step at a time
– anticipation of difficulties.

Less able pupils may be unable to see ahead, or lack the skill of perceiving the relationships between the stages in a learning task. Therefore we give them short-term goals, and help them verbalise clearly the way they will deal with it. It is not willpower, but knowing what one should do and how it is to be done. They have to talk about their strategy for coping, almost learning it off by heart. Gradually, we can extend their views of how they can behave, accepting that self-control has to be gradually acquired. Self-control is not restricted to restraint – the ability to inhabit an impulsive response – but will include the acquisition of positive new behaviours.

Trainers should ask one or two imaginative year heads to experiment with these ideas and those given in the source cited above. Anticipation is useful. If they experiment well in advance of the training sessions they are able to act as credible sources of influence.

Finally, I offer two amusing problems derived from one of the Clwyd cadre of trainers' packages of work.

27 High Street,
Colwyn Bay

Dear Teacher,
       My son John was absent from school yesterday because his grandfather died.

Yours Sincerely.

J Williams (Ms)

This is the 3rd time !!!
he's died this term
Please check
RH

How would you initiate action?

3 Gower Street
Wrexham,

Dear Mr. Evans,

My darter Tracey is having truble with Micky Maths, I dont know his reel name - sorry. I am sick of him pickin or her for somethink she hasnt done.

If this is not sorted out her nan says that she will sort Micky Maths out herself

M Williams (Mrs)

The ultimate threat! But seriously, there is clearly a problem which has to be sorted out. How do you go about it?

Summary

1 This chapter recognises that the caring or welfare activities of the head of house or year may be ineffective, despite real concern.

2 The skills of counselling are set out in a simple training programme which incorporates a realistic behavioural approach.

3 The need for clear thinking is stressed, perceptions and judgements are carefully considered, and fallacies and self-defeating behaviours are examined.

4 Heads of year or house are given techniques which will improve their counselling and guidance.

3: The skills of head of year or house: leading a team of tutors and developing tutorial activities

We have seen that the caring aspect of middle management's role is problematical in pastoral work, but even more insecurity is aroused by the need to lead a team of tutors. Trainers must recognise this, adapting their approach to the experience and skill of the heads of year/house. No recipes can be given, because there is no necessary connexion between length of experience and level of skill.

Vulnerability to criticism and anxiety inhibit innovation, therefore training begins with examination of the attitudes and actions which foster development. Utopian aspirations have little worth; instead we have to think about the *strategies which will work in a specific context*. Persuasive communication based on accurate assessment of the current staff power structure is a pre-requisite for extending tutorial work. Trainers should begin by stressing the need to:

- code information for opinion leaders, who shape the responses of certain colleagues;
- anticipate the responses of the 'resident cynics' who pour cold water on enthusiasm and block initiatives. This means learning to give weakened forms of their objections, showing the fallacies involved, before they produce them.

This anticipation does not deny the voicing of doubts – it is crucial that they are aired – merely that habitual forms of resistance to change should be interrupted.

Heads of year or house unnecessarily fear failure. This is a product of their desire for both consensus and an Utopian state of affairs. Causes of underfunctioning in pastoral work have to be assessed, but so do strengths and potential supports. We will never have consensus – neither would this be desirable. Complacency and inertia might result. It is sensible to focus on sources of support and consolidate them before dealing with the negative. Focus on opposition gives it an importance that is undeserved.

Trainers must also stress the advisability of:
- stating goals in a concrete way;
- giving tutors a choice between activities and materials whenever possible.

The latter point is often forgotten. There is no reason why tutors in a particular year group should all be doing the same thing at the same time. We would hesitate to suggest this in subject fields, yet we do it in pastoral work without appreciating the infringement of professional autonomy. The tutor knows best – or should know best – what will be productive for his tutor group at a particular time.

The pastoral curriculum and adolescent development

Marland (1980) succinctly outlines the content of a pastoral curriculum. From the viewpoint taken in this book, the basic considerations are the same as with other curricula. Content in isolation does not form a curriculum. We must give sufficient attention to *process*, asking *how* skills and knowledge deemed to be appropriate will be taught. There must be a visible progression; the activities must stretch pupils and have worthwhile intellectual content. The basic principles trainers should endeavour to meet are:

1 It must be significant, and not trivialise topics such as body image, social anxieties, study skills or trust. The latter is especially important for the 16–19 age group who are deeply concerned with trust versus mistrust.

2 Methods must incorporate respect for the individual. We cannot push pupils towards activities because we believe they will be helped by participation. Personal space must not be violated, feelings about touch and dislike of role play must be registered, therefore we must react sensitively to pupils' vulnerability and fear of exposure.

3 Cognitive aspects of problem-solving have to be stimulated. The aim is to integrate thought and feeling, which means helping individuals discriminate more accurately in stress and achievement situations. Spivack *et al* (1976) showed that training in personal problem-solving aids adjustment. Cer-

tainly the ability to relate means to an end, anticipating the outcomes of action, is a skill which many pupils need to acquire. Tutor work should allow discussion which enhances pupils' capacity to analyse problems, detect ways of coping and of evaluating the costs of actions.

Strong emphasis has to be given positively to processes which constrain and lower pupils' performance. In addition to those given on page 3, embarrassment and audience anxiety, rigidity in thinking and perceiving, inadequate problem-solving, and maintaining self-control are stressed. The pastoral curriculum therefore focuses on mastery learning and constructive self-discipline. A balance has to be achieved between the social, moral, intellectual and vocational elements. There is no ideal or right way, but a sustained, and progressively more complex approach, is necessary over the years.

Consumer research and, eventually, evaluation is neglected. Pupils can contribute in two ways: by giving their ideas about their needs and what would be helpful; and by producing materials for use in tutor periods. The first-year sixth form have given help in fifth-year study programmes or have produced materials for the first-year induction programme. Pupils taking art and drama have produced cartoons, diagrams and tapes for use in tutor periods.

In developing a pastoral curriculum, a module or unit approach may be sensible and economical. It allows one to 'home-in' gradually on topics. More immediate feedback can be given, tutors can be involved in revisions, and a greater sense of involvement can be developed. This greater flexibility allows heads of year/house to overcome reservations and to avoid overwhelming tutors with an intimidating large scale programme. Note, however, that each year head or house head must spell out gradually his intermediate objectives.

It is never too early to consider storage and retrieval systems. Basic questions are:

1 Will there be one central system on which all houses or years draw? If so, who will over-see it?

2 Is there a separate bank for each year? In this case, we must ask, if heads of year move up with the pupil group, what problems are created.

Taba's (1962) steps in curriculum development provide a foundation for the trainers who are devising units for tutor work:

1 Diagnosis of needs – including consumer's perceptions of what their problems are.
2 Formulation of objectives.
3 Selection of content.
4 Selection of learning experiences.
5 Organisation of learning experiences.
6 Determination of what to evaluate, and ways and means of evaluating.

Steps 2 to 4 interact – a certain amount of oscillation between them is productive. Step 6 involves decisions about the timing and form of feedback.

The unit approach allows one to develop materials under broad headings, e.g.
   – positive discipline and tension management;
   – study skills, achievement motivation and learning about learning;
   – social anxieties and social skills.

Trainers must raise questions about the philosophy underlying their pastoral curriculum. What are we preparing pupils for in life? Do we unthinkingly assume stability in the future when we should be questioning? Are we preparing pupils for a dynamic, essentially unstable, and therefore unpredictable future? Can we forget that they are living life now in our emphasis on the future? Somehow we have to emphasise the value of commitment, and provide the tools of learning, without foisting on pupils over-rigid definitions of what has to be learned, and to what one should be committed.

The concept of development is crucial. Trainers would do well to incorporate the ideas of Erikson (1968) and Wall (1948) into tutor work if it is to be developmental rather than to reinforce mediocrity. In the first three years of life, individuals learn to walk, talk, keep themselves clean and dry, and adopt behaviours currently associated with gender. Only in adolescence have so many developmental tasks to be faced, e.g.
   – gaining a positive sense of identity;
   – learning to make a truly intimate relationship of integrity – *not* to be confused with erotic behaviours;
   – the construction of *selves*:
      – as a learner;
      – in terms of a world view which permeates interaction between the individual and his environment, incorporating beliefs about the nature of causality;

- socially;
- sexually, including beliefs about the appropriate expression of masculinity and femininity;
- vocationally, incorporating adaptation to unemployment.

These developmental processes need to inform tutor work explicitly if positive mental health is to be fostered within the school. Entry to the secondary school brings expansion in the volume of social relationships, whilst adolescent development brings increasing complexity of those relationships, and the need for more precise discriminations. Vulnerability to comparisons with others, the tendency to self-derogation or defensive omnipotence and disregard for others are complications to be dealt with in tutorial work.

A caveat

We must beware exaggeration and stereotypes in thinking about adolescent development. Differences in age of entry to puberty and rate of development exist between boys and girls – the latter tend to be one to two years ahead of boys in early and middle adolescence – but there seem to be few, if any, gender-based differences in aptitudes and abilities. Such differences are probably a product of cultural influences, or are self-imposed. Self-imposition of gender-based limits applies as much to boys as to girls – many boys falsely crystallise an identity based on family pressures as scientific or practical, and then experience intra-personal conflict.

It is easy to exaggerate the stresses of adolescence. Tensions with parents undoubtedly occur as adolescents strive for autonomy, yet Kandel and Lesser (1972) show that parental values are generally reflected in adolescents, and that parents wield influence in important areas such as careers.

Physical development brings problems, but most adolescents are able to cope with sexual issues. There must not be illicit generalisation from the few who experience maladjustment and disturbance to the total population. *Body image and presentation of self are topics with which tutor work is concerned positively.*

Peer relationships

Peer groups have positive functions for their members. Values in peer groups are not so much antagonistic to those of adults as different. One usually finds no evidence of alienation or segregation from the adult world. More usual are premature or ill-fated attempts to enter it. Peer groups provide a breathing space from the demands of school and home. Within them, inadequacies and failures in those areas are irrelevant. In the period of increasing demands for achievement and social competence, the peer group

78

allows a temporary regression and gives support. Role confusions can be aired, some sense of control of environmental pressures achieved, whilst fashion and other symbolic activities state their awareness of generational identity.

Trainers should be aware that parents thrust their children into undue reliance on peers when:
- acceptance is conditional on achievement;
- there is little reward incorporated into the interaction between children and parents;
- their values are grossly inconsistent, hypocritical or unrealistic;
- they have eroded self-confidence, and the ability to act autonomously without excessive concern for the reactions of others.

There is no inevitable conflict between involvement in the family and involvement in the peer group. Kandel and Lesser found that intensive interaction within the family did not interfere with, but facilitated peer group interaction. Friends reflected similar values, attitudes to homework, school success and educational aspirations.

Adolescents, therefore, look to peers for immediate gratification and companionship. They differ from adults in emphasis on immediate, rather than future rewards. Trainers must open up development of tutor work with exploration of these questions, showing their practical importance. There is little point in producing neat packages of tutor activities with apparently clear objectives which ignore these fundamental developmental questions.

We can therefore:

a QUESTION the 'exclusive theory' of either high family interaction and low peer-group involvement or low family interaction and high peer-group interaction.

b ASK if coercion to conform exists within the peer group.
   Pupils can be encouraged to ask:
   i Because I find the group attractive, has it the right to impose identity on me?
   ii Do I need to do everything that the others do?
   Have those others the right to make me do something if I don't want to?

c EXPLORE these issues as part of diagnosis:
   i What needs does the peer group meet for this pupil?
   ii What is the balance between the costs of belonging and the costs of giving up membership?
   iii If necessary, we can ask what pressures are driving her/him into exclusive reliance on the peer group.

iv What positive or negative sanctions hold him there, despite his desire to leave the specific peer group?

d CONSIDER the importance of the peer group as a reference group, i.e. a group from which he draws his values, and whose members he uses as a source of valid comparison.

The self concept

Tutorial work emphasises self-knowledge and the salience of the self-concept in achievement. Trainers need to create awareness of the issues. Crites (1968) cites research which suggests that mid-adolescence is marked by a period of doubt and uncertainty. Premature crystallisation of interests, beliefs about aptitudes or career plans will be unhelpful. It is usually claimed that the acquisition of more positive perceptions of oneself are a prerequisite for improving competence. True, but in practice it can be an over-simplification which ignores the contribution of the environment to behaviour. Holland (1977) argues that many problems and contra-dictions exist in the work of 'self' theorists. Difficulties are ignored, and change is made to appear easier than it is. Pastoral workers should be aware that it is an area bedevilled by many problems, e.g.

– the relationship between the self as perceived and the ideal for which the individual may be striving;
– the self as the object of perception by others, and the self as experienced;
– reliance on individual's self-reports and doubts about their validity.

Tutorial work could be a healthy counter response to the fact that the self is taken for granted, if not ignored in instructional processes. The focus is on the subject matter, rather than the pupils and their style of learning. As a working hypothesis it is useful to begin with the possibility that the purpose behind transactions with the social environment is that of enhancing or maintaining some definition of self. Behaviour may make sense only when viewed in such terms. The danger lies in accepting such an explanation as a final one.

Let us be clear that the self-concept of pupils can be an object of concern, because it limits and restricts the individual. Even the adolescent has to shed outworn conceptions of himself. Conflicts potentially exist as Young (1972) argues between self and society. Sugarman (1973) claims that socialisation compels pupils to put on a false front – i.e. pleasing teacher by giving the appropriate answer – resorting to secretive, deviant behaviour. The expression of self is therefore false. A façade self is imposed through social interaction and experience.

Heads of year or house must debate these themes:

1 Part of the pupil's self is a defensive process set up to meet the expectations of others. *But* this meeting of expectations distorts and stunts personal development.

2 How does this relate to the moral development we hope to induce? Is choice possible for the individual? Yet moral and ethical behaviour implies willingness *and* freedom to choose.

3 Does this mean that sociocentric behaviour is necessarily restricting in its personal impact, or that crude self-expression is essential for personal development?

Tutorial work loses credibility with colleagues if such issues are ignored. Over-reliance on questionnaires and ticking boxes are in collusion with apathy and pretence. Materials for tutor work are in short supply, therefore availability is more critical than content. Trainers must help heads of year or house ask what assumptions have been built into the activities unnoticed. Some games and simulations may reinforce a model of man nearer to Adam Smith's economic man than is desirable. Life is more than the rational maximisation of satisfactions. Hamblin (1974) argues that role play can be used in an authoritarian way to suggest a single right answer exists or to over-simplify reality.

Maslow (1970) suggests that a complex attitude exists in the 'self-actualised' person towards himself. When ego strength is high, there is a tendency to forget or transcend self. There is an ability to centre on others and the world, rather than being egocentric or solely orientated towards self-gratification.

Tutorial work benefits from consideration of the following questions:

1 Do we confuse self-esteem with the total self-concept? It is only one element, albeit an important one. We can reinforce false confidence. In study skills and achievement orientated programmes of guidance, some students experience a reduction in confidence as they realise they were deluding themselves.

2 Do we assume a single unitary self rather than multiple selves? The selves implicit in situations may be disregarded, or we may be conscious of them only in extreme negative situations, e.g. football hooliganism.

3 We may not help pupils discriminate between the self as object and the self as subject sufficiently clearly. Self as object means we can view ourselves in a detached way – separately from our bodies and environment – and evaluate ourselves. Self as subject means that we are referring to ourselves as experiencing, although this is not totally satisfactory because we cannot be certain what belongs to the self and what belongs to areas of conditioned or autonomic response.

It is desirable that tutors should discuss these matters, but crucial for heads of year/house and senior management. We not only ask if we are providing the tools for self-assessment, but if they are being used competently. Provision of activities is insufficient, the result may merely be time-filling. What concepts are developed to help pupils understand themselves and their world? Early closure or triviality in the field of self-evaluation is harmful.

Tutorial work often stresses the management and presentation of self in social situations. Goffman (1959) produces a 'dramaturgical' thesis of group presentation of self. Individuals in group situations – e.g. pupils and teachers during a general inspection, or teachers at a parents' evening cooperate to maintain a single definition of a situation. A performance is given to an audience who respond to the pictures of self projected by the performers, and the lines of action initiated. The presentation of self is seen as a dynamic process of creation of impressions and manipulation of inferences. Behind the definition of the situation, lie certain definitions of the motivation and intent of participants. My description is inadequate, doing scant justice to a complex and persuasive analysis of interaction. The point is that similar assumptions are built into relevant areas of tutor work.

Goffman's work reflected reality as he observed it in a socio-anthropological study. Tutorial work does not merely observe, it teaches. Is there a danger in the current emphasis in tutorial work on life skills and self-presentation of creating the cool, calculating manager of impressions? Does the stress on interaction and transactions carry an unrecognised danger of encouraging Machiavellianism? In later discussions of interaction, Goffman examines face work, creating a picture of individuals orientated towards gaining advantages and producing inferiority and shame in others. The impression is that of a player in a ritual game, coping with honour and dishonour. The same impression is given by some programmes of tutor work. Trainers should ask if there is danger of reinforcement of these elements in the life and social skills sessions, particularly for the able and articulate who may be very sensitive to praise and blame, and whose parents have taught them to strive for advantages over others.

If the possibilities mentioned above are valid, then larger questions arise. If self is not only internal, but also diffusely located in the flow of events, becoming manifest only when events are 'read' and the appraisals contained in them are interpreted, what is the significance of self-awareness activities in the tutor periods? *Do they actually operate as devices for distracting attention away from the significant contribution made by organisational factors and teaching methods to identity?* The school is a signal system, bombarding individuals with messages about their value, and incorporating predictions about their future. If the bias in messages is negative, will positive tutor-period activities encouraging self-awareness be potent enough to overcome this? The pastoral heads must see that system-based expectations and interaction can stunt or reinforce development of full personal potential. Is there any point in self-awareness activities if harsh labelling processes operate and teaching methods are ineffective? Note that I come to no conclusions and see the question as an open one.

The self as a learner

This, one of the most salient elements of the school's output, is often neglected. Study skills can be reduced to ineffective prescription, when attitudes, defences against learning and achievement motivation need to be tackled. Insufficient opportunity is provided for pupils to assess their learning styles and develop their strengths appropriately. Hamblin (1978) points out that the true failure of the secondary school may not be in relationships, but in the failure to create an adaptive learning environment. Elements of self-management and internal versus external control are also important. Acceptance of responsibility for success, the incentive value of success, and the attribution of blame for failure are key concepts in the self as a learner. Some externally orientated pupils with a negative self as a learner tend to react to frustration in learning by blaming others. They are the pupils who say, 'The school is no good', 'The teachers say they care, but they don't really', or 'They don't teach you properly here!' For trainers, the message is that processes exist which constrain pupils, and make our teaching ineffective, therefore tutorial work must tackle them. The able are as liable to adopt such passivity as the less able, e.g. O-level and A-level candidates rely on teachers to tell them the meaning of questions rather than ferret it out themselves.

Be clear that self-evaluation of school work is useful, but that this is not exploring the self as a learner, although some forms of self-profiling could achieve this. Learning about learning accompanies awareness of the self as a learner. Tutorial activities must be accompanied by opportunities to talk about learning strategies within the classroom. Marland (1981) (Ed.) points out that more than learning in context is required – pupils need to have the skills explained and opportunities to discuss them. The didactic and the contextual are both necessary.

Investigation of the self as a learner should encourage the abandonment of rigid concepts of 'the right answer', and the assessment of the assumptions about what works in problem-solving. Rigidity, as Rubenowitz (1968) shows, can permeate attitudes to music and art; and the rigid pupil denigrates the unfamiliar. Behind rigidity may lie predictions of failure and humiliation. Tutor work in this area should tackle self-defeating assumptions held by pupils and develop more sophisticated ideas of causality, probability and the use of evidence.

Only then does tutor work contribute dynamically to achievement. We break into the resistance to change in thought patterns, the concrete thinking and the striving to do the done thing in a somewhat rigid and compulsive way found in pupils coming from homes where the intellectual climate is limited and emphasis on respectability of a restricted type constrains creativity.

The sexual self and body image
An anonymous survey of adolescents would reveal that many of them were dissatisfied with their bodies and the picture they present. Hamblin (1980) writing on adolescent attitudes to food found that a large number of boys and girls, aged fifteen, would welcome change of weight and regretted that their bodies were not more attractive. Attention needs to be given to this as part of tutor work, stressing ways of making the best of oneself.

Wide variation in age of entry to puberty is statistically normal. Late-maturing boys are at a disadvantage, particularly if they come from a background where physical prowess is important, and have mothers who are over-protective. Writers, e.g. Conger (1973), report studies which suggest that such boys tend to be less popular with peers, to indulge in more attention-seeking behaviour, and are clumsily assertive. Some feel rejected and inadequate, therefore being sensitive to apparent threats to their autonomy. Tutors should be alert to the possibility that these physical factors in conjunction with situational features contribute to the problem.

84

(Note the qualification implied in the word 'possibility'.) What is important, is the provision of activities which build constructive coping behaviours. Early entry to puberty, although generally advantageous, creates problems for some. Activities will focus sensibly on such issues as the impact of being the tallest in a group – how does it affect what people expect from you?

Obesity, skinniness and height are sensitive issues. Boys dislike being short, while some girls dislike being too tall. Obesity for both sexes lays them open to ridicule, feelings of guilt and shame, and the temptation is to cope by clowning, bullying or escapist behaviour. The importance of pre-menstrual difficulties is now recognised, but the reactions to lack of preparation for menstruation, parental inadequacy in dealing with the girl's feelings and consequent ambiguity lead to difficulties we cannot ignore. A girl whose first menstruations are difficult and painful, may, if the above are present, find it difficult to accept her femininity. Boys can be tied to limited and rigid definitions of masculinity which make it difficult to accept that, in the future, it is just as likely that the male will stay at home and undertake domestic duties, as the reverse is today. Units of guidance which cope with sexual stereotypes and the factors which lead able girls to deny their capacities or to avoid success, have to be part of tutor work from the first year.

Acne and other physical defects can cause a pupil's perception of his body to be almost entirely negative. He notices only the unattractive features and becomes vulnerable to the evaluations of adults and peers. Trainers will obviously realise that this can lead into work on handicap and stigma.

The social self
Buss (1980) describes audience anxiety. This is closely associated with evaluation and the experience of being a social object, e.g. a girl, alone, walking past a group of workmen, or a boy in school uniform face-to-face with a group of 'skins'. The three major areas of social difficulty are fear of:
- losing control in the presence of others;
- the limelight;
- creating adverse impressions in others – authority figures as much as peers.

Tutor work should provide activities which elucidate solutions, not only giving the steps to be taken, but bringing out the importance of 'one step at a time'.

This brings us to the associated concept of 'learned helplessness' where the individual feels that nothing he can do will change the situation. Garber and Seligman (1980) show the importance of learned helplessness in subjects such as mathematics, but it also applies to social situations and personal problems. Adolescents are sometimes keenly aware of their marginal position in society and of the conflicting demands made by adults. This, in conjunction with the tensions between the demands of adults and peers, activates tendencies towards learned helplessness. Failure to see this and to help individuals examine the consequences, reduces the head of year/house to impotent exhortation or ineffective reassurances. Yet decision-making and other tutor group activities can help. Let us, however, be alert to the complex interaction between achievement motivation, learned helplessness, internal or external sense of control, and the pupil's predictions of the outcome of action.

The vocational self

Knowledge of unemployment and work is a prime demand, especially in the later school years. In some schools, even first-year pupils are sensitive to the career implications of particular subjects. It may seem that long-term structural unemployment reduces the importance of the vocational self. Life style and the satisfactions sought from life, however, will always need clarification. New forms of exchange relationship which give the individual self-respect may have to be given pride of place in guidance. Work may have to be disentangled from traditional notions of unemployment. Be that as it may, the need to equip pupils to take up a responsible role – not to be equated with unthinking conformity – is paramount in an age of uncertainty. (Further discussion can be found in Hamblin (1983) and Watts (1983).) Decision-making, risk-taking related to entrepreneurial skills and investment in oneself should be at the forefront.

The philosophical self

Wall's (1948) ideas about the philosophical self form a framework for tutor work, which I see as involving questions such as, 'Am I a pawn to be pushed around or can I make an impact on a malleable world?' 'Is the world a jungle or has altruism validity?' Basically, it is concerned with the interpretation of the transactions between the individual and his world. We should also think about:

1 *Identity by opposition* Many adolescents are clearer about what they are not than what they are. They are strong in opposition, but sometimes weaker in affirmation. The experienced teacher knows this and accepts it constructively. Condemnation merely hardens resistance and could make permanent what

would otherwise be transitory. The pastoral system help exploration, tolerates ambiguity, doubt and the guilt that arises from the upsurge of impulses and sexuality.

2 *Trust versus mistrust* This is a major issue in the 16–19 year group. They are asking questions about relationships:

a What can I give and what can I take?

b If I let somebody come close and reveal myself, how do I know they will not abuse my trust?

c If I enter into a deep friendship, do I have to be what the other person wants me to be?

d Do I run the risk of disillusionment in a relationship because I may turn the other into what he/she is not?

Doubts about the possibility of attaining self-set goals in life often result in a superficial cynicism and distrust of others. Contradictions are sought out, failures in teachers and parents stressed, and positions are taken up from which the young adult finds it hard to retreat. It is in these issues that the deep morality of pastoral work is embodied: that we should judge, not so much by the nature of the act itself, but by its meaning to the people involved.

A final note

An urgent task may be that of examining key concepts in the school which shape our reactions to pupils. The concept of normality needs urgent attention in the post-Warnock era.

a Are we talking about statistical frequency, i.e. equating normal with the modal? If so, what does it say about the creative or very able person? Are there unsuspected links between the 'normal' and conformity or mediocrity?

b Do we pay sufficient attention to the possibility that one man's deviance is another's custom?

c Is 'normal' used to imply moral goodness?

d Are multiple meanings incorporated in the term, which we do not make explicit?

e Is normal seen as healthy or not pathological? If so, is there a fallacy in equating health with frequency of appearance?

f The naturalistic fallacy equated what is desired with what is desirable. Is the normal confused with the desirable in pastoral work?

Pastoral workers will find it profitable to debate these issues in depth as a preparation for change in education.

Development of tutor group activities

In the many short training courses I have led, my fellow teachers have shown that they can produce stimulating and effective materials which meet realistically the needs of their pupils. The following simple principles have guided their work.

1 *An effective tutor period has a clear structure*
   OBJECTIVES of each activity must be given to the pupils. This ensures that they do not misinterpret our intention and allows them to orientate to the task accurately.
   ACTIVITY must be simple, getting to the heart of the problem, catching the interest of pupils without postulating a threat.
   APPLICATION should be explained. We cannot assume pupils will either see the full relevance of what they have done or will know how to apply what they have learned.

Notes for trainers
   1 The objectives must be given in a simple, practical way, couched in terms that are meaningful to the pupils.
   2 The activity must incorporate an interesting stimulus which breaks into apathy or boredom, focusing attention on the problem.
   3 Tutors must help heads of year gain the skills of using small group activities. This means that instructions must be given precisely and strict timing observed.
   4 The application section must be carefully planned, sharpening what has been learned, as well as stressing application.

Example
This suggests the way in which a topic can be handled without resort to vague encouragement.
Tutor Group First year at entry.
Topic Teasing and fear of bullying.
Objectives You are probably feeling a bit strange – you were the biggest in the primary school, now you're the smallest. You knew your way around the primary school and what was happening – here you aren't very sure about things yet. When you feel uncertain like this, and meet somebody who is bigger and teases you, you can feel there is nothing you can do. Today, we're going to learn that there are lots of sensible things to do. Listen to this.
Activity A tape has been prepared in which two pupils speak to the teacher.

Pupil 1	Miss, Jim Brown has been calling me names all the week, and today at break he took my crisps off me!
Pupil 2	Yes, Miss. That's right, Miss.
Teacher	Well, I'm sorry. I can do something and will, if necessary, but what do you think you could do?

The tutor stops the tape saying, 'Yes, what do you think you could do that is sensible. Work it out in groups of four for ten minutes.'

Application   The tutor gets feed-back from the form, building up a blackboard diagram of ways to cope, reinforcing the sensible without being negative about the unhelpful.

(*Note* This basic structure will not be repeated in discussion of the principles.)

2 *The stimuli and activities must reflect reality and appear authentic to pupils*

Trainers   Note that this is often ignored. In the example above, the tendency to carry on with primary school habits is used to give reality, i.e. in the first term or so, children still tend to come up to the teachers in pairs.

3 *Humour should be employed to get the message across, breaching habitual reactions of apathy or inattention*

Example   In introducing homework skills, the tutor suddenly reveals a cartoon which is on a flip-chart and has not been visible.

Pupils laugh – the tutor *quickly* asks them to fill in a check-list of the conditions for doing good homework, e.g.

Having a box in which you keep your things.
Getting an elder brother or sister to check it.
Checking your bag when you finish, to see you've got everything for tomorrow.
Having a regular time to do your homework.
A good discussion then follows.

Trainers The more emotive the issue or the more likely pupils are to feel they are 'being got at', the more essential is constructive humour.

In looking at self-defeating behaviours connected with achievement, I often use some version of the cartoon opposite. The children laugh – then I can get to grips with the equivalent of 'cutting off your nose to spite your face' in learning behaviours.

4 *We must accept and use in a constructive way negative factors often associated with development*
Example We can use identity by opposition helpfully. In fifth-year work on revision I prepare a tape on a pupil's revision strategies. It looks at his balance of effort between strong and weak subjects, patterns of revision, proposed use of the Easter vacation and techniques. It lasts about six minutes. Pupils tend to listen passively. After playing it, I say, 'Well, I'm sure you think I'm going to say that's how you should do it. I'm not! Listen again – this time take notes and criticise it. As soon as the tape stops, work out your own way of revising. Don't rely on the tape.' They work with a will. The tape acts merely as a bench mark and the tendency to oppose is harnessed constructively. The initial playing of the tape was essential to allow constructive criticism.

Trainers Alert house/year heads to the possibility of using apparently negative factors. For example, pupils tend to compare themselves negatively with others – misery seeking out misery to reinforce it – yet we can use those comparisons as the basis for coping.

5 *Tutor work is seen as a message system, reinforcing positive images both of pupils and teachers*
Example Certain pupils attract unwittingly bullying and teasing, quickly acquiring identities which are not easily modified. Unhappiness in school becomes their lot, and teacher time is used in dealing with incidents such pupils unintentionally provoke. A tutor

I QUITE LIKED THIS GIRL UP THE ROAD, SO I WENT TO TALK TO HER ....

... BUT WHEN I GOT THERE I WAS SO EMBARRASSED I COULDN'T SAY ANYTHING TO HER !

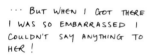

SO I HIT HER !

activity consists of a questionnaire which helps them identify individually the type of individual who attracts teasing and the type who does not. The positive, self-reinforcing element follows. 'Work out with a partner what advice you would give to that kind of person so that they don't attract teasing.' This is just one activity where the latent message is 'We believe you are mature and can deal with these matters sensibly.'

Trainers Teach your heads of year/house to scan the activities they offer for their cumulative impact. Outcomes depend partially on unsuspected orientations imbedded into a sequence of activities. One emergent outcome of school interaction is the image of teachers created in the eyes of pupils. Unsuspected forces can make this negative despite our deep concern. Note how the example under 1 above gave responsibility to pupils but indicated the teacher's concern. We can give the impression that we are rejecting, when this is far from the case.

6 *Tutor work must involve pupils as helpers and sources of ideas*
Example In some activities pupils can be involved in the application stage, e.g. before the tutor period two opinion-leaders in the class are given a simple briefing, and they take the final section. A simple blackboard list of points is made. I have found pupils' ingenuity surprising, which adds a freshness to the period.

Trainers The importance of pupil involvement must be stressed. Unilateral pastoral care can be interpreted as imposition or lack of understanding. Pupils must be allowed to contribute ideas, evaluate activities and sometimes take tutor periods. The contributions of the sixth form, and of pupils taking art and drama, has been mentioned elsewhere.

7 *Tutor activities must challenge constructively negative attitudes and defences*
Example By the fourth year, negative and defensive attitudes diminish involvement in school work and produce unwilling ritual performances. These must be challenged. The tutor begins by writing on the board, 'If you did all the teachers want you to do, you would have no life of your own!' The tutor asks the group to examine the reality of this statement. Each pupil produces a check-list of the 24 hours of yesterday, from midnight to midnight, filling in each hour precisely – sleeping, eating, working, enjoying them-

selves or just drifting. Each category is totted up and the implications for self-management are examined. (I still have a sneaking affection for the youth who yelled out, 'My God, Sir, I wasted eight hours yesterday!')

Other aspects of self-management follow if one uses Stevie Smith's poem, *Not waving but drowning.* The implications of bravado, false confidence and pretence are analysed honestly, but acceptably.

Trainers Tutorial periods must cope with the factors of self-deception and ineffectiveness. Pupils resort to expedient responses which stifle initiative, maintaining an uneasy equilibrium between them and their environment. Tutor work isolates these mechanisms and shows their debilitating effect. For example, a pupil in the second year predicts failure in mathematics. He also predicts that even the teacher who is 'all right' (high praise from a second year) will ask him questions he can't answer, and that this failure will make his friends laugh at him. On the basis of these predictions he may cope by misbehaviour, distracting the teacher's attention from his alleged mathematical inability. If he is lucky, the teacher will eject him from class, allowing him to escape a noxious situation with some prestige. I find pupils can derive benefit from simple case histories or decision-making exercises, appreciating the limitations of such ways of coping, and, in a supportive climate, adopt new behaviours.

8 *Tutorial activity must 'stretch' pupils by its intellectual demands and call on their imagination*

Example Fifth-year pupils need to think about adjustment to work in depth. One topic might be conflicts between the generations and antagonistic standpoints. A basic situation is presented.
'You have gained a technical apprenticeship. The first week consisted of a high-powered induction course conducted by the personnel department. It included guidance on promotion possibilities, safety procedures and many other matters which interested you. Your basic on-the-job training, however, consists of learning from a skilled worker. When you meet him, he says, "Now lad, I've been with this firm thirty years, man and boy. Don't take any notice of that lot up in the office, they don't know what they are talking about. Just let me catch you doing any of that, and you'll be for it!" But you've seen the point of the induction course and know the personnel department evaluate your progress. How do you cope?'

Simple situations promote deep thought if they are relevant, and tutors sharpen pupils' understanding of their import, e.g. 'Four of you are at the disco. You have been friends for a number of years. Towards the end of the evening, although you have all enjoyed yourself, three of you notice that one hasn't danced all the evening. You try to make him. Have you the right to make him?'

Exploration of the limits to membership of a group, the right of a group to foist an identity on its members, and whether the attractiveness of a group implies blind obedience will often emerge. The pupils can then relate their observations to their current experiences.

Trainers Tutorial activities must lead to cognitive gains. The raising of questions and the sharpening of judgemental, decision-making and problem-solving skills provide legitimacy for pastoral care as a developmental activity. Pupils, as much as tutors, should be able to say *why* they are tackling a topic, *what* they are learning, and *how* they will use it.

The construction of tutorial activities by heads of year/house

A trial unit

Participants list topics which they feel are relevant to a particular year. From this they select 4–6 topics which interest them.

In planning the activities the structure of objectives, activity and application is used. Simplicity is emphasised.

A key element in this trial unit is the requirement that participants should explain and justify their activity to the training group.

When the unit has been developed, participants should test it out with a form themselves. Pupils should be invited to comment on each activity, making suggestions for its improvement.

Written comments could be invited. A session should be given to 'reporting back', sharing experiences.

Trainers may find a check-list makes a useful start on the evaluation, which can be undertaken in pairs. More will be achieved and any threat of exposure diminished.

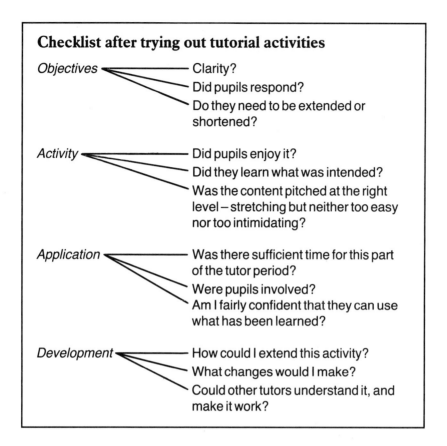

Checklist after trying out tutorial activities

Objectives — Clarity?
Did pupils respond?
Do they need to be extended or shortened?

Activity — Did pupils enjoy it?
Did they learn what was intended?
Was the content pitched at the right level – stretching but neither too easy nor too intimidating?

Application — Was there sufficient time for this part of the tutor period?
Were pupils involved?
Am I fairly confident that they can use what has been learned?

Development — How could I extend this activity?
What changes would I make?
Could other tutors understand it, and make it work?

A basic principle of training is that participants work in small groups as soon as possible. Experience taught me that even a well motivated group, if allowed to function too long as a total group, becomes the equivalent of a committee, a prescription for inaction. Patton (1982) described a committee as a 'group of the unwilling, picked by the unfit, to do the unnecessary.' Trainers could create this climate!

A climate of creativity and confidence probably requires a graduation of complexity in the activities on which heads of year/house work.

1 Simple questionnaire and paper/pencil activities.

2 Decision-making activities.

3 The use of tapes.

4 The introduction of role-play and other standpoint-taking activities.

5 More complex activities concerned with subject choice, study skills or adjustment to work and unemployment.

The danger of loss of control in the classroom, undue excitement or noise, too great demands on teachers for preparation and violation of pupils' privacy and expectations have to be kept in mind.

Questionnaires and paper/pencil activities

Pupils assiduously placing ticks in boxes have become a common sight in tutor time. But how much is this an advance on the previous state of affairs, when tutors marked and pupils did homework? Such activities are as good as the follow-up. In planning and developing materials we must be able to justify our actions – if a questionnaire is used, we must be prepared to state how pupils benefit from its use. There was a spate of work books after the war, and pupils loved filling in the missing words but, strangely enough, there seemed to be little transfer to other contexts. Paper and pencil activities could be as ineffective in pastoral care.

First, we can examine the first-year exercise on page 97.

Training exercise 1 Solving simple problems or 'Stopping myself getting in a sweat'

What to do

   a Here are some situations that bother us when we are in a new school, a time when we don't feel sure of ourselves. These little things can upset us, so it is a good idea to think about them before they happen. Then we can deal with them sensibly.

   b Fill in the answers in the boxes *after* you have talked about the problem in your small groups. Try to help each other find a sensible solution.

   c When you have done this, your teacher is going to talk about some of your suggestions. Compare your ideas with what the teacher suggests.

The tutor must handle this questionnaire in the way he feels suitable. He could, for example, select certain items. Simple key principles are present – pupil discussion precedes teacher suggestions, to avoid precipitating socially desirable responses. Next, why bother with this approach? Why not just tell them? Well, we usually do, but it doesn't seem to have much impact. More important learning may develop from this exercise, especially if the tutor carefully draws attention to such factors as the consequences

Problems which occur because I am new in school		
Problem	What I should do	a Who could I ask? b Where would I find them?
1 Getting lost when I sent on a message.		a b
2 Not knowing where to go for my next lesson.		a b
3 Losing my coat from the cloakroom.		a b
4 Feeling sick or cutting myself.		a b
5 Losing my dinner money or forgetting to pay it.		a b
6 Arriving late		a b

Problems about other people

1 Being bullied.		a b
2 Having my PE kit stolen.		a b
3 My parents want to visit school to talk to my teachers.		a b
4 Missing the bus after school.		a b
5 Returning to school after having been ill, or away.		a b

Other problems (One will make you laugh, until it happens!)

1 Having to take tablets regularly.		a b
2 Splitting my trousers.		a b
3 Breaking a window accidentally.		a b
4 Having to go to the dentist or doctor during school time.		a b

of certain actions, or ways of avoiding panic reactions, reinforcing his suggestions by simple cartoons.

Example 2 Help! I've lost my satchel
Basic situation   Form groups of four. In each group one of you has lost his satchel, which contains books, pens and PE kit. Having checked the various places where you could have left it without any success you feel anxious and upset. Your main thought is, 'What's Mum going to say?' You start talking about it to your friends.

The groups try to work out a sensible course of action. The first step in the follow-up is to ask two or three people from different groups to tell the form what they decided. The small groups then discuss these strategies. Finally, the tutor looks at tendencies to panic, blaming others for one's misfortunes, and sharpening the good ideas. Application can be stressed by getting the class to give ideas about similar situations, e.g.

1 Having difficulty in interpreting the timetable.

2 Lending a pen to another pupil, later finding that your attempts to get him to return it result in bullying on his part.

These simple materials reflect the concerns of pupils in the first two years. Our failure to register with them that we appreciate their existence and can help them cope, is to facilitate dissociation from school. Pupils must be secure, and security comes from knowing how to tackle situations.

Example 3 Bullying
Objectives   To explore reactions to a minor bullying situation, and to allow discussion of alternative ways of coping. (This situation could be put on tape. There is no reason why it should be restricted to paper presentation.)

Situation   Before school starts in the morning, Brian proudly shows off his new football boots to friends. Two third-year boys are watching and are obviously making remarks about them. They are no teachers around. Then the third-year boys push their way into the group, snatch Brian's boots and run off.
Brian's reaction:

1 He runs after them, and asks them to give the boots back. They refuse. Brian gets very upset and tries to grab them. When he fails to do so, they laugh at him. He begins to cry, so they call him names. The third-form boys throw his boots away, blocking his path and pushing him about as he tries to reach them. Eventually, he runs away, crying, to his friends.

2 He asks them politely for his boots. When they refuse to give them, he shrugs his shoulders, turns back to his friends and goes on talking, pretending not to care. The third-year boys return, trying to provoke Brian, who takes no notice. They soon get bored, throw the boots away with a rude remark and go off. Brian then collects his new boots and puts them in his satchel.

Application Discussion is usually intense. Form tutors will not only look at refusing to give practical jokers their pay off, but at loss of face. Exploration of the impact on friends of an inadequate response to this type of situation is important. Friends can be embarrassed and tensions can enter the friendship.

Questionnaires There is nothing wrong in questionnaires as such; the fault lies in over-use, inadequate content and failure to develop the implications. We should be cautious about questions about families and family matters. Parents resent it and pupils can find these questions intimidating or impertinent. A lack of sensitivity is displayed to likely reactions. We must know that some parents train their children to be evasive in answering questions about home. Even if pupils answer them, they give socially desirable, rather than genuine replies. What, therefore, is the point in activating such attitudes and responses? The use of questionnaires is to be carefully considered, therefore let us look at this one taken from Hamblin *Guidance: 16–19* (1983).

Study difficulties: a brief check-list

		Like me	Not like me
1	Find it difficult to get started on my homework at night.	☐	☐
2	Get bored quickly in lessons.	☐	☐
3	Don't know how to make good notes.	☐	☐
4	Worry about making mistakes.	☐	☐
5	Can't take in what some teachers say.	☐	☐
6	Put off revising for exams.	☐	☐
7	Read rather slowly.	☐	☐
8	Often seem to forget things I need to bring to school.	☐	☐
9	Rarely test myself when I have finished reading.	☐	☐

---

10 I often don't answer examination questions ☐ ☐
    in the way the teachers want.

11 Find it hard to remember what I have read. ☐ ☐

12 I don't make a revision timetable. I revise ☐ ☐
    when I feel like it.

13 I never seem to have enough time to finish ☐ ☐
    an essay.

14 Teachers say I go off target and don't put ☐ ☐
    down the key points in essays.

15 If I meet a difficult bit when reading, I skip ☐ ☐
    over it.

16 Can't make my books look neat and ☐ ☐
    attractive.

Pupils could merely fill it in, with the implicit question being, 'So what?'. Follow-up exercises would be important, e.g.

1 Select the three things that seem to cause you most difficulty. Now in groups of three, discuss whether you want to change them and how you would attempt it. If you don't want to change them, can you explain why?

2 Writing a self-report on oneself as a learner. One asks pupils to write about their strengths and weaknesses as a learner, writing as if they were someone else – somebody who knows them better than even their best friend does. They are asked to begin in the third person. 'Sue's strengths are' or 'The interesting thing about John as a learner is . . .'

3 Information could be quickly gained about the whole form. Tutors could select five or six relevant items, getting the endorsements by a show of hands and then presenting the percentages on the blackboard. Interesting discussion follows. (This activity opens the way for more work on looking at the form as a whole, and discussing the significance of existing attitudes and patterns of behaviour in a mature way.)

4 Helping activities can be developed. Consider items 9 and 16. The tutor may introduce the topic of diagrams and give some training in their use, but then stimulate peer help as a response to item 16. After examining the factors leading to attractive work, friends work together to achieve better results.

5 The analysis of trends in the class may be followed by a series of decision-making exercises, coping with the issues involved.

Trainers A warning: the currently popular open-ended sentence technique is not appropriate for tutor work unless it is related clearly to a topic such as study skills. The more general approach should be restricted to individual counselling and, even then, the procedures suggested in Hamblin (1974) should be followed. Inappropriate use of this technique can create anxiety and embarrassment in vulnerable and sensitive pupils.

Decision making

Trainers Decision-making activities need not be complex, but we should understand the underlying issues. Take this simple example which can be very productive.

Basic situation It is Thursday night. For homework you have two subjects to do: one you like a lot, and are good at; the other is one you don't like very much, and are not good at. Which will you do first? Why?

This simple situation requires us to be aware of many things. First, there will be no right answer. Even in such apparently simple matters, truth is conditional, propositional and relative. Personality will influence reactions, therefore we have to see that anxiety will play a part. Anxious pupils often feel they must do the 'bad' subject first because 'it will be on their mind'. This means examination of the likely consequences of their strategy. Some equivalent to Hullian stimulus generalisation could occur, i.e. the good subject becomes contaminated by negative feelings because the pupil is frustrated and tired when he approaches it. Then we get the beginning of deterioration in the good subject. Underfunctioning can begin in this unsuspected way. A more general strategy for coping, involving form tutor, subject teacher and possibly parent, will have to be worked out. No recipes are possible, pupils have to think it out for themselves.

The analysis could be taken further, but it would be wearisome. Trainers must help the year/house heads sharpen their model of decision-making, demonstrating the need to focus primarily on one issue, e.g. source of influence, in the activity. Reflection and follow-up are at least as important as the experience.

Many pupils face weighty decisions with a limited repertoire of responses – often just blind avoidance or impulse. The elements to which we pay attention are:

1 The preference for risky decisions, founded in the desire for excitement, maintaining prestige with friends or ignorance of

the risk involved. This lack of prudentiality may be supported by neighbourhood and family influences.

2 The probability of outcomes, and the satisfaction they yield – both may have to be considered subjectively as well as objectively.

3 Perceived and actual desirability of courses of action, reflecting the values and preferences of the individual.

4 The preference for immediate or deferred gratification. Note that unemployment may be eroding the importance of long-term gratification in those for whom it was formerly a prime motivator.

5 Knowledge of the possibilities.

One aspect of adolescent development is the crystallisation of a style of decision-making. Some pupils already display undue caution or the tendency to make instant decisions based on minimal evidence. Personality operates within a specific set of conditions, however, and we must never forget that decisions are also shaped by specific situations. Decisions made by the same person vary with the degree of visibility and responsibility. Where anonymity is possible and accountability a group affair, even the virtuous kick over the traces.

Within a group in the later years of adolescence, teachers have to cope with those who emphasise the outcome without thought of costs and probabilities. A high level of risk is incorporated, but not detected. Such pupils are not necessarily unrealistic, but may be immature. Contrasting with them, will be those who appear to be motivated by anxiety, fear of creating adverse impressions in authority figures or fear of failure. Others will take a more balanced approach, evaluating, and weighing factors against one another.

Activities should call attention to:

1 The danger of immediate response based on minimal information and automatic allocation to a category.

2 Undue procrastination, which can hide the hope that the need to make the decision will go away if the individual waits long enough.

3 The source of influence – teachers, friends, parents or the mass media. Pupils have to learn to ask, 'Who makes up my mind? Do I delude myself when I say that *I* made the decision?'

Two dangers are ever present. First, pupils remain unaware of the obvious. They discuss, perhaps agonise, searching diligently for information to help them decide to take the available job or stay on at school. Then, a chance remark from a valued source or an emotive pressure triggers action in which all preceding information is forgotten. Second, *trainers must be alert to the possibility that, in giving the experience, we lose the meaning – an ever-present danger in experiential methods.* The elementary framework below provides some safeguard.

Decision-making exercises

1 What do I intend the pupils to learn?
2 Which aspect of decision-making is to be stressed?
3 In what situation, meaningful to the pupils, can I imbed the learning?
4 Does this situation contain possibilities that pupils will learn things irrelevant, or in opposition, to my intent?
5 What type of follow-up will clarify the learning and highlight the principles and values behind the decision-making?

Training exercise 2
Heads of year should construct a series of three or four linked decision-making exercises centred on a theme of interest to the age group, e.g. disco, 'outward bound' emergencies, planning a holiday, or vocational choice. Continuity of this kind evokes more interest and allows emphasis to be placed systematically on one component of decision-making. At the end of the series, tutors can summarise, and reinforce what has been learned. The simplicity of this approach is shown by the example below, which is the second activity in a series of four, entitled *The Paper Round*.

The Paper Round

Your interview has been successful, and you got the job. You dislike dogs very much, indeed you will normally do anything to avoid them. You are being shown the round by the person who is giving it up. You come to a house where there is a very fierce dog, yet papers have to be delivered. The garden is large, and it is quite a long walk from the gate to the front door.

You really want the job, but you hate that dog. How will you cope?

Discussion will focus on the *'approach–avoid'* conflict, possibly moving to the need to face the fact that, if we want something, we may have to do something we find unpleasant. Moralising is to be avoided in the follow-up – imaginative discussion of the unpleasant things that have to be faced in achievement in sport, pop music or science will be productive. The links with career and subject choice can be mentioned. (*The Paper Round* is often used in the last term of the second year to sharpen decision-making skills, which will be applied in the third-year subject choice programme.)

Stop – Wait – Go is an effective activity devised by Bradbury (1981).

Stop – Wait – Go

This is a decision-making game which can be adapted to various topics for discussion and to different levels of ability and age-grouping. It was originally developed for encouraging independent thought and decision-making in a situation where two close friends seemed seldom to 'think apart' and who normally came to a decision made by the dominant member of the pair.

The objectives of the game
Structure, presentation and objectives are important:

1 to encourage independent thought and decision-making, which can be recorded on paper for the discussion which follows;

2 by use of familiar traffic light signals, to catch interest and to give structure to the game, so that it may be played purposefully and in logical sequence;

3 to provide the opportunity for individual, personal decisions to be made, as well as presenting alternatives for choice;

4 in the discussion to view the possible alternatives of choice, to evaluate them, and to see if there is general agreement, or difference, in the group.

Attractive presentation stimulates effort as well as interest. It is also important to note that this game can be a *quiet* as well as a *spoken* activity. In part it can be completely *silent*.

The game
20–25 minutes. Groups of four recommended. The game can be played between two people, or involve an entire class when sub-groups join together to present their decisions and evaluations.

The STOP card presents a situation in which a decision has to be made. The WAIT card gives the chance to think and consider a choice of possible courses of action. Apart from the selection provided, there is a chance to make an independent decision. The GO card involves the written activity, in which each individual records his or her decision privately. Each of these stages can be carried out silently.

The discussion which follows is based upon decisions which are written down. This enables the discussion to keep on target. Small group discussion precedes the class discussion.

One situation is provided on a sample STOP card. Three alternative solutions and a space for own choice are provided on a sample WAIT card.

The following may be useful in providing material for three situations related to the topic of truancy. There are other possible 'starters'.

Stop situation

Your dog is ill and no-one is at home during the day to look after it. You are worried and find it difficult to concentrate at school, although your parents say the dog will be all right.

Wait

Do you:

1 Stay at home with the dog, without telling your parents?
2 Get your register marks and then go home, twice during the day?
3 Seek some advice on what to do from friends?
4 Own choice?

Stop situation

Mum has asked you to look after your baby sister for the afternoon. She has an appointment to keep. Next day you go to school, without a note.

Wait

Do you:

1 Say you felt unwell, and promise to bring a note?
2 Tell your mother, if you get into trouble, you will come home?
3 If Mum says she is too busy to write a note about your absence and you know you must have one, forge a note?
4 Own choice?

Stop situation

In a rash moment you truanted. You hear a check is going on.

Wait

Do you:

1 Hope the fuss will die down and wait, hoping you will not be found out.
2 Invent an illness to cover the reason for your absence?

3 Go and own up, although you may risk getting your friends into trouble?

4 Own choice?

This activity need not be confined to the card method described. Each phase can be put on a separate sheet of a flip chart, the tutor revealing each traffic light in sequence. Six linked situations could be contained in a single flip chart. Pupils taking art could prepare the flip chart in an attractive way. Responses which are socially desirable should not be included in the possibilities given as they would kill discussion and build in the type of dishonesty referred to by Sugarman (1974).

Training exercise 3
Objective To orientate heads of year or house towards decision-making in the field of social demands, dilemmas and skills.

The framework is given by the social skills scale set out below. This can be used in a number of different ways.

1 It can be given to fourth- or fifth-year tutor groups, so that pupils can select what they think is of prime importance. Heads of year/house then develop activities and test them out.

2 Heads of year/house can work directly with a tutor group, getting pupils to devise activities in small groups. They can then take the ideas away and build on them.

3 Items 6, 11, 13, 14, 18, 19, 21, 24, 26, 28 and 29, provide a basis for selecting situations for a unit on this theme.

Social skills scale

What this scale is about

As we grow up, the social skills which allow us to work constructively with other people become more important. There is nothing mysterious about getting along with people – although we may be unaware of what we do which makes it unnecessarily difficult. Once we have identified the causes we can do something about them. This simple scale will help you to do this. The statements are made by people of your own age or older than you. They should start you thinking.

What you do

1 There are three columns headed:

LIKE ME   NOT LIKE ME   DON'T KNOW

Read each statement carefully and then place a tick in whichever box which you feel is the right one for you.

2 When you have finished the scale, you will be given the opportunity to discuss the results with either your teacher or friends.

	Like me	Not like me	Don't know
1 I try to avoid reading aloud in class.			
2 I can't help saying the wrong thing and upsetting people.			
3 People always seem to be looking at me when I walk down the street.			
4 I'm not very good at telling jokes and making people laugh.			
5 I find it hard to talk to adults outside the family.			
6 I find it hard to decide to go out or stay in when my friends call for me.			
7 I tell my classmates about the things I have and what I can do.			
8 I don't like being asked to do something in front of other people.			
9 I don't seem able to make friends of my own age easily.			
10 I often agree with people, although I think they are saying something stupid.			
11 I find it hard to go to a party where I don't know many people.			

12 When I start to say something to adults it often comes out differently from the way I wanted it to.			
13 Ringing up someone I don't know very well is something I dislike.			
14 When I am embarrassed I cover it up by getting angry.			
15 I avoid looking at people when I talk to them.			
16 I sulk when things don't go my way in a group of friends.			
17 I worry a great deal if I am going to have an interview with a teacher and don't know what it is about.			
18 I find it hard to start a conversation if I don't know the other person well.			
19 I get confused when somebody unexpectedly asks me for directions to a place, even when I know it well.			
20 I rarely seem to praise my friends.			
21 When I am unsure of myself I tend to boast.			
22 I don't seem able to answer questions very well.			
23 Mixing with people at the youth club seems hard for me.			
24 I am afraid I will let the team down if I play and that they will be annoyed with me.			
25 I find it hard to explain to adults what I want.			
26 Teasing and joking by my classmates often upsets me.			

27 I stay as far away from people as I can when I talk to them.			
28 When somebody says I have done something that I have not, I get very angry with them.			
29 I am always telling my friends what they ought to do.			

Getting on with the job

Now write down the *two* things you would like to tackle in the near future.

1.

2.

Many items could lead into a sequence of activities, e.g. 13 could develop into dealing with different telephone situations – receiving a complex message, or telephoning your youth leader to explain that, although you promised to play in the match, you can't make it.

Trainers
1 It will be particularly important to encourage those concerned with the fourth and fifth years to involve pupils by:
getting their ideas about topics and activities;
evaluating and making suggestions for improvement of activities.
2 Decision-making for these years must realistically recognise that often the most pressing feelings are about '*avoid/avoid*' conflicts. This is illustrated in the cartoon on page 111. Pupils will produce the ideas for decision-making related to this dilemma themselves.

Training exercise 4
Objective To stimulate decision-making in the field of subject choice, career preparation and unemployment.

DILEMMA!

Trainers Hamblin: *Guidance: 16–19* (1983) will provide material that will help you. Decisions about job attributes and values are essential. One technique involving decision-making is given below.

A list of qualities associated with job satisfaction is written on the board, e.g. good pay, promotion opportunities, pleasant workmates, responsibility. The topic is introduced and a ladder is drawn on the board. Comments are invited about which qualities are crucial and which are unimportant. The tutor says that pupils could be giving him the answers they think he wants, rather than what they really think. Therefore he wants them to talk about the qualities before filling in the ladder individually. After 10–15 minutes' discussion in triads, each pupil makes his own decision about priority by filling in his own ladder. General class discussion follows.

The important technique of using a peer judge should be introduced. Each small group should include a peer, chosen by them, to evaluate their decision. Preliminary briefings or a checklist provide sufficient guidance. I find that the peer judges are responsible, and that the small groups listen to them attentively.

The number of qualities should not exceed twelve. Follow-up work can look at the way ranking can be tackled. The extremes can be allocated first, then the middle items thought about in an effort to resolve uncertainty. Pupils are often unclear about the method of coping. Social desirability can also be examined. It is an aspect of authority relationships that is neglected.

A few examples of typical activities follow.

Example 1

Jim works in a large discount store which has its own repair department. His last job – a washing machine – has been collected by the customer. As he clears his bench at the end of the day, his eye falls on a brass screw. He realises he has not connected the earth wire to the frame of the machine. Nothing may happen, but there is the possibility that one day somebody will get a serious shock. Decide what he should do.

Here are some possibilities, but there are others.

1 Take a chance and say nothing.

2 Go round to the owner's house and fix the machine tonight.

3 Telephone to warn him.

4 Explain it to the boss, asking his advice.

Example 2

You are a secretary in a small firm. Business, however, is growing, largely due to your boss's initiative. He was getting along nicely, negotiating part of an important contract by telephone when he was disconnected by you. It was carelessness. You know he was very angry, but neither of you has spoken about it because it was lunchtime.

In the afternoon, another client has arrived, but he has no appointment. He claims that he made an appointment by telephone and that you must have forgotten to enter it into the diary. Your boss is busy. You are quite certain no appointment was made.

How would you cope? Discuss in groups of four – look closely at what is likely to happen. Share your decision with another small group.

Example 3

Imagine that the numbers of those taking the O-level French course are restricted. Your head of year has said that only one of your group of four can take it, but that you can make the decision for yourselves who it will be. The other three will have to take German.

The basic case for each pupil is given below. After reading them, work in groups of three or four to come to a decision. You must be able to justify your decision to the member of the class who will question you. While the group is reaching a decision, the peer judge examines the information sheet, drawing up a list of questions. Tutor briefing will help the evaluators.

1 *Sue* wants to be a courier and recognises that she will need a second language in which she is really fluent. She is a bright girl, doing well in all her subjects, but the only language teacher she can get on with is the French teacher. She feels she will be unable to learn from the German teacher.

2 *Steve* is the son of an international business man who attends many conferences abroad. Steve feels he would like to work in the E.E.C. because he enjoys the trips he has made with his father when he was on business. His ambitions are clear and realistic. His progress in French has been good, but he doesn't get along very well in German.

3 *Alice* is now keen to take French because her widowed French grandmother is coming from the East Indies to live with the family. Alice is not very good at languages but wants to improve her French so that she does not feel left out. She hates German.

4 *Derek* doesn't know what he wants to do, but feels that he has the right to take French if he wants to – and he does! He goes on holiday to many countries with his parents and enjoys trying to make himself understood.

Role play and simple simulations

These activities often cause concern to tutors who invest them with an aura of mystery they do not deserve or see them as violating their beliefs about the nature of teaching. It is imperative that trainers should consult and enlist the aid of the drama specialist, if role play is to be used soundly in tutorial work.

First, let us be clear that role play is the mirror image of the importance given to the self picture in changing behaviour. The technique is based on the belief, supported by some experimental evidence (Berkowitz, 1980), that overt behaviour can influence attitudes. Moreno (1946) encouraged patients to undertake role play in order to gain insight into their own problems and to understand the perspectives of others. Studies gathered together by Elms (1969) amply demonstrate the complexity of the questions associated with the technique, and also the unresolved issues. Role play can delude the pupil into believing that reality is simpler and easier to modify than it is. It can be used unwittingly to make the pupil believe there is one right answer, so reducing the technique to a form of pleasant coercion into conformity. The enthusiasm for role play might have unsuspected links with our tendency to approve the amiable extrovert in the secondary school.

Triviality rather than actual harm is more likely to exist in tutor period role play. It will be helpful if trainers stress the following points.

1 Role play is a skill which has to be acquired by the pupil. Competence will develop slowly. For this reason, and because middle adolescence often brings a tortuous self-consciousness, it should be introduced in the first year.

2 It is most effective when incorporated into a supporting framework. At first, it should be brief. Two minutes is often sufficient. Simplicity is also important in the initial stages, not only in the topic, but in the number of role players. Partner work is the most rewarding introduction.

3 Role reversal is crucial, i.e. if the role play is concerned with a parent–child negotiation, each partner must play the parent in order to understand the perspective.

4 Preliminary stimulation of ideas is helpful, especially in the early stages. Pupils do not necessarily have ideas about a situation – they may have given it no thought. The pooling of ideas from which pupils can select gives structure without undue limitation because it usually triggers off their own ideas and interpretations.

5 Careful thought has to be given to the follow-up, if learning is not to remain implicit and probably unused.

Training exercise 1

Heads of year begin by developing a series of four-partner role-play exercises for a particular year group. The usual structure of objectives, preparatory discussion and follow-up is used. Simple suggestions are made below as the point of departure for the first attempt.

First year   Two friends are on the bus on the way to school. One says he has his birthday money with him, so why not drop off in town and spend it? The second says he prefers to go to school. The first responds by name-calling and saying that the second is showing

114

he isn't a real friend. The second wishes to stay friends but also intends to go to school.

(Pupils have to try to achieve a solution satisfactory to both.)

Second year Two pupils meet at break on Monday. Last week, one bragged about how well he was going to do in the soccer match on Saturday. Reality was very different. The other begins to send him up. The 'bragger' has to cope constructively.

(Pupils have to learn to deal with such self-imposed loss of face without making the situation worse.)

Third year Pupil stays out late without permission. Father gets anxious, but questions the pupil tersely. (Basically, when is concern communicated as distrust? This situation could be played twice, once with a positive outcome, the other with an unhelpful state of tension. Follow-up explores escalation of tensions and reactions to positional control, 'I'm your father', etc.)

Fourth year Two friends are talking. Both are achievement orientated, but one feels he made a mistake in choosing a particular subject at O-level – another might have been better. He blames the head of year/house, but is asking the friend for advice. (Objectives are to look at the tendency to blame others and to create awareness of the difficulties of advising someone.)

Fifth year A student has splashed out on tapes and records – now he asks a friend to lend money to finance a trip to hear a pop group, which the friend detests. The friendship is strong and lots of mutual support is given, but the potential lender has definite ideas about what is proper expenditure – and it isn't for going to hear this group, live! (Consideration of the criteria for lending is relevant, but also examination of the limits to imposition of one's tastes on others.)

Sixth year Two friends have just heard the latest unemployment figures, which are grim. One expresses anxiety, feeling cheated and wondering if it is worth striving to obtain a degree. The father of this student is a graduate, but has become redundant. The other feels he should pursue his intentions, but also feels that school does not do enough to prepare students for unemployment. (Searching discussion can occur of personality factors which shape reactions to such signals of future uncertainty, and of what the school can, should, and is able to do.)

Training exercise 2
Trainers should encourage the use of tapes as the basis for role play. Pupils taking drama produce excellent material with minimal guidance. The suggestions below could be developed by heads of year/house in various ways.

Situation 1: Leadership skills and relationships
The tape presents an emergency on Snowdon. Despite precautions, four of the party have got cut off. A blizzard – not forecast – develops. One of the party has sprained his ankle. It is clear that a night has to be spent on the mountain. The other three respect the fourth one's physical capabilities and trust him, therefore they allocate him the leader role. How will he cope?

Trainers Role play can be developed in a number of different ways.

1 Pupils can discuss what happens. Scripts could be written or acted to the class.

2 Discussion of the qualities needed for leadership in this situation of physical emergency will produce new insights.

3 The first taped situation may be followed by one where a youth club is producing a Christmas play. Things have become tense, accusations are thrown around and the main player, together with a group of friends, is about to walk out. The producer has to cope. What is the best way?

Procedures are the same as above, but a fresh dimension is added by looking at:

a The difference between task leadership (getting things done) and social-emotional leadership (enhancing positive relationships within a group).

b The different skills needed by the leader in the two situations.

Training exercise 3
Trainers Extensive and elaborate preparation for role play is impossible for the tutor. Pupils can be involved in tutor group projects. Role play can be built into activities associated with that

major concern – employment. Parents often become interested in these projects, providing valuable support. The following material was produced and tested by my students, and I have found it extremely useful.

Work on your doorstep

Form groups of three or four.

1 Divide up a map of your local area, so that there are the same number of sections on the map as there are groups. Each group studies one section in detail.

2 Make a large-scale drawing of your section of the map.

3 Plot on the map any places of work, e.g. factories, offices, shops, banks, schools, farms, hospitals, surgeries, public services, gardens, etc.

4 Obtain an estimate of the number of people employed in your area – don't forget the milkmen, postmen, window cleaner, etc.

5 Try to find out how many school-leavers are taken on in your area each year. The local paper may be useful here, but don't forget employment agencies and personal contact with employers.

6 For which type of work are there the most vacancies for school leavers?

7 Present your findings on the map and in the form of histograms.

Project on researching occupations: Choose an occupation!

1 Choose an occupation you think you would really like.
   ....

2 Name the occupation that you think you are most likely to follow when you leave school. (This may or may not be the same as 1.)
   ....

3 Form groups of 3–4 individuals who have chosen the same or similar occupations, so that each group is researching a different occupation.

117

4 Discuss briefly in your groups what you think this occupation involves – it may be interesting to make notes at this point, to be compared with the information you find out during the course of the project.

5 Now, as a group, find out as much as you can about the occupation you have chosen.
Possible methods: writing for information
        newspaper articles
        advertisements for jobs
        careers room at school
        local careers office
        interviews
        job centre
        radio and television

6 Use the check-list opposite to record your progress.

7 Present the information you have gathered in an attractive form, in a folder.

8 Devise an imaginative method of reporting your findings to the rest of the class. The report should last between 5–10 minutes.

These activities have often led into small group simulations presented to the whole class, e.g in an investigation of a near-by building site, scenes were written which involved interaction between plumbers, carpenters and electricians about the sequence of jobs and the•difficulties associated with bad weather. Conflicts between the 'brickie' and his hod-carrier, who was not on piece rates, were brought out. The functions of the clerk of work were shown. Involvement of the class was obtained by the group teacher's stopping the simulation and setting a problem or topic for discussion, 'Do you think he should have done that?' or 'What do you think will happen now?' Audience participation, useful in theatre, is crucial in such use of simulation, if it is not to degenerate into boredom.

Pupils take their tape-recorders and interview workers, making their interviews the basis of simple simulations. The same has been done with the elderly or handicapped and insight gained into their problems. Heads of year/house, in conjunction with relevant departments, will find such projects make sense of the claim that pupils should be involved in their own guidance.

Check-list

Information	Tick when found
Qualifications needed	
Personal qualities desirable	
Number of employees men/women	
Working conditions:	
Pay	
Overtime/bonuses/discounts	
Hours worked	
Shift work/weekends	
Pension	
Uniform or overalls	
Age on entry	
Holidays	
Canteen facilities	
Rest room	
Games room/sports club	
Medical facilities	
Transport: bus services, car parks	
Locality	
Training programmes	
Promotion prospects	
Security	
Vacancies	

Case studies Older pupils benefit from the case study technique. As teachers, we possess a fund of experience which we could put at the disposal of our pupils more effectively. We have more to give than we realise and, despite our doubts, pupils want it, provided we put it into an acceptable form. Case histories are well received because they neither threaten nor moralise. A simple example dealing with study problems is given overleaf.

Study skills

In the following case-study you will find some of the difficulties encountered by pupils during the course of their O-level work.

Objectives

1 To alert pupils to the difficulties encountered at O-level.
2 To help them develop the skills needed to cope with these difficulties and so achieve success.
3 To develop in them a positive and practical approach to fifth-form work.

Case study: Terry

Terry, a fifth-form boy, is the oldest of a working-class family of five children, the youngest of whom is ten months old. His father is a miner in the local colliery and his two younger sisters are in forms 3 and 1 of the school he attends. He has a younger brother in primary school. The family lives in a terraced house on a very busy street. Terry's father has had a hard life and he is insistent that all his children are going into white-collar jobs. Terry appreciates his father's efforts to support him but sometimes wishes he were left alone, especially when the pressure of work builds up in school. Besides, he is not a strong boy and suffers from bouts of asthma.

His teachers' comments on his school reports have usually been positive with high marks for effort, but frequent remarks like 'has difficulty in organising his ideas', 'often fails to complete home-work', 'complains that he cannot get his reading done', 'writing very poor' are giving him cause for concern. Besides, his father tried to be helpful by giving him a lecture after each report on the need to organise himself, saying that he wouldn't survive for a day underground. Terry is quite good at maths, presenting his work neatly.

Terry is taking English, history, geography, maths, physics and chemistry at O-level and he is taking CSE in art and technical drawing. He enjoys maths and could spend hours working on a problem. He finds he always does maths, physics and chemistry homework first every night and works right through until the 9 o'clock news and supper. If he has work to do in the other subjects he does it after supper. He often falls asleep while reading and his mother insists that he goes to bed, otherwise he will not be able to get up in time to catch the 8 o'clock school bus next morning. He has difficulty in recalling what he reads and finds that the notes he makes are inadequate when it comes to revision.

Terry is afraid of exams. Teachers say he should do better. He knows himself he could do better but he wishes someone would show him how. His writing becomes illegible after the first page of the answer sheet and he is often left with a whole question to do with only ten minutes left. Last summer he panicked in the end-of-term tests and got only a bare pass in Maths and English.

Now note down the areas in Terry's work which need attention. Special care should be given to the home situation, the attitude of his father and the teachers' attitudes. In what order do you think they need to be dealt with?
Use the spaces below.

What do you think is Terry's basic difficulty?

Reading is a key element in learning. At O-level it is important that the pupils should be able to read with a considerable degree of speed and accuracy.
In what ways can Terry improve his reading ability?
How do you think he will put your ideas into practice?

Note Have you thought about seeking extra information on a topic, improving the ability to recall the substance of what has been read, use of index cards, summaries, use of coloured pens, alphabetical lists of ideas, structural diagrams?

Terry finds it difficult to recall what he has read. Can you suggest how he can help himself?

His tackling of examinations suggests an inefficient use of time. How best can he use the time available to him?

   a In school
   b At home
   c Immediately before examinations
   d During examinations

Can he do something about his handwriting?

Note-taking, both in school and at home, is an important aid to recall when done efficiently. Can you help Terry to develop better note-taking skills?

Remember that

1 Ideas relevant to a topic can differ in importance.

2 Notes ought to be a stimulant to further thought.

3 Notes may not always express accurately what has been read.

4 Notes can be used to indicate what has not been said in the text.

5 Notes can be revised.

Another equivalent of the case history is given below.

In pairs

1 Discuss how the pupils 'avoided' the challenge of the examinations.

2 Why do you think they did this?

3 Talk about what may stop you doing your best in the next examinations.

4 Work out with your partner:
   a The steps you will take to deal with the problems.
   b Your target for the next seven days.
   c How you will help your partner.

A final note on simulations and games

Trainers should remind themselves that training is a continuous process, not a once-for-all event. Skills will be acquired slowly, and too early an insistence on more elaborate games and simulations will be counter-productive. Four to six years may be required to reach the optimum level of skills, and during that period adaptations will have to take place. The work by Taylor and Walford (1972) and Davison and Gordon (1978) will be of great help, as will the discussion by Watkins (1981).

Summary

1 Immediate attention is given to the difficulties inherent in leading a team of tutors. The developmental aspects of adolescence which form both the context and focus of pastoral activity are discussed.

2 A brief training programme for heads of year or house is introduced. It is seen as a point of departure rather than a final product. Attention is paid to:

   – the construction of activities and materials for tutor work;

   – the necessity to graduate the demands for new skills and to build tutors' confidence;

   – decision-making as a key part of tutorial work.

3 The principles of tutorial work are stated and illustrated by simple activities. Practical expression of the limits imposed on teachers by pressure and lack of skill is present.

4: The skills of head of year and house: training and leading a team of tutors

The context of the task

Concentration on the alleged opposition of colleagues to the tutorial task, conceals the fact that uncertainty, questioning the legitimacy of pastoral work and ignorance of its nature have to be met by a carefully planned strategy for enlightenment. Middle managers in pastoral care feel devalued – perhaps inferior – yet perpetuate this state by failing to work together as a team engaged in an educative endeavour. Taking the role of revelatory prophet or adopting heroic stances invite rejection, yet there must be a steady attempt to refute misconceptions and crippling expectations which stem from the limited disciplinary and expedient perception of pastoral work. Common sense and adaptive strategies are required, with the determination to work on the training consistently for three to four years. Like other high achievers, heads of year or house have to learn to defer gratification!

Antagonism may be partially the product of resistance stimulated in an over-stretched and stressed profession by any type of change. This has obvious implications for the way we code our messages. Sensitivity dictates that the trainer appreciates the significance of his colleagues' rigid ideas of order, relationships between teachers and pupils, and beliefs about which teaching methods work. Credibility will be diminished immediately by making extreme statements which increase resistance and polarise attitudes.

Trainers must allow expression of anxieties and opposition rather than stifle them. Why? Resistances which have an emotive base lose their compulsive hold when rationally examined. A more constructive climate is promoted in which cooperation can develop as a result of teachers feeling better because they can speak and are *listened to.* The most anti-growth situation is where people believe, rightly or wrongly, that they cannot express criticism about pastoral care. Wholesale adoption of programmes and compulsion without negotiation, leads to ritual performance and eventually abandonment of tutorial activity.

Adaptation to what exists differs from the tendency to focus almost exclusively on opposition. After creating the climate for negotiation, heads of year or house focus on strengths in the tutor team, showing what can be achieved. We do not give the unthinking malcontents an importance they do not deserve. We should be realistic and acknowledge that some individuals predict that, if they can delay long enough, pastoral care will go away or that the senior staff and middle management will give up the effort.

Leading a team of tutors and training does *not* imply a single head of year or house working alone with a training group. It should be a cooperative effort. Division of labour then occurs within the group of heads of year/house and deputy head. Strategies of training are based on answers to the questions:
- Who does what?
- What are the strengths of individuals?

In developing training skills, I found that some individuals can quickly create an atmosphere of warmth and induce cooperation, whilst others are better at the technicalities. Contrast of personalities and approaches can be productive, but meticulous planning and timing is crucial.

Negotiation plays a part even within a training group of heads of year or house. We negotiate:

Tasks

What training tasks will be attempted? On which areas is effort to be concentrated? Is a particular sequence of training (e.g. study skills, followed by decision-making) more likely to be productive with a particular group?

Time

What time can be invested by heads of year or house? What demands can be made for time on those already concerned by the demands of after-school meetings? Good planning involves realistic assessment of what can be covered in a given amount of time. Breach of time limits may convey an impression of incompetence.

Audience

Leading a team of tutors does not mean that every tutor will be present if training occurs outside the normal hours of school. The idea of training as a long-term process allows this. The audience should not be too large, allowing trainers to gain confidence and reinforce the tutors' strengths. The cynical and uncommitted may be more susceptible to the indirect influence of those who attended the training and found it profitable. Rather than try to overcome resistance, it is crucial that the trainers present models of competence.

Topics

Teachers tend to display a tendency to wait to be told what to do and to expect simple prescriptions, evidenced by the frequent question, 'What do I do if . . .?' Negotiation can occur, but it is wise to have a programme based on themes which people will probably welcome because they are concerned with recognised problems.

Presentation skills Heads of year or house need to emulate the proficiency found in presentations given in industry or other organisations. This is based on understanding of persuasive communication. The following points have proved important in developing training skills.

Variation

Vary the methods, carrying the tutors along with you. Move from the visual to the verbal – the latter can include recorded comments, brief interview or dramatic excerpts, e.g. parent/form teacher confrontation. This includes using males and females as contrasts – differences in pitch, warmth and rate of speech can provide positive stimulation.

Structure

Have a number of focal points which provide the basic structure for the training session. In planning, recall the importance of primacy and recency: both are associated with retention, but initial statements shape later reactions and interpretation of activities. The final activities are equally important. A concise recapitulation is essential. Tutors must have the reward of feeling they have learned something useful and not wasted precious time.

Structure means using different ways of giving and reinforcing information, e.g.
- use of the flip chart with diagrams;
- gradually building a summary by adding points to a transparency as the presentation proceeds;
- audio-tape or video-tape illustrations.

Involvement

As soon as possible, get the tutors to do something. This does not mean vague discussion, but a precise task, e.g.
- planning a tutor period activity;
- discussing a set problem, working out ways of coping.

Beware loose discussion, which can reinforce prejudices or encourage negative pairing, where two individuals combine to reject what is happening or provide mutual support for destructiveness. Movement between total group discussion is essential if problems are to be attacked vigorously.

Fears

Trainers will have to look at tutors' fears about the use of small groups. Questions must be anticipated about:

1 The composition of groups. Anxiety will be expressed about those students who cannot write or who are less intelligent, as if these difficulties existed only in tutor groups. The best response is to stress the way these pupils gain from discussion about concrete situations or from decision-making activities.

2 Tutors sometimes behave as if the composition of groups is immutable, due to unfamiliarity with methods. Stress the variations possible:
- same-sex groups versus mixed groups;
- friendship-based groups;
- tutor-selected groups;
- informally selected groups which are changed after 3 or 4 weeks to prevent habitual patterns of interaction occurring, i.e. completely new groups are formed 3 or 4 times a term.
Trainers should stress that pupils were accustomed to working in small groups in most primary schools.

Preparation for introduction of activities

Self-analysis provides some safeguard against ineffectiveness as trainers. Heads of year or house have found the simple analysis below helpful, provided that it is followed up by honest discussion. If openness cannot be achieved in the training group, problems will be evaded, to the detriment of all.

Training situations where I might feel embarrassed.	My strong areas of competence as a trainer.
Training elements where I feel especially uncertain.	Supports available within the school or authority which I could use.

Rehearsal of ways of dealing with difficulties is sensible. Many of us who wish to innovate allow ourselves to be put off too easily. Negative individuals rely on the innovator being non-plussed by simple-minded disapproval or rejection which brooks no discussion. Insulation against change is unfortunately achieved by such measures.

Activity

a Discuss with a partner how you would cope with the responses set out below:
   i I'm paid to teach!
   ii I'm not here to molly-coddle them.
   iii We are doing it already.
   iv Are you saying pastoral care will solve all our discipline problems?

b Strategies should avoid aggressiveness. Where possible, take the wind out of their sails by agreeing, as the first step in helping them look at their position. Statement *i* would lead into a discussion of good teaching and creating a productive climate for learning. Statement *ii* brings one to look at giving pupils the skills of coping. Statement *iii* would be dealt with by getting them to explore what they *are* doing. You gradually make suggestions for extension. Statement *iv* could be reflected back and they should be asked if they believe that anything

128

> could achieve this. Reality is then brought in. An appeal to common-sense can be made with humour, e.g. 'I'm sure you don't really believe I'm so foolish . . .'

> *c* Now make a list of remarks that could disorganise you. In small groups share ideas about constructive replies or responses which divest the remarks of their sting.

Presenting your material constructively is helped by:

1 *Using a step-by-step approach.* Don't overwhelm. Choose an activity which you think will interest participants, but which does not make too many demands, e.g. *Stop – Wait – Go,* described earlier.

2 *Anticipating difficulties or objections by introducing them yourself in a weakened form,* then refuting them. You can make use of the typical approach of teachers: 'What happens if . . .' which makes you appear down-to-earth and increases your credibility. You should try to reinforce the idea that there is no single right answer. Beware giving an easy response to requests for advice without further exploration of the beliefs of the questioner about what works in such situations. A hasty reply invites the rejoinder, 'But that wouldn't work for me!'

3 *Collecting tutors' ideas for activities.* Take one and show how it could be turned into a tutorial activity. Then ask tutors to work in pairs, developing the other ideas in the same way.

4 *Discussing how pupils' resistances can be coped with.* Discussion of pupils who say, 'What's the point?'; or refuse to participate; or complain, saying, 'Why do we have to do this? They don't in other schools!'

Tutors can be discomfited by pupil reactions which reflect the fact that tutorial activity does not possess the legitimacy of subject-based activity. The climate for acceptance has to be created when pupils have limited perceptions of, or hostile reactions to, the functions of the form tutor. Rigid ideas about what ought to happen in school can be reduced only by sensitivity to pupils' embarrassment and by carefully phasing the introduction of activities.

An alternative approach to involving tutors

1 This is the best way of coping with resistance and, more positively, of getting a sense of commitment.

2 Trainers should prepare a model decision-making exercise and also a tutor-group activity.

3 The training session should begin with a brainstorming activity, in which tutors' ideas are written on the blackboard or sheets of paper without evaluation.

Groups are then formed (not more than four people), which work on a selected activity for 20 minutes. The framework should include:

a objectives

b activity

c follow-up designed to sharpen ideas and induce transfer to the classroom or peer group.

4 Each group then joins another group. In turn, they describe their activity, inviting helpful appraisal and suggestions from the other group. Opportunity is therefore provided for evaluation of ideas in a constructive way.

The use of video-tapes and audio-tapes

The best way of over-coming resistance is to show those who advocate tutor work undertaking it. In a different context – styles of learning – I noted in two schools the respect induced by tapes made by the deputy heads, showing them at work. Weaknesses and the occasional error did not destroy the impact. This manual will be supplemented by a series of six video-tapes, but this does not remove the need for trainers to make their own video-tapes. To ensure reality, the person making the tape should have a relationship with the group – tutorial relationships can be illustrated as well as techniques. It may be helpful to:

1 Ensure that the objectives of the activity are given to the viewers and also presented to the pupils.

2 Highlight issues of classroom management, e.g. forming groups and distributing materials without losing the momentum of the activity.

3 See that instructions to pupils are given precisely and clearly.

4 Demonstrate the way the tutor moves around the small groups, encouraging without unnecessary intervention.

5 Stress the order and sense of purpose which must be achieved in moving from small groups to the final stage where the whole form is concerned with application. Blackboard diagrams, group reporting and tutor presentation of relevant situations could all be used to illustrate the point.

Audio-tapes have also proved useful. Problems can form the basis of recorded illustrations, and confrontations and dilemmas can be given dramatic form, to give the immediacy essential to good training. In tutorial-activities training, the objectives, preparation for the activity and the instructions can be recorded directly. For the small-group or partner activity, the 'observer' approach is used, in which the activities and reactions of pupils are described. Pupils' comments and evaluations can be introduced at this point or form part of the conclusion.

Another use of video-tape is to show – with the help of the drama specialist – the use of role play and the need for a planned extension of it. We might:

- show the need for brevity at first, coupled with the use of familiar everyday situations;
- gradually increase the intellectual demands for problem-solving and imagination;
- stress the importance of role reversal, linking it to standpoint-taking;
- illustrate ways in which pupils' ideas can be stimulated through partner discussion or a brief 'warm up' or trial activity;
- show follow-up activities which highlight the value and purpose of preceding role play.

Demonstrations should include decision-making exercises, exploring subject choice, coping with frustration, leaving or staying on at school and career matters. Tutors can try them out, reporting back to trainers. Concentration on *one* aspect of decision-making is urged, e.g. the level of risk, sources of influence or ethical issues.

The tutor

Training the form tutor begins with discussion of the job specification. Heads of year or house will find the exercise below illuminating. Where it has been done with tutors, it has led to rewarding insights and a working consensus has emerged.

Initial activity

You have been asked to construct a *basic* job specification for the form tutors in a school. It is therefore irrelevant whether the system of pastoral care is based on the house or year system. As you think about this task, you begin to note down some points including the following:

Job specification for form tutor

a Concrete and specific behaviours necessary, e.g.
  i responsibility for following up absences
  ii undertaking periodic homework reviews (how often?)
  iii carrying out a programme of tutor work.

b Basic questions

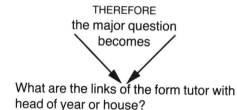

What action can he initiate?   What information must he pass on
What information has he   and to whom?
access to?

THEREFORE
the major question
becomes

What are the links of the form tutor with
head of year or house?

c Now sketch out a job specification which states

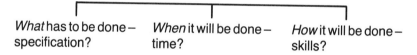

What has to be done –   *When* it will be done –   *How* it will be done –
specification?   time?   skills?

Problems which are unexamined professionally exert a powerful influence on perceptions and actions, eroding confidence. The deputy head responsible for the training must provide opportunities for analysis and clarification. Exercises of the type illustrated below have proved profitable.

Discuss this situation

Mr Gregson, who is in his late fifties, is a very good, indeed, excellent teacher of chemistry. His pupils' examination results at O-level and A-level are outstanding. He finds it difficult to relate to pupils, but his lessons are extremely competent and logical expositions. Pupils can follow him easily, and a few are inspired by his obvious devotion to his subject.

The school has been reorganised and a pastoral care system has been devised in which all teachers are to participate. Mr Gregson is horrified by this and says he has nothing to offer. What happens?

a Should he be persuaded?

b Should he be coerced?

c Should negative sanctions be used?

d Could an alternative contribution to the system be made by Mr Gregson? If so, what form could it take?

Thought should also be given to the issue of accountability. A simple exercise of the type below crystallises the issues.

Accountability

Background factors

1 Research indicates that a pupil's chances of getting adequate guidance depend, not so much upon the system as upon the willingness of the teacher to take up this responsibility. (See M. Reid *et al* (1974) *A Matter of Choice*, Slough: N.F.E.R., which suggests that accountability must be built into the pastoral care system.)

2 Accountability is indirectly associated with legitimacy – if an activity is seen as legitimate, it is likely that procedures exist to ensure that the performance of individuals in that activity reaches a minimum level. If pastoral care is seen as an optional activity, indeed perhaps as illegitimate, then procedures for ensuring that the task is being done probably will be absent.

On what does accountability depend?

a In the box below, list the factors which you think influence evaluation and assessment of the *form tutor's* work.

3 Consider the simple diagram below.

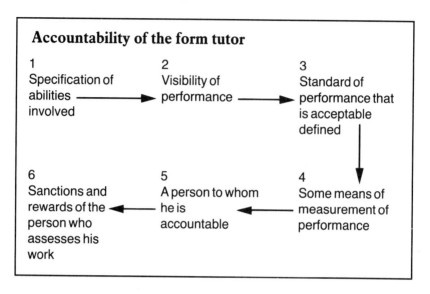

Accountability of the form tutor

1 Specification of abilities involved → 2 Visibility of performance → 3 Standard of performance that is acceptable defined

↓

6 Sanctions and rewards of the person who assesses his work ← 5 A person to whom he is accountable ← 4 Some means of measurement of performance

4 Now please comment on:

 a The ways in which the performance of the form tutor is visible or how it is possible to make it visible in a constructive fashion.

 b The criteria that can be employed to decide whether the form tutor's standard of performance is acceptable.

 c The possibility of measuring performance. Do not be limited to obvious types of measurement.

 d The sanctions and rewards of the person to whom he is accountable.

5 Does the concept of accountability include the pupils and their parents? Discuss this.

6 Spell out ways in which the principle of accountability should be applied to the year head or house head. After discussion with your partner, please construct your own diagram which shows this. Ensure that the links upward and downward are shown.

7 Accountability also involves knowledge of results and feedback. How would you build these into your scheme for:

 a the form tutor?

 b the head of house and year?

 c the deputy head and headmaster?

8 *A note on the fundamental processes*

 This exercise on accountability has tended to emphasise the

need to assess a specified performance, but in the school, perhaps especially in the classroom and pastoral care situations, we need to be aware of underlying processes. There are two strong mechanisms at work which can distort the judgements involved in accountability.

a The attribution process is fundamental to all situations of interaction. We go beyond a person's behaviour to attribute intention and motives to him. In working with pupils we can move almost unwittingly from thinking about an annoying piece of behaviour to making judgements about their emotional stability or character.

Discuss the ways this occurs or can occur in the pastoral care system between colleagues.

b Most interpersonal judgements are based on unthinking, stereotyped responses. It has been shown that interpersonal judgements are fundamentally a response to minimal cues which trigger off a sequence of automatic responses, in a way which is unrecognised by the judge. These cues are characteristics of personality or behaviour which are very important to the self-picture of the judge.

Discuss the form this process might take when the performance of a young male member of the pastoral care team who is in his first year of teaching is being assessed.

The role of the form tutor

Evaluations suggest that the tutor's role becomes biased towards the negative or is seen as trivial by both staff and pupils in some schools. Tutorial work partially rectifies but does not guarantee elimination of this state of affairs. Interesting activity cannot undo the damage caused when complaints about uniform, nagging about misdeeds or sterile emphasis on rules contradict claims that the tutor's relationship with his form is crucial. Irrelevant or poorly planned tutorial activity makes matters worse. Trainers should not lose sight of this or under-rate the tensions created by a discrepancy between the tutor's habitual teaching style and activity-based tutorial work.

The wider aspects of the role have to be given attention if tutor work is not to become merely another lesson or give rise to token performance. Areas to be tackled are:

1 Developing the skills of monitoring the progress of pupils constructively and writing helpful reports.

2 Fostering observational skills, e.g. acting as 'an early warning

system', noting the growth of anxiety and changes in appearance or behaviour.

3 Applying the skills of guidance and counselling, especially:
   – clarification of the problem;
   – establishing effective communication with the pupil;
   – using simple behavioural approaches;
   – mobilising peer support within the form;
   – implementing and changing a programme of guidance for success so that it becomes meaningful and relevant for both tutor and pupils;
   – detecting information which should go immediately to head of house or year.

Monitoring of progress

Training could begin as an exercise in self-evaluation based on questions such as the following:

1 How satisfied am I that I know how every pupil in the form is progressing?

2 If I were suddenly asked to write a report on all the members of my form, which individuals would present difficulty? Why? (This draws attention to the fact that the difficult or extrovert assume prominence, whilst we ignore the withdrawn or non-committally polite pupil who insulates himself against involvement in tutor group relationships.)

3 Can I spell out in fair detail the criteria I use in deciding whether:
   – a pupil is 'at risk'
   – preventive or remedial action is necessary if there seems to be underfunctioning, anxiety or maladjustment?

4 Profiles are one element in the move towards wider assessment of achievement. They may also be seen as a step towards greater pupil involvement in education and self-evaluation. The latter is not confined to profiles: check-lists and other simple scales can be used. Points at which pupils profit from self-assessment of learning skills, e.g. subject choice or entry to the sixth form, should be a focus for exploration of the dynamic aspects of monitoring where a dialogue ensues from consideration of pupils' self-assessments and tutor judgements. Techniques such as writing references for oneself and comparing them with the references written by others is often neglected as a form of monitoring which involves pupils. In the fourth and fifth years this can be related to leaving school. An example is given opposite:

136

At some time in the future it is very likely that you will have to use the school as a reference. Imagine that a reference has to be written now, and try to complete it for yourself.

NAME:	
1 Date of birth:	
2 Dates attended:	
3 Subjects studied and predicted examination results:	
4 Details of any positions of responsibility, sports, clubs etc:	
5 Is the candidate *a* honest	
b reliable	
c industrious	
6 How many days' absence has the candidate had in the past year?	7 Main reasons for absence?
8 Please comment upon the candidate's punctuality, manner and response to discipline.	
9 Is this candidate suitable for a post requiring co-operation with others? Please give reasons.	Yes/No
10 Is the candidate capable of working without supervision? Provide details.	Yes/No
11 Is the candidate suitable for a course of training involving academic work?	Yes/No
12 Please comment upon candidate's general personality and suitability for employment.	

Pupils' ability to take the standpoint of others can be stimulated by the following questions related to this self-reference form.

1 Put yourself in the position of a busy employer who has a large number of applicants for a job, but wishes to interview five people only. Which questions might he pay special attention to in coming to his decision?

2 Assess the importance you think an employer might give to the following points. Rank them in order of importance, starting with the most important.

Appearance
Dress, speech, health, physique, mannerisms.

Knowledge of job
What the firm does, the tasks involved in the specific job, understanding of the difficulties of the job.

Ability to relate to others
Manner, confidence, friendliness.

Personality
Reliability, initiative, honesty, helpfulness, leadership qualities.

Experience
Relevant part-time work, hobbies, involvement in youth organisations.

Responsibility
Good time-keeping, regular attendance, presents a good picture of firm to the public, getting on with job when others are busy.

Trainers should alert tutors to the need to link this activity to the skills of self-profiling by pupils. People talk as if self-assessment is an undemanding, unproblematical activity when it, in fact, involves not only honesty, but accurate discrimination, a sense of causality and some understanding of complex processes of social interaction.

Monitoring progress is a basic tutor task that can either develop constructively or be a relatively meaningless operation. The pastoral team will have much to contribute to the social and personality aspects of reports. Let us begin by asking what is the significance of reports to parents and pupils. Steps may have to be taken to increase their importance. Format may be improved, bearing in mind that the report card or form reflects a picture of the school to parents. Many reports fail to involve parents and pupils because they lack constructive suggestions for remedial action or building

NAME _Smith_   CHRISTIAN NAMES _John David_   FORM _20_

SUBJECT	SET	%	GRADE	REMARKS	Teacher's Initials
English Literature ⎱ English Language ⎰	4	65	B–	Shows imagination in composition and an adequate grasp of grammar. Spelling and punctuation weak.	A.
Mathematics	6	13%	C	Quite good progress made.	A.D.G.
Physics ⎱ Chemistry ⎰ Gen. Biology ⎰ Science	5	50	C+	Keen but clumsy. I doubt whether we shall have enough apparatus for next year.	LHJ
Art	4	65	B+	Reasonably competent.	DR.
Craft	3	73	A.	A good lad. He made a very good job of his letter rack. Well done	JR.
Needlework					
Home Economics					
French					
German					
Nursing					
History	5	52	C	Satisfactory	CHL
Geography	6	48	D	Has not made much effort. I want to see more homework required in this subject	M.C.
Religious Education	6	32	D	Is not really up to the standard required in this subject.	E.V.
Shorthand/Typing					
Commerce					
Music	4	65	B+	Should be a good C.S.E. option later.	JS.
Physical Education				B+	Has good athletic ability and ought to be in the 1st team under 14 rugby team next year.	W.J.R.
House Activities				Rugby team and work on props for school play.	

ATTENDANCE _Good._	PUNCTUALITY _Good._	NEXT TERM COMMENCES _1st September 1984_

A - Very Good	B - Good	C - Average	D - Weak	E - Very Weak

GENERAL REMARKS

FORM TUTOR   John is a friendly boy who gets on well with adults and other pupils. He is always ready to help, especially in the form project with handicapped young people. He needs to work harder in some subjects.

HEADMISTRESS A reasonable report, but more effort would help John.

PARENT'S COMMENTS

on strengths. Some actually deceive unintentionally, parents then react with disbelief when the school feels unable to enter their child for O-level. Comments such as 'lazy' evoke resentment, whilst 'idle' or 'misbehaves in class' provoke the comment, 'Well, they should be doing something about it.' Tutors could be helped to rewrite comments which are negative or puerile, e.g.

   – could do better
   – reasonable progress

- trying
- always late
- never gives his homework in
- average effort
- weak
- disappointing results.

A simple exercise is to prepare a report form as shown on page 139, asking tutors to assess how useful it would be in placing a new pupil. Questions of allocation and interpretations of grades will arise. Tutors will focus on the lack of information related to possible underfunctioning and the reasons for the clumsiness in science, when the student seems to have good manual coordination in craft. An outcome could be clear specification of what is needed from feeder schools. The outline on page 216 can be referred to as a point of departure.

Recording should imply action. We do not wish to have fully completed records and reports which become an end in themselves. Monitoring homework need not be mechanistic or monotonous. Recognition of a problem developing leads to action by the tutor, involving the following type of exercise.

Objectives To reinforce the sense of being in control of learning and to stimulate planning of homework and use of time.

Activity A brief tape-recording is played, in which pupils complain about the amount of homework and the erosion of their spare time. Pupils then draw up a timetable for the week, indicating the balance between homework and leisure activity.

Application Pupils discuss with a partner. A record card is prepared, in which they enter comments nightly, discussing them next day with the tutor.

Registers are records to be used. Not only must tutors regularly scan for patterns (i.e. the consistent half-day absence every Tuesday afternoon, three or four days away at monthly intervals, or pupils who are absent together) but more subtle factors are to be considered. In the extract below this is evident:

- The admission number shows that Elaine Gordon joined the school after other pupils. How well has she settled?

ADMISSION NUMBER	AGE	DATE OF BIRTH D M Y	CLASS No.	NAME Of SURNAME	NUMBER	WEEK BEGINNING 5th. JAN. M T W T F	WEEK BEGINNING 12th. JAN M T W T F	WEEK BEGINNING 19th. JAN M T W T F
335	13	23 2 67	1	ARGYLE	1			
336	13	12 6 67	2	BENNETT	2			
337	14	19 9 66	3	CLARK	3			
482	13	18 4 67	4	GREEN	4			
340	13	8 5 67	5	LOW	5			
376	13	3 3 67	6	MORRIS	6			
377	14	11 10 66	7	NORTON	7			
378	13	20 4 67	8	PIERCE	8			
379	14	3 12 66	9	SMITH	9			
380	13	29 8 67	10	A THOMAS	10			
			11		11			
			12		12			
			13		13			
			14		14			
			15		15			
383	13	7 6 67	16	BARNES	16			
386	14	14 10 66	17	DAVIES	17			
387	13	6 7 67	18	EVANS	18			
624	13	12 3 67	19	GORDON	19			
390	14	22 11 66	20	JAMES	20			
391	14	24 12 66	21	KING	21			
393	13	8 5 67	22	MORTON	22			
394	13	19 2 67	23	SHUFFLEBOTHAM	23			
402	13	30 4 67	24	SOUTHALL	24			
403	14	12 11 66	25	TARIQ	25			
			26		26			

- Alan Thomas is almost 12 months younger than Andrew Clark. How important is this?
- John Argyle is away every Tuesday afternoon. How is this to be approached?
- Melanie Barnes is frequently late. What will be the tutor's response?
- Some surnames obviously invite teasing.
- Elizabeth James's sickness shows an interesting regularity.

Ethical and legal questions have to be debated. It appears that in the final analysis no records have privilege in law. Another parameter is parental access to the records held by the school about them and their children. Administrators, when pressed, usually say that parents have the right to see school records. Confidentiality is not made irrelevant by this. If information is recorded, who has access to it? Schools sometimes have a special pastoral file containing information about the home and the past history of the pupil. Child abuse, clashes with the law and sexual misdemeanours may be noted. Alleged parental difficulties and abnormalities may not only be written down but, even more alarming, may be commented on. Trainers should bring the morality and prudentiality of this to

141

the forefront of discussion with tutors. As professionals, we are primarily concerned with the best interests of the pupil, but we have responsibilities to others, including the local authority. Heads of year or house should emphasise:

1 The need for accuracy. In one small project my students found that much information entered on records was inaccurate and that the validity of data about home background was often suspect. In some cases, it bore little relation to what the counsellors had discovered in working closely with parents. Hearsay, gossip and guesswork rather than evidence underlay many statements.

2 Schools sometimes operate closed and open records. The former contain details of home background and problems to which access is restricted. Is this divisive? Is it legitimate in a profession to exclude fellows from information? Tension there-fore seems to exist between the protection of the pupil and the rights of colleagues. Crucially, does this state of affairs suggest pastoral care is concerned with pathology rather than edu-cation? What is being said about the professional standards of those from whom information is withheld? Is there moral justification for holding such information without telling the pupils and parents.

3 The tutors and their trainers should debate the conditions under which information is given to other agencies. Social workers are hesitant to share knowledge with the school because confidentiality is violated. Good tutors learn much through the pupil's trust of the tutor. Should we not be clearer about the conditions for giving information to other agencies about those for whom we bear professional responsibility?

Phrasing the topic as questions has been deliberate as each team has to find its own answers. Prudentiality and ethics may make good bedfellows.

Profiles

This discussion is restricted to issues that are of special concern to the pastoral team. It is not intended to be a full discussion. Balogh (1982) and Schools Council Committee for Wales (1983) have proved particularly stimulating to thought. Profiles are based on concern for the less able, incorporating Daunt's (1975) principle of the equal value of all pupils. Pastoral workers must maintain vigilance to detect divisiveness or the gradual emergence of 'profile pupils'. The assessment of personal qualities and life skills is

142

commendable, but assessment depends on opportunity to display them. Balogh raises the question of the relationship between what the school wants, reinforces and assesses. What type of initiative is fostered by the school? Profiles imply the rethinking of educational objectives and learning experiences. It cannot be taken for granted that measurement of life skills means that schools feel compelled to foster them in a planned way.

Long-term debate of the reward power and motivational benefits of profiles must be initiated by the pastoral team. Pastoral care has been accused of diverting blame from the school as an organisation to the individual by labelling him as maladjusted or inadequate. Reality may differ from the ideal, if the mechanics and morality of judgements remain unquestioned. Self-profiling and the associated counselling may make the pupil feel the school sees him as significant, but curriculum structures may be sterile, preventing the motivation engendered by involvement in profile-recording reaching fruition in learning.

One of the helpful things undertaken by the pastoral team could be closer examination of the ethical and psychological issues. It was not unknown in the days of rigid streaming to hear the reprimand, 'I didn't expect that of you, an A-stream boy!' as if there was a necessary connection between virtue and placement in a stream. Matters of taste acquire a sense of 'rightness' which obscures their subjectivity. Unfamiliarity or distaste is not sufficient grounds for condemnation. Yet profiles open up the unwary tutor to such dangers. Judgements on personal appearance may be related to prejudice or inhibitions in the judge about dress. Adherence to school uniform coupled with politeness may create an aura which conceals weaknesses. Pastoral workers should question whether distasteful or unusual appearance is necessarily undesirable. Reflection on the anxieties created by the change in male hair styles provides orientation to the problem.

The Schools Council Committee for Wales (1983) stress that the profile monitors and records development, rather than predicting future performance. But is this proper viewpoint likely to be the reality? Profiles are often constructed with an eye to the employer's needs. Imperceptibly, description may give way to prediction, credibility then being given to the illegitimate shaping of school experience by the imagined or stated needs of employers. The uses made of profiles may lead to selectivity of content, which is as distorting as the public examination system.

Problems abound in the assessment of personality and character, because despite the stress on description, insufficient attention is paid to the contribution of the situation. People are reliable in some situations and not in others. Honesty and initiative are other characteristics which can be context dependent. A static picture of personality can be incorporated or initial judgements can shape later ones unnoticed.

Unquestioned assumptions about the nature of personality dimensions can be present in a profile. In one trial profile it was suggested that the following be assessed:

- flexibility/adaptability;
- perseverance/reliability;
- leadership;
- self-confidence;
- social relationships;
- initiative.

An alert pastoral group would immediately raise questions, e.g.

- A dictionary will throw light on the differences between adaptability and flexibility. Is there an unjustified assumption of similarity? Is adaptability conceptualised as a general attribute or related to particular situations? Is flexibility unthinking bending to situational demands, and is there an intended pay-off?
- Perseverance/reliability are two related, but partially independent, qualities to be assessed. The situational factor can be strong – pupils judged unreliable at school have behaved very differently at work.
- Leadership judgements may be especially vulnerable to the assessor's beliefs about the genesis of leadership. It may be seen globally as personality-based rather than skill-based, and unrelated to the needs of the groups in which the individual functions. Different situations demand different leadership skills, but our assessments may be based on an inadequate analysis of them. Task leadership may need to be supplemented by the skills of social-emotional leadership.
- Self-confidence needs justification. Is it realistic or does it operate as a defence against recognition of doubt and the need for change. Some adolescents cling to non-growth through unwarranted confidence. Study skills programmes have a 'two-way' effect – confidence is boosted in some, while others realise their defects in study, thus becoming more uncertain. Confidence is therefore diminished productively, eventually to be restored on a valid base.
- Many questions enter into evaluation of relationships with peers. It may be sufficient to start discussion by suggesting that

we too often unquestionly endorse the desirability of amiable extroversion.

- Initiative is one thing, but initiative taken on intelligent assessment of the characteristics of a situation is another. We ask whether the general tendency of the pupil is to pursue the initiative to a successful conclusion, but also whether than pursuit involves proper regard for the rights of others.

Trainers therefore need to help tutors examine the foundations of their judgements. It is tempting to think in terms of continuua, e.g. reward/punishment or permissive/controlling, ignoring that it is not so much a matter of degree as of discrete categories. Certainly reward and punishment are independently structured and operate differently. Professionalism demands that the pastoral team does not succumb to the pressures created by current shortage of resources, but vigorously examines these issues.

The assessor's characteristics must be taken into account. Well confirmed tendencies exist: some habitually make central judgements; others use the extremes. Concern is no safeguard against unwitting personal bias created by a limited frame of reference. Dispositional qualities can be judged from a moral – possibly moralistic – point of view. Assessments emanating from a number of teachers provide a partial corrective, but new problems are raised if such judgements are averaged or combined, because useful discriminations are lost and the meaning becomes doubtful.

Some of us may be unknowingly vulnerable to the 'halo effect'. One salient characteristic strongly influences the judgements made of other aspects of a student. More serious still is the failure to see the subjectivity of judgements. I have had to take myself to task because I structure tasks by setting objectives and then assume that the objectives justify them. In fact, I have to question my assumptions and accept that a spurious objectivity could be present – that the face validity conceals the questionable. This means that emphasis on behavioural anchorages does not mean much, for what is competence to one person is not so for another. What is initiative for one, is aggressiveness or domineering behaviour for another. The same behaviours are interpreted differently and create difficulties that are glossed over.

'Caring', if it is to be a reality, demands investigation of issues such as the accuracy of observations. Training is necessary, and also the opportunity to observe. The question of the meaning of intervals arises when scales are incorporated into the profile or other records. Sometimes I have found that assessors behave as if there was greater distance between the negatives (E and D) than between the positives (A and B). But they have never recognised this, so the validity of the assumption remained unchallenged. Is the assumption, sometimes found, that all the qualities and abilities conform to the normal curve of distribution justified? Certainly we must ask if tendencies or behaviours appearing in different contexts can be combined in a single judgement defensibly. Examination of one list of descriptive behaviours alleged to indicate introversion strongly suggested that assessors identified introversion with social anxiety. This identification could be a product of poor skills rather than of the personality under examination.

Profiles should be formatively orientated and, hence, descriptive; and an alert pastoral team guards against their being used predictively and against the greater danger that the pupil comes to be regarded merely as the sum of the attributes assessed (for much has been left out).

Trainers should raise the questions:

a How can I write reports that are honest, and yet invite cooperation?

b How can I make suggestions for improvement that are constructive?

Trainers may find it useful to prepare videotapes which help tutors relate better to parents at open evenings and similar occasions. Parents sometimes leave feeling disappointed or resentful that they were not allowed to ask the questions about their child that they wished to ask; that words have been put into their mouths; or that not much is really known about their child. Tutors may not appreciate the anxieties of the parent, even when they have secondary-age children themselves. The result is sterile communication, despite the tutor's good will. Tapes could examine:

1 Ways of helping parents who holds unrealistic expectations of their child.

2 Coping with an aggressive parent without either passively agreeing or provoking a major confrontation.

3 Involving the parent in various ways as a support for the school. (Cave (1970) offers very useful suggestions.)

Tutors could be involved in activities with parents related to progress in school, e.g.

1 Helping parents of first-year pupils:
   – to understand the purpose of homework. Some tutors have never systematically assessed the reasons for it and are therefore unconvincing advocates;

146

- to focus on the purpose of an assignment, giving their children sensible support;
- to make it as enjoyable as possible by expressing approval, when relevant, and by making it a time for positive communication between them and the child.

2 Creating awareness of the ways in which their attitudes and remarks impinge on performance at school.

3 Involving parents in subject choice in the third year (see Hamblin, 1978).

4 Helping them cope with pupils' stress at O-level and A-level. Impatience, over-zealous vigilance, moving from urging achievement to the 'It's up to you' approach, and restricting contacts with friends, all make pupils rebel or increase anxiety unhelpfully. Parents and child then get locked into conflict from which neither can escape.

Activities

Homework: Parents as supports

Trainers encourage first-year tutor to produce a presentation leading into activity and discussion by parents. Materials would include:
- overhead transparencies;
- taped situations for discussion;
- decision-making activities;
- a booklet which helps to understand learning and study skills;
- the rationale for homework.

Parents can be given the opportunity to discuss their aspirations and beliefs about their child's ability. The aim of the exercise is to help them express concern and interest positively. Some issues of adolescent development and management of behaviour difficulties are brought in by parents. Tutors should be taught how to facilitate exploration and encourage parents to work out their own strategies rather than give trite – and suspect – recipes.

Third-year subject choice

The activity can profitably centre on a programme of guidance which is wider than many current ones. In *Teaching Study Skills* (1981) I argued that the processes through which pupils learn should be part of an active dialogue, not only between teacher and pupil but between pupil and pupil. The importance of introducing self-evaluation and pupil target-setting in the first year was stressed. First-year pupils can discuss preferences, style of learning and presentation competently if given the chance. Too rarely do they get it!

Third-year guidance challenges apathy and stereotypes. Awareness of structural changes in industry and the need for constructive risk-taking should be created by beginning a programme of guidance in which *increased* emphasis on internal control, the skills of entrepreneurial activity, responsible use of opportunities and self-assessment plays a major part. Harding (1983), Ormerod and Duckworth (1975) show that girls see physics and chemistry, not only as difficult but *too* difficult for them, despite abilities and aptitudes at least equal to males. Dweck and Licht (1980) stress learned helplessness as a factor influencing achievement. Many signals may be given to girls that they are not expected to do well in science and mathematics. I have found that girls taking physics and chemistry in the sixth form feel that they are not being taken seriously by teachers, or by their male peers in the co-educational setting. Girls seem more vulnerable to negative expectations incorporated into teachers' feed-back. Boys are more likely to receive messages that failure is due to lack of effort rather than ability. Girls may be constrained to a more passive approach by a constellation of forces, including their own unquestioning acceptance of negative stereotypes about their ability. Concern should be given to both sexes. Harding suggests that boys choose science and girls reject it equally unthinkingly. Tutors should be taught to question their own attitudes: conflict may exist between their subject interests and the need for objective guidance; and tutorial materials may incorporate stereotyped assumptions about boys and girls.

Tutors concerned with subject choice should devise a programme based on the following guidelines.

Suggestions for content of third-year guidance unit

Success

We must encourage exploration of feelings about success, e.g.
- what it means to them;
- beliefs about why people are successful – success, like science, may have distasteful, although unjustified, implications for the thoughtful pupil;

- discussion of what they would *like* to achieve, comparing it with what they *expect* to achieve;
- what are the incentives which lead them to strive for success.

Self-evaluation and life style

The concept of 'field' can be used as a basis for self-exploration. A field can be defined as a broad area of activity to which one is drawn, and which seems to offer personal satisfaction, e.g. the computational, scientific, mechanical, practical, medical, literary, social services. Aptitudes as well as personality will be taken into account.

Then they can examine the 'level' at which they wish to work within that field. Effort, toleration of anxiety, the challenge of investing in themselves and doing something they find intimidating can be raised. Boys can be asked to consider whether they define themselves too rigidly as practical, mechanical or scientific, ignoring other aspects of self. Questioning of crude concepts of masculinity and femininity should occur – occupational stereotypes can then be challenged.

Subjects

Exploration can raise questions that they must ask about a subject. What are the later demands and stages of a subject? What is its likely career importance? What qualities are possessed by the successful student in the subject?

Activities

- Partner assessments – friends evaluate one another's capabilities.
- Assessing the impact of micro-technology on life styles.
- Examination of good or poor choices presented as decision-making exercise or case history.
- Matching self with occupation – a tentative exercise.
- Assessing how one would cope with frustration or failure in a subject.

Trainers

The careers officer and career department within the school should be involved in constructing the above unit. Failure to consult may produce an ineffective division of labour.

There is little point in study skills, profiles, learning about learning and achievement-stimulating activities, if they are not steadily developed and seen as long-term processes. Equally, if what is learned in tutor periods is not applied in the classroom, energy is being misapplied. Pupils must, from the moment of entry to the secondary school, be encouraged to discuss the way they learn and evaluate their success and failure within the classroom. Tutor work prepares pupils for involvement in learning. A vital use of speech is to employ it as a tool through which the pupil accurately analyses his learning strategies and develops better ways of coping.

In developing profiles as an aid to learning, trainers will find Mansell (1982) and Dockrell (1982) thought-provoking. Let me again warn trainers of the danger that profiles can be mis-used. Self-evaluation could become potent self-labelling which reinforces helplessness or the *status quo*. Let us never forget that profiles should encourage acceptance of responsibility and stimulate change, assisting the pupil to defeat any implicit negative predictions. This emphasis on purpose should be reflected in the construction of the learning profile. For example, assessment of listening skills means specifying the purpose of listening – selection of salient facts or distinguishing between fact and opinion. The suggestions below are merely illustrative and not exhaustive.

Ideas for a third-year learning profile for use by pupils

Talking and using speech

How good am I at describing something I have observed?
(An experiment in science or a film or TV programme?)
(Tutors could launch discussion of the purpose of such activities and the skills involved.)
Can I tell somebody the main points of something I have read without putting in unnecessary things?
How well do I answer questions in class?

Trainers

Tutors could provide experiences as the basis for assessment. Pupils could then observe themselves during the next two days, reporting back in a tutor period. Some discussion by tutors of the questions they tend to ask pupils will be useful in alerting them to the possibility that questions can limit learning or encourage it. They can help pupils explore possibilities, or suggest there is a clear-cut answer, even where this does not apply. Questions often stress passive statements of what was taught, rather than encouraging application or extension of ideas. Profiles must lead us to consider the experiences we provide!

Note-taking

Do I have a sensible way of making the key points stand out in my notes?

Can I use diagrams as a way of making notes?

Do I stop to ask myself how I am going to use my notes?

Trainers

The suggestions above provide a starting point for developing a learning profile which institutes an active dialogue between tutors and pupils. Constant discussion of learning tasks has to be fostered, including pupils' self-management. Simulated tasks, such as preparation for a geography or history project, can be associated with the profile. The attitudes towards writing of those interested in science can be discussed. The skills of report-writing, précis and logical presentation can initiate lively debate, as will the question of evaluating discrepancies between intention and the final product.

Observational and counselling skills for the tutor

Heads of year or house will build on what has been laid out in earlier chapters. Simple assessment skills need to be developed. A basic model which incorporates the interaction between situation and personality is given below. Systematic observation is involved, and trainers will find it useful to set tutors the task of observing a pupil whose behaviour causes problems.

1 In what situations does he behave in this way?
2 In what situations does he *not* behave like this?
3 What are the relevant differences between the situations where the behaviour occurs and where it does not occur?
4 What seems to trigger off the behaviour?
5 Is there a pay-off, of either a direct or indirect type?
6 What part do friends, peers, teachers or other adults play in maintaining the behaviour?

The results could then be discussed and a plan for changing the pupil's behaviour be worked out. A slightly different approach, which appears less technical, is given below.

Observation and assessment of a pupil presenting problems

1 Spend as much time as possible over 3 days in observation; then describe as fully as possible his behaviour and reactions. *Do not speculate* on the reasons for them. Confine your description to what was observed.

2 Now speculate on the reasons. Justify your statements by reference to your observation and other available evidence.

3 List the behaviour(s) he needs to *acquire* if the difficulties are to be resolved. Rank them in a hierarchy of difficulty.

4 List the behaviours he needs to *modify*, arranging them in the order in which you feel they should be tackled.

5 What strengths has he got, and what supports can be enlisted?

6 Work out a realistic strategy for helping this pupil. Present it in a step-by-step way, showing that you recognise change will not be instantaneous. State any difficulties you will need to anticipate.

Tutors should be encouraged to discuss:
- the significance of changes in behaviour: apathy replacing interest; tension and irritation at the beginning of the school day; fatigue or hyperactivity where it had not previously been present; sudden deterioration in physical appearance.
- signs of stress, carefully questioning the significance of nail-biting, bed-wetting or a speech defect.

   (Trainers should note the need for caution and avoidance of early closure on judgements. Involvement of the educational psychologist or child guidance clinic staff should be considered.)

Counselling skills have been dealt with in some detail. Repetition would be wearisome. Heads of year/house should select what seems appropriate for their team of tutors. Some points can be stressed helpfully. Training should create constructive evaluation of the tutor's tendencies to:

i support others;

ii attack others by being destructively critical;

iii build on what has been said;

iv bring out the ideas and opinions of other people;

v take a defensive attitude when questioned;

vi gain dominance by asking questions;

vii give praise and convey warmth.

Three practical elements can be given salience:

1 Helping the pupil see how he contributes to the problem, e.g. 'What could you do to stop other pupils from picking on you?' This leads to the realisation that he may be provoking the others or giving them a reward, e.g. he goes berserk, which has entertainment value.

2 Helping the pupil identify 'triggers', i.e. the point where difficulties begin, teaching him to behave differently at that crucial point.

3 Assessing the likely costs and consequences of actions and inoculating pupils against them, e.g. the emotional blackmail of friends, or appeals based on potential loss of face.

Tutors can make global prescriptions for change which are meaningless to pupils. The earlier discussion on discipline implies that trainers should help tutors see that change is a gradual process based on success. The use of friends as helpers is to be commended. After a period of absence – not always illegitimate – pupils can be re-integrated quickly when a peer is charged with giving them support. Thought has to be given to the limits of the responsibility of the peer helper but, if gradually introduced, the support system can reinforce a positive climate within the form. Tutors will find it useful to think of other ways of stimulating cooperation, discussing the nature of friendship, social influence and group interaction, which lead to increased effectiveness as managers of learning experiences.

Summary

1 Presentation and other training skills are discussed. The issue of accountability is brought to the reader's attention again.

2 A discussion of reports and profiles touches on psychological and ethical issues as well as practicalities.

3 The tutor is seen as an 'early warning' figure; therefore his observational skills are stressed.

4 Counselling skills are seen as part of the tutor's armoury.

5: Other aspects of training

The pastoral team and the probationary teacher

Attitude changes induced by a costly teacher training are largely reversed or eroded in the first year of teaching. These findings by Oliver and Butcher (1968) are still relevant. The Machiavellian and authoritarian personalities tend to make expedient and superficial adjustments during their course. The combination of change reversal in those who responded to their training, and lack of change in others, makes it likely that innovation in education may be more difficult to achieve than we hope. Pastoral workers should be concerned that child-centredness, radicalism in approaches to methodology, and positive perceptions of innovation are sometimes destroyed in the first year. The rejection of caring and of tutorial activity of which we complain, can be system created – a product of limited survival skills rather than of personality.

Heads of year have a responsibility for supporting the new teacher, understanding his position and ensuring he gets as great a measure of job satisfaction as possible. Why is the probationary year stressful? Skills have been acquired, but not consolidated. They have also been practised in a sheltered position. Students see only how protected they were when they begin their first job. Many share the sentiments of the young woman who said bitterly, 'If I'd known teaching was like this, I would not have come into it!' Probationers in the school system are in a marginal position in terms of professional identity. They are developing professional self-concepts, but during a period of evaluation by others, of which many probationers are keenly aware. This insecurity is worsened by the fact that they sometimes have insufficient knowledge of the procedures and criteria involved, other than a superficial level. Labelling and stereotypes flourish in these conditions.

The first year of teaching is marked by fatigue. The burden of preparation is worsened by restriction of social life. Conflict begins between the need to boost professional competence and the need to lead a life of one's own. Inability to get adequate or helpful feed-back from supervisors guides the conscientious into a process of self-evaluation which can become unnecessarily defensive or negative and lead into later problems. Disillusionment then takes some into limited performance.

What are the pressures?

One of the strongest pressures is to gain acceptance by colleagues. Two factors complicate this. First impressions given to others seem to have a permanence. Therefore, the probationer has to learn initially to ask task-related questions rather than give opinions. Unsolicited expressions of opinion create resentment towards the newcomer in any institution. These pressures make some probationers feel that acceptance can be gained only by rejecting what has been taught during training or by displaying attitudes and behaviour incongruent with inner self and personal values and beliefs about teaching. For the marginal, this produces doubt about the realism of methods advocated at college. Retreatism begins.

How then does one help probationers avoid the sterility of becoming teachers who merely survive? They have to learn to avoid instigating negative labelling by building up their credibility. The head of year/house helps with emotive and attitudinal issues. They need to come to terms with feelings about uniform, their own dress, and other disciplinary elements. Help with control, order and classroom interaction will be needed. The full import of lectures and seminars has often not been grasped, and a number of probationers find themselves unable to translate research and theory into practice without aid. Feelings of 'not coping' appear. They must be accepted, but evaluated rationally. Most painful is the impression not just of no movement but of 'getting worse', which activates negative comparisons and self-punitive reactions in some. All this is accentuated by conflicts about autonomy and independence – teaching for the young teacher may seem to insist on his stifling his initiative. Exploration of these issues is crucial – feelings must be recognised and analysed professionally.

Insecurity leads to faulty solutions. Occasionally, the probationer identifies with the pupils, playing the game of 'I'm different from all the rest'. Creation of psuedo-distance, or the 'hard man' approach, creates unncessary difficulties. The old 'Is it safe to smile at them after Easter?' is amusing, yet one does meet some approximation to it. Some probationers have to be encouraged to express their difficulties, although it is equally important to alert them to the dangers of indiscriminate discussion of problems. Labelling of young teachers on minimal evidence or hearsay is a feature of school life to be questioned and eradicated.

A *programme of coping strategies*

On the first day, probationers should be given as much information as possible about minor routines, because pupils and colleagues form impressions of the newcomers on their ability to cope with such things. They must be taught to mark a register quickly and accurately and to develop a way of dealing with the 'travelling register', where this exists. Procedures for getting new books and essential supplies and for dealing with forms often remain a difficulty, reminding colleagues and pupils of their newly qualified status. We teach them to demonstrate competence. Colleagues usually have to rely on such simple cues in forming judgements. Basic organisation is even more vital in 'teaching nomad' schools, where teachers move from class to class. Timing is crucial – failure to end a lesson on time means an irritated colleague waiting for entry, a class elsewhere having to be quelled and vulnerable pupils experiencing unnecessary anxiety.

School rules have to be explored in conjunction with the inter-relationship of classroom management and positive discipline. The views of first- and fifth-year pupils reported in Chapter 1 provide discussion material. Idiosyncratic classroom rules about entry, routines for setting pupils to work quickly, giving instructions and packing up are part of creating a safe, predictable environment. Avoiding unnecessary confrontations, yet being firm, poses a dilemma for probationers. Control is signalled by the 'eyes like a hawk' technique, where at the end of the lesson one praises appropriately or points out that certain minor misbehaviours have been noted and will not be expected next time.

Heads of academic departments have the major part to play in developing teaching skills. Probationers, however, often wish to discuss their doubts about standards more generally. They may be clear about O-level standards, reasonably clear about CSE, but expect too much or too little from the less able. Homework presents similar difficulties in evaluating how long it will take, selecting the right amount and giving clear instructions: probationers have to be trained to anticipate difficulties, because pupils cannot ask at home as they do in school.

Unbelievably, after an intensive course of teacher training, probationers still run into difficulties because they use moral blackmail or punish the whole class for an individual's offence. Pupils respond with hostility to 'own up or the rest suffer'. Enmity is the result, and the unforgiving pupils exploit every weakness. Inevitably, tempers are lost, but often the probationers have not been taught to reduce the significance of their mistake. Humour, getting on with the activity rather than dwelling on the incident, and ending the lesson positively are simple skills often conspicuous by their absence. The insecure individual feels caught in the situation, not seeing it can be changed by minimal action. The sensible thing is to ask, 'Why did I allow this to develop?' and 'How can I change such situations?'

Property is an issue to be tackled. Some teachers have insufficient respect for their own property, let alone that of others. Carelessness with handbags or placing money in open drawers, which leads to loss, is reprehensible. More senior members of staff then have to interrogate and tensions are created for the probationer. More sinister effects occur when the probationer conceals the loss. Pupils know of it, evaluate the response of the loser and manipulate the situation.

A warm glow comes when a pupil asks the teacher to look after a personal possession but care is needed. The teacher should say that he cannot guarantee its safety or that he will be available when it is needed. If the responsibility is accepted, the property must be looked after with the care that the responsible person gives to his own belongings. Confiscation leads the unwary into trouble. It is justified by the teacher's being in *loco parentis* and acting in the best interests of the pupil, but responsibility for the confiscated property is still necessary. The pupil's property must never be destroyed, and at some stage it must be returned to the pupil or his parents. If drugs or stolen property are involved, the probationer must refer *instantly* to the head of year or house.

Aspects of discipline of special concern to probationers
Pupils have reputations allocated to them, and so do teachers! Once acquired, they have a compulsive hold on the individual and credibility has been lowered. Heads of year/house should stress the need for accepting support *and* the dangers of over-reliance on others for discipline. There is no point in building a reputation of not being able to cope. Punishments should be just and never break regulations. If parents have to be informed of detention, then this rule must be observed. School buses run to strict timetables, therefore to hold a pupil for reprimand, causing him to miss the bus, puts the probationer at risk. Some probationers have found themselves driving a pupil home in areas with a poor public bus service! The outcome was positive in these instances, but perhaps such situations are to be avoided!

The remedial department contains a fund of expertise on the teaching of the less able which may be neglected. The conscientious probationer in a mixed-ability teaching situation may feel he is not reaching the less able members of the class. Understanding of attitudes, anxieties and the response to learning can emerge from discussions with the remedial team. Insufficient attention is often given to the withdrawn pupil. If a pupil appears to be immersed in day-dreams or shows signs of isolation, consultation with the head of year or house is essential. Some discussion of anxiety reactions in the classroom is a helpful part of the programme.

Probationers need to be aware of the ritual elements of staff-room communication, understanding that it has a cathartic or expressive function for hard-pressed teachers. Trouble begins when the probationer assumes that staff-room talk is an accurate indicator of colleague's beliefs about pupils – in other settings their views will be more balanced and objective.

Some discussion has to be given to the problems posed by the older, sexually provocative girl or boy. Males have always been at a disadvantage in controlling girls, especially those from disadvantaged homes, who are prone to resent patronage or who have had to fight for recognition within the home. A common solution is the creation of a joking relationship which eases interaction. This can incorporate, unnoticed over time, a sexual element, which the girl resents or exploits. Young men may fail to see that they are promoting sexual phantasy. Realism points out that they do find the fifteen to seventeen year-old attractive. There is nothing wrong with this, but the problem begins when they communicate their sexual interest without realising they are doing so. Some males regard cautions about touching or being alone with a pupil as evidence of sexual frustration in those who warn. But many teachers with promising careers have learned to regret disregarding similar warnings. In counselling, girls have said to me of such teachers, 'One day, he'll go too far, and I'll get him!' Occasionally, I have met the situation where several girls set out to test how far the male teacher can be induced – perhaps seduced – to go.

Female teachers can be at risk when the male sixth-form student misinterprets or turns to his own account innocuous warmth and interest. Preservation of professional boundaries and ways of coping with the situation without reducing the self-respect of the pupil or teacher have to be discussed. No recipes are available, but a strategy of gradual modification of behaviour, accompanied by distancing which is friendly rather than rejecting, has usually worked.

Sources of stress

Many probationers are unaware of the stress they create by living too far from the school. Time is eroded by costly travelling. Heads of year/house can explore the issues of management of time, economical working and target-setting. Procrastination about marking and writing reports seem to add to the burdens. Even in these days of contraction, teachers' centres offer valuable facilities which are under-used by probationers. Preparation of materials can be eased if full advantage is taken of the centre's resources. Probationers have to learn quickly and observe carefully the school's regulations about reprographic materials. Some do not realise that the close scrutiny is due to the high cost of reproduction and the inadequacy of capitation. Tensions are generated because they do not take the standpoint of others, or are unsystematic and unreasonable in their demands.

Authority relationships can be a source of stress. Unresolved conflicts about authority are not always accessible to their possessor. Working with adolescents precepitates immature feelings which normally we hide or have no wish to resort to. Transition from student to probationer creates insecurity and defensive reactions. Colleagues can, unhelpfully, be made to feel out of date, or be provoked through criticism based on partial understanding. Pressures are not appreciated by the newcomer; therefore anger and rejection are generated in the older colleague. Dress symbolises generation values and makes statements about identity. Occasionally, a probationer adheres to unsuitable dress provocatively, alienating colleagues who would prefer to be cooperative. The observer might justifiably suspect disguised immaturity on both sides. Decision-making exercises and discussion allow sensible anticipation and some degree of inoculation against these situations.

Opinion leaders in the staff-room should be accorded a healthy respect. A few thoughtless probationers fail to see the importance of secretaries and caretakers. Relationships with ancillary staff form part of the programme provided by the pastoral team. Secretaries have the ear of the head and can ease the path of the entrant. Colleagues as well as secretaries can be irritated by the sending of messages. Teachers always dislike interruption of lessons, and the over-frequent sender of messages soon acquires a poor reputation.

This brings the discussion to coping with classroom visitors. Anxiety is often high, which causes the probationer to act defensively or incompetently, leaving him with a legacy of self-recrimination. Pupils scrutinise the behaviour of the probationer closely. Even if the visitor has an evaluative role, he will still appreciate a warm welcome. The image of competence created initially inclines the assessor to interpret ambiguous cues favourably. The ability to admit mistakes, ask for advice and formulate problems provides evidence of maturity. I have found that the presence of a visitor evokes reactions associated with the visits of tutors during teaching practice. Educational method is moving away from the closed classroom, which was the individual's jealously preserved territory, but visibility of performance is seen as distasteful and threatening. My experience suggests that insulation against observation is a ploy arising from ill-developed skills of self-preservation – the pastoral team can help the new entrant cope more adequately.

Materials for work with probationary teachers

A programme for a course for probationary teachers is set out below – I am grateful to Ms A. Silcox for providing this outline of a well-established course.

Programme of in-service training and induction 1983–84

Duties	How to avoid trouble.
	Areas to patrol.
	Danger areas.
	Materials Accident forms.
	Pattern of authority in the
	school.
Classroom management	Mark books.
	Where to get help/support.
	Medical list.
	Rewards available.
	Marking – phasing, purpose.
	Disruption, analysis of 'What is going on'.
	Mark book sheet.
	Classroom situations. What to do if . . .
	Merit marks.
	Merit certificates.
	Suggestions for successful classroom management.

Tutor group management	Marking registers and looking for patterns.
	Records – folder, cards.
	    Materials Confidential files – purpose, access, how to use them.
	        Registers, holiday forms, some suggested letters.
	        Avoiding self-fulfilling prophecies.
	Things to look out for – what to do and see, signs of disorientation in pupils.
	Parents' evenings.

Mark sheets and reports	Timing. What is required. How to fill them in.
	    Materials Report sheets and slips.
	        Copies of mark sheets.

Pastoral care in lower school	Records. Interviewing. Study skills.

Taking a pastoral lesson	Demonstration.
	    Materials Test to indicate whether we follow instructions.
	        The new football boots.
	        Induction course.
	        Research papers on what worries children transferring to Tavistock School.

Evaluation	Questionnaire on probationary programme. Last year's probationary teachers.
Outside speakers	School nurse, epilepsy, asthma – looking for change. School peripatetic teacher of the deaf. Staff governor and safety officer. Educational psychologist. Educational welfare officer. Social services. Deputy Head, i/c pastoral care in upper school.

Duties: 'What do you do if . . .'

Situation	What would you do?	What is the likely result of your action?	Where would you find help?
1 It is morning break and you are on duty. As you go down a corridor a third-year girl comes and takes you to a classroom where her friend is crying and bleeding from a large cut in her arm.			
2 You are on bus duty and just as the last bus is leaving the school a first-year boy comes running up to you and says he has missed his bus.			
3 It is just before first bell and you are walking along the back of school. You see a fourth-year girl smoking. When you tackle her she is very rude to you.			
4 During the afternoon break, when you are on duty, some second-year boys come up to you and tell you that while they were playing football they broke a window.			
5 It is after school and you have just finished playground duty. You are walking through the cloakroom and you see a boy obviously upset and bruised about the face. He tells you that two bigger boys came up and knocked him about for no reason.			
6 You are patrolling and several small second-year boys are running around the school. They take no notice of when you call after them. They disappear, only to return after a few minutes.			

162

Director of sixth form.
Teacher of the gifted childrens' class.
AV teacher.
If time – Basic accounts, commerce
department.
Police liaison officer.
Teacher of primary school
special unit.

Decision-making exercises

Situation 1

You are an alert tutor, and therefore note that Phil and Dave, who are close friends, are sitting apart and exchanging hostile looks. You overhear Phil making an angry remark as they leave. You wonder if you should speak to him, but you decide against it as you are in a hurry.

Next morning, there is obvious tension between them, but no trouble occurs and they do not speak to each other. You consider investigating, but you get absorbed and so forget.

That afternoon, the head of fifth year comes to tell you that both boys have been suspended from school. Dave has been spreading rumours about Phil's girl-friend, trying to stir up trouble. At dinner-time things boiled over. Phil lost his temper, and a fight broke out – a serious one. The head sent them home, refusing to have them back until their parents visit the school. You wonder why you did not realise the urgency of the situation.

Discussion questions:

1 If you had spoken to Phil and heard about the problem, how would you have dealt with it?
2 Could you use such an incident as part of tutor work?
3 What will you do when the boys return to school?

Situation 2

As a form tutor you are having discipline problems with your new form, and now other members of staff are complaining about their behaviour. So you know it is not just you. The following behaviours have begun to appear regularly. Your head of year expresses sympathy, but little is done. So you have to deal with them yourself if things are not to get out of hand. Work out a way of tackling them.

163

1 They take longer and longer to settle down for registration.
2 Several pupils have begun to drift in late, with excuses about having been to see other teachers.
3 There is persistent noise while you are marking the register.
4 A number of pupils leave for the first lesson before you have dismissed them.

Situation 3

The Truant

Pupil is 14 years of age. He is of average ability, attainment and physique. Indeed, the word 'average' seems to sum him up in every way, except for the fact that he has been truanting badly during the last nine months. His attendance was never very good before, but it is now abysmal.

Warnings have had no effect on Paul, and he appeared in court last week. The magistrate, impressed by Paul's apparent penitence and shame, adjourned the case for ten weeks, asking the school to help the boy. (This had to be done before, with success in several cases.) The parents agreed to co-operate.

It is one week after the court appearance and Paul has attended school for one half-day – the morning after the court. The head of house has called a case conference and you are attending it. The object of the exercise is to find ways of helping Paul attend school.

You have, in common with the other participants, the following information:

1 There is marital discord at home, indeed divorce or separation are very likely.
2 Father is away at work for several days at a time, sometimes even for as long as a week. Mother nags him. Paul loves his parents and they still want the best for him.
3 Paul has only one friend in school and he is a delinquent character. His other friends go to a near-by school when they are not truanting. They will invite him to join in, calling for him at the house.
4 Paul is afraid of the PE master, although he does like games. He also has a dislike of mathematics.
5 He is always losing his books and certainly is vague about his homework assignments, yet his attainment is average in an average class.
6 Paul is not delinquent, although some of his friends have stolen

from shops. He has managed to keep clear of this, but is obviously at risk.

What can be done to help him? Decide as a small group the way you would approach the problem.

a Work out an order of priority for your helping efforts. List it below.

b What support could be given in school. (Be both realistic and concrete.)

c What could be done about his lack of friends? (Be careful not to underestimate the difficulties involved.)

d What, if anything, could be done about the home situation? (Be clear there are limits to the task of the teacher.)

Further brief decision-making situations

1 You are a form tutor. You have been trying to get a truant to return to school. The day he returns, you find out that a more senior member of the staff has sent him home because he does not have a proper uniform.
What would you do?

2 A boy is sent to you because he refuses to take a shower after PE or games. He says that boys are slippered if they do not get changed quickly enough.
What action would you take?

3 At the end of the school day on a Friday a hysterical girl pupil who is in your form comes to you and says that she is going to run away from home because of fighting between her parents.
What do you do?

4 One of your form pupils is repeatedly late. You speak to him about it, but there is no improvement.
What action do you take?

Style of interaction

The following scripts can be recorded. The objective of the exercise is to help probationers realise the vulnerability of pupils, the existence of negative ways of responding to pupils' problems which create further difficulties, and the way in which they can build an image of themselves which is at variance with their professed desire to help.

Trainers

The two interviews should be taped and played. Tutors should have copies of the script for discussion of individual items.

Interview 1

		Process
Knock at the door.		
F.T.	Come in. (Enter Mary.)	
Mary	Excuse me, sir.	
F.T.	Yes, what do you want? (Irritated tone.)	Interrogation Distancing
Mary	Well, er . . .	
F.T.	Come on, girl. I haven't got all day to listen to you. What is it you want to say?	Interrogation Assumption of superior role
Mary	(Hesitation.) Well, sir, I'm worried.	
F.T.	Worried at your age? Don't be ridiculous.	Rejection
Mary	But I am, sir . . . (Begins crying.)	
F.T.	For goodness sake, girl, pull yourself together and stop crying. A girl of your age shouldn't have worries, should she?	Further rejection Interrogation
Mary	No, sir, but . . .	
F.T.	There are no buts about it. Now stop crying, pull yourself together and go to your next lesson. All you need is a good dose of hard work. That's the way to stop worrying. Cut along now and don't waste my time.	False reassurance Early closure.

Discussion points

1 What might make a form teacher behave in this way?

2 Is this type of approach ever justified?

Interview 2

		Process
Knock at door.		
F.T.	(Moves over to the door and opens it.) Hello, Mary. Come in and sit down.	Relationship-building

	(F.T. shows Mary to her seat). It's nice to see you Mary. How are you getting on?	
Mary	(Hesitates.) Well, er . . . not very well, sir.	
F.T.	Not very well?	Reflecting back
Mary	No, sir, I'm worried about my exams next term.	
F.T.	I see you're worried about the exams in some way.	Reflecting back
Mary	Yes, sir. I don't think I can cope.	
F.T.	Most people feel a little nervous about tests so you're in good company. But there are ways of helping yourself. The first thing to sort out is what particular aspect of examination preparation worries you.	Realistic reassurance Clarification
Mary	(Hesitates.) Well, sir, you see, I can't remember what I've done, so that when the examinations come, I'm hopeless.	Clarification Catharsis Acceptance of feelings
F.T.	Yes, Mary. I can see you feel unhappy about this, but let's look at what subjects you are good at for a moment. Could you tell me about those?	Emphasis on strengths
Mary	Well, in the last tests I got 70% for French and 65% for English.	Emphasis on positive aspects
F.T.	Well, now, that looks as if you're not hopeless. They are quite respectable marks . . . but you're worried about something else . . .	Exploration
Mary	(Interrupting.) Yes, sir, but it's not those subjects I'm worried about – it's geography and physics.	Clarification
F.T.	I see – go on.	
Mary	Well, when I do those subjects I get poor marks for my homework, and even worse ones for the exams.	Catharsis
F.T.	Yes, I understand. How do you cope with the work in class? That might be difficult for you.	Clarification Relationship-building
Mary	(Hesitation.) My friend Sue lets me copy her book.	Catharsis

F.T.	Yes, you copy from Sue's book, but then you don't understand the work, is that right?	Acceptance Clarification
Mary	Yes, sir.	
F.T.	And the whole thing is worrying you?	Clarification
Mary	Yes.	
F.T.	I see . . . Now, let's see how you are tackling the work in the subjects you are finding difficult at the moment . . .	Relationship-building Analysis of problem Skill development.

Discussion points

1 Teachers often act as interrogators. What other modes of interaction can you envisage using which might be less intimidating to a child displaying anxiety?

2 How would you help Mary to begin to solve her problem?

A follow-up exercise is given below:

1 Boy aged fifteen: 'Mr. Jones has it in for me! We haven't got along from the start. I don't do anything different from the others, but when there's trouble, I'm the one who gets the blame. I wish he'd stop picking on me.'

Discuss the responses below with a partner, deciding which you feel would be most profitable.

a You feel he's being unfair to you?

b You've been in trouble with other teachers before. Are you being really honest with me?

c You could play it cool in his class. Why get thrown out for something so small?

d You know I can't listen to tales, especially about others teachers.

e OK – let's sort it out.

2 Write sensible accepting responses to the following:

a I worry a great deal about coming to school. I often feel quite sick when I wake up on a school day.

b I wasn't able to do my homework last night.

c Bill Jones has been calling me names all the week, and today he took my crisps at break-time.

d I couldn't help being late.

Interaction and communication

The head of year/house will find it profitable to include fairly detailed consideration of the above as preparation for tutorial work. It provides a safeguard, preventing tutors becoming despondent or feeling inadequate. The following could be covered:

1 *The tutor's leadership style*

The following diagram can be presented as a transparency or on a large sheet of paper. It acts as the basis for discussion which examines the need for a balanced approach.

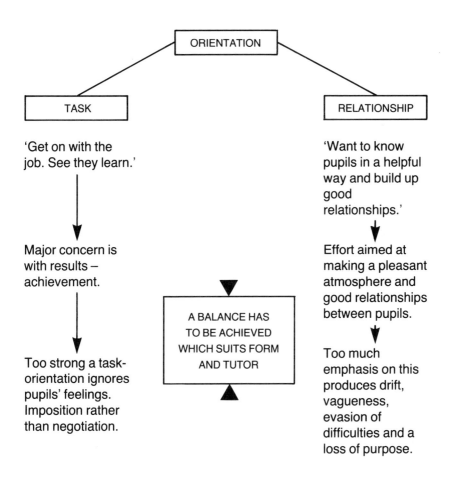

Questions to be explored:

    1 What factors may push the tutor towards unproductive emphasis on the tutorial tasks?

2 How will he assess his own effectiveness?

3 What considerations should he hold in mind during his first few weeks as a tutor, which may be vital to success?

4 What *is* success as a tutor?

Heads of year/house could explore methods of dealing with routine administration quickly and efficiently without letting them take pride of place.

2 *Interpersonal perception*

The objective of this session is to alert probationers to the factors which can distort teacher–pupil interaction and reinforce a negative self-picture.

    a Preliminary discussion, in small groups, of:
- How do teachers judge pupils?
- How do pupils judge teachers?
- What expectations do teachers have of pupils?
- What expectations do pupils have of teachers?

The two-way interaction is stressed by these questions. People who are uncertain tend to look at one side of interaction only.

    b These statements are then considered:
- Well-dressed pupils are well behaved.
- Pupils who do not wear school uniform show disinterest in school.
- Pupils who truant come from bad homes.
- Pupils who wear jeans are likely to be those who are always in trouble.
- Neat handwriting is an indication of a well-motivated pupil.
- Good-looking pupils tend to be arrogant.

These statements are crude, but they are not too far away from what underlies much interaction. Tutors can explore the implications of such statements for the building of positive or negative relationships between pupils and teachers.

    c Tutors consider the statements at the top of page 171:
Teachers write reports on pupils, based upon their perceptions of those pupils.

Discussion follows:
- What types of behaviour do you consider dishonest? Why?
- What purposes might aggression serve for a pupil?
- What behaviours do *you* see as disruptive? Why?

170

What situations haved proved him to be like this?

John is dishonest, disruptive and enjoys playing the clown.

What specific behaviours does he display?

Who is he aggressive towards and what function does his aggression serve?

He can be aggressive and difficult to deal with.

What approaches have been tried and what responses obtained?

He would do better at school if he . . . etc.

3 Aggression and threats to status

a A well-built boy of fifteen – taller than you – continually comes without pens, pencils, books, etc. He extracts them from other pupils in the tutor period using threats, verbal abuse or by hitting the pupils.
– What rewards is he getting?
– How will you cope?
– What potential difficulties exist for you in this situation?

b You are on playground duty. You see pupils converging at the farthest point from the school. You suspect a fight is going on.
– What will you do?
– Could intervention make it worse?
– Is non-intervention justifiable?
– What supports could you muster without drama?

c A girl in your form is refusing to participate in tutor work. She says that it is stupid when you question her. How will you deal with this?

4 Provocation of anxiety

Tutors should be able to take the standpoints of pupils. The concept of 'boomerang' is important. This is the situation where the teacher's actions or statements are intended to help or reassure but actually make matters worse, e.g. 'I'm sure you will do well in the test, Bob. But don't worry if you do badly. They let you take it again.' or 'This piece of work isn't very good, Jane, but I'm sure you did your best!' First present the chart overleaf:

	Tutor response which might increase anxiety	Tutor response which would build confidence
Reading aloud in class		
Pupil has forgotten to bring homework		
Teacher giving out marks		
Pupil makes a mistake in answering a question		
Pupil's friends are not working when he is		
Teacher praises pupil		

5 *Standpoint-taking*

The object of this activity is to help tutors see the teacher from the viewpoint of the pupil. The focus is on the general impression created by the teacher, although some attention is given to the 'ideal teacher' and 'ideal pupil'.

1 Consider the two teacher types on this page. Discuss how the appearance of the teacher (dress, stance, non-verbally communicated signals, etc) may send 'messages' to the pupils, which will affect interaction. What 'messages' do you think would be sent by the two teachers pictured?

TEACHER A

TEACHER B

Teacher A ....
....
....
....
Teacher B ....
....
....
....

2 Consider yourself as each of the pupils described below. How would you react to the two teacher types shown on page 172? Discuss, and write down your ideas; show also how you think each teacher would react to the pupil.

PUPIL 1 You have no friends in the class. You dislike the other pupils, refusing to sit next to them. You hate one pupil in particular and take every chance to annoy this pupil in a sly, 'undetectable' way.

Teacher A

Teacher B

PUPIL 2 You are the leader of a group of boys/girls who have a reputation for being 'hard'. You are anxious to maintain your reputation in front of every teacher.

Teacher A

Teacher B

PUPIL 3 You are usually cooperative, but you find this subject boring and do not want to work at it.

Teacher A

Teacher B

PUPIL 4 You are keen to do well in this subject but find it hard to understand. You ask as many questions as possible to try to improve your work.

Teacher A

Teacher B

PUPIL 5 You are a bright pupil who is a bit fed up with some of the messing around which happens in class. You want the teacher to 'control' the class so that you can learn.

Teacher A

Teacher B

PUPIL 6 You are a withdrawn pupil. You are very frightened about reading aloud in class and sensitive to the teacher's comments about your work. You dislike being asked questions.

Teacher A

Teacher B

3 What characteristics do you think will be most appropriate in a teacher to cope with the range of pupils considered? Make a list.

4 *a* What is your opinion of what constitutes an 'ideal' pupil? Describe such a pupil, in terms of behaviour, attitude, appearance, etc.
  b Discuss whether you feel this concept to be valuable.
  c In what ways will your concept of the 'ideal' pupil affect your reactions in the classroom? List your ideas below.

The importance of initial support by the pastoral heads
The concept of staff development is firmly established in good schools. Heads of year or house can immediately create a climate of exploration of attitudes and evaluation of action within a context of support. The long-term aim is to help those in a professionally marginal position to develop the intelligent imagination prime in job satisfaction in an era of uncertainty, where traditional anchorages have been lost and previous solutions are inapt. Initial failure to resolve underlying emotionally and developmentally based conflicts activated by the nature of teaching, coupled with failure to

174

acquire ways of expressing concern constructively contribute to low job satisfaction and professional underfunctioning. Rigidity and lack of involvement may be seen in the older teacher, but it is not restricted to them. Entrants to the profession develop these behaviours as a means of survival in a stressful situation. Attempts at helping misfire. It is all too common to attempt to help the probationer ease himself into the tutor role by including him in the first-year team. Doubtful assumptions underlie this: probationers do not necessarily find it easier to relate to the first-year pupil; nor have they always the ability to appreciate the difficulties of adjustment facing the first-year pupil. Some find it easier to interact with the fourth- or fifth-year students, bringing a refreshing spontaneity and vitality into tutor work. (The evaluations reported earlier show that the need exists.)

The pastoral heads' contribution to professional socialisation is essential in an age of blocked promotion and stress, but it is insufficiently clearly articulated. This situation must be improved, if current underfunctioning in pastoral systems is to be rectified. Stress therefore is a relevant consideration for the heads of year/ house. Dunham (1978; 1980) has done valuable work in this field, and his articles should be consulted.

Stress is prolonged tension, and, although it is not identical to anxiety, some overlap between them exists. It is a state of pressure – a feeling that, if we relax, things will get out of hand. Stress is always accompanied by a fear of loss of control, hence the colloquial phrase, 'losing one's grip'. The sense of being powerless is strong. We have already seen that positive mental health can be viewed as positive attitudes to oneself and others. Active attempts to master one's current environment should be accompanied by realistic optimism about the future. This statement explains why stress is so evident in a contracting and devalued profession – although this manual is in some ways an attack on the devaluation of teaching.

People under stress therefore feel held in a position in which little change can occur. They then:
– predict that nothing can be done;
– go on to predict, that even if it could be, nothing will be done;
– have no anticipation of things improving.
Negative predictions dominate their thought and actions and are expressed in a context of passivity and blame-pinning.

Factors to be considered by those dealing with stress
Those taking a helping role must be aware of the stressed teacher's latitudes of acceptance and rejection for encouragement and re-

175

assurance. Clumsy approaches or the insensitive use of praise tend to 'boomerang', leaving the helper with diminished credibility. The helper's strategy may have to be indirect, and based on 'one step at a time'. A direct, business-like approach not only encourages premature closure on the problem and a false diagnosis, but leaves the more subtle emotional issues untouched, so that no real change occurs in dealing with the pressures of professional life. Initially, one encourages the individual to talk, whilst keeping a critical eye on oneself by asking, 'What am I reinforcing?' Talking about the problem can occur in a way which makes the reinforcement stronger.

We can assess:

1 Where the stress lies.
   – With colleagues or pupils?
   – Within the family (but the teacher cannot separate home and school)?
   – Within the individual, appearing as guilt or anxiety?

2 The functions served by stress in the colleague's life. Is it a device for evading problems of a deeper and more personal type? Does it provide a structure to life for them? *Cautious* speculation on how they would be different if the stress were removed can be enlightening. Would they need to find something else to worry about?

A caution

Do not make illicit assumptions. Look for the evidence. Raise the questions constructively and allow the stressed person to look at the possibilities. Do not impose your definition of the situation on them.

The helper encourages the stressed teacher to compare situations which are stressful with those which are not, working out the implications for themselves. Stress falls into two areas, usually:

a PROFESSIONAL, e.g. discipline, teaching ability, promotion or colleague relationships.

b PERSONAL, e.g. family, sexual or monetary problems.

There must be discussion and eventually an agreed policy about the scope of problems dealt with in staff development. This area of work is unrewarding and therefore avoided. It seems to me that the female deputy or senior mistress often has the task foisted on her in a way foredoomed to failure. But personal problems do impinge on school: the teacher with pre-menstrual tension, who punishes irrationally, marks harshly or creates destructive confrontations, and who does not cope with the aftermath; the male in his mid-fifties, who suffers from exhaustion and becomes apathetic or, more obviously, the one who compensates for fading virility by making provocative remarks to female colleagues and pupils.

Areas of stress

Mixed ability teaching seems to be a source of stress for many teachers. The benefits of mixed ability teaching have been discussed by Ferri (1971), Newbold (1977) and others, but insufficient attention is given to the stress associated with it. Some teachers have not acquired the necessary skills, and so feel guilty or resentful. The burden of preparation is increased, causing the conscientious teacher distress. Threat also emanates from the feeling that the teacher is unable to 'reach' certain pupils in the mixed ability situation. The rigid beliefs about what works in teaching also prevent some individuals from adjusting. The issues above should be considered by the pastoral heads – a debate on stress and teaching style integrates the pastoral and the curricular realistically.

For some, the management style of the head has resulted in stress. There are teachers who desire close direction and find autonomy disturbing. Let us be clear that distorted perceptions of the head's motives and intent are common. Teachers often cannot understand the perspective of the individual who has to accept the final responsibility. Stress flourishes when there is:

- a legacy stemming from misuse of the 'points' system as a way to induce personal loyalty or to divide the staff and rule;
- over-reliance on paper directives;
- a tendency for the head to delegate work without responsibility;
- conflict based on vacillation of the head between the demands of parents, staff and local authority, possibly accompanied by a refusal to make a firm decision;
- marked drift or undue restriction.

A profession should be involved in evaluating the causes of stress and removing them.

One source of stress is a lack of promotion. Teachers frequently report a feeling of lack of recognition for effort. Deployment and potential redundancy lead to the belief that expression of views is frowned on, or that views will not be listened to with respect. A pattern of alertness to signals of devaluation emerges, and tensions escalate. Such teachers need to be helped in staff development to look at possibilities, to develop strategies for exploiting opportunities and to plan for the future.

Teaching as a form of 'policing' is no longer confined to twilight urban areas. I find, however, that stress is often related to the inability to deal with passive and psychological aggression. Pupils use passive aggression to force teachers into the role of nagger, using their nagging to justify further rejection of the values of the school. Understanding of such mechanisms and the way that stress causes us to provoke unwittingly the hostility of which we complain increases our power. Isolation and visibility are strangely intermingled in many cases of teacher stress. Teachers work to reduce the visibility of their performance (ask about reactions to glass panels in classroom doors) yet they feel threatened because they cannot communicate difficulties. A curious ambivalence exists, where they desire openness and yet feel compelled to hide their difficulties with a class or individual. Strong statements and reactions cloak doubt. A constructive strategy is to begin by helping the stressed teacher identify points of vulnerability, e.g. the last lesson of the morning, a particular reaction of a class, or tensions associated with Friday afternoon. Coping may include learning to make fewer immediate decisions, avoiding confrontations or dropping abortive patterns of interaction. One insufficiently recognised source of stress is more numerous meetings. Time and energy are scarce resources for both sexes, although the impact of meetings on females is greater. Job and home demands have to be met, yet the promotional rewards and professional future seems bleak for them.

General pointers for helping a colleague under stress
Convey respect, whilst looking for ways in which demands can be legitimately reduced, *and* the teacher can behave competently. Help them assess the validity of their perceptions. Do they see a situation of no change, when change is actually possible? Depression brings the sense that one cannot predict or control the outcomes of actions, or resolute prediction that no change will occur. Starting the day is often difficult; help in structuring this often is the first step in change.

Be aware realistically that communication with stressed teachers is difficult. Defensive reactions protect them against realising their contribution to their predicament, e.g. investing energy into confrontations or adopting 'gallows humour' to keep colleagues at a distance.

Difficult questions are faced in reducing stress. Energy may be invested in a custodial approach to the less able, which creates a host of minor disciplinary situations. The teacher may retain frameworks of judgement which are no longer appropriate to a changing society. Is there a rigidity of approach which further exacerbates stress? We urgently need to tackle the problem of incompetent teachers who create burdens for others. The margins for absorption of the difficulties they create steadily decrease. Stress is therefore a total school problem which the pastoral heads can illuminate.

The application of counselling skills to staff development and interaction with colleagues: Notes and an activity for the heads of year or house

The major elements

1 *The professional self-concept of the individual*
This alerts us to the fact that, despite official prescriptions and delineations of role, the individual *interprets* it in an idiosyncratic manner. If the other person holds a different definition of the role, communication becomes less effective, if not counterproductive. Unawareness of the professional self-concept, e.g. of the elements of performance which a person holds to be salient, prevents one from coding communications to them in an acceptable way.

2 *The attribution process*
A key element of the process of interaction is the attribution of intent, motives and purpose to the other person. This is, of course, a two-way process in which the person instigating the interaction – disciplinary, staff development, or dealing with grievances – has to be aware not only of what intentions and motives the other person is attributing them but also of the need to examine their own pre-judgements of the other person, rather than taking them as given. Unawareness of this inferential process, which is often masked by convention and professional etiquette, can cause mutual misunderstanding or render the interaction abortive.

3 *The predictions of the individual*
This calls attention to the fact that people bring sets of expectations to a situation and that these shape their reactions and largely determine their behaviour. Their past behaviours are a causal

element in current behaviour and predict certain outcomes which limit their future actions. Failure to identify the predictions and expectations held by the other person may lead one unwittingly into making statements and acting in ways which create resistance and destroy our credibility as a source of influence.

4 *Personality factors*

This does not imply a so-called 'deep' analysis, which would be beyond the skills of most of us, even if this were to be professionally acceptable. Within the practical limitations of time it means some assessment of:

- the tendency to close early on problems, imposing meaning or a definition of the situation which is then adhered to rigidly;
- the degree of anxiety which seems to mark the individual's habitual interaction with superiors, even when it is disguised by a superficial impression of confidence;
- the tendency to avoid challenge and to see events as lying outside their personal control, so that they remain passive and inactive.

5 *The social comparison processes*

All of us scan our social environments constantly, evaluating ourselves by using the performances and actions of others as a basic measure. Some individuals see themselves unnecessarily negatively, whilst others deny the reality of the signals from others, which indicate that they are not doing as well as they might. In some colleagues one may meet a defensive denial of the validity of the comparisons contained in reports. Others often manage to depress themselves – and others – by their pessimistic self-comparisons.

Final note

The factors mentioned above have been selected because they contribute to constructive interaction. Many of us will be required to modify the attitudes and behaviour of colleagues. Consideration of these factors allow us to make the necessary adaptations to the individual which avoid unnecessary confrontations and situations of stalemate.

Personal difficulties and professional competence

This exercise touches on the crux of the problems aroused when one helps a colleague: the conflict between concern for the individual and the needs of the job.

The situation

You have had to interview a colleague because he is frequently absent for unsatisfactory reasons. His absences are never longer than three days, indeed, they usually tend to be single days off. His explanations are vague – sickness, headache or something physical.

Because of your competent approach he reveals that his basic reason for absence is a mentally unstable wife. Her condition is not severe enough to require hospitalisation, but she is receiving medical attention. She tends to be obsessional, having fantasies that she will do something 'bad' to the children. She alternates between depression and aggressive suspicion of others. Your colleague feels he has to stay at home on his days off, either to provide his wife with support or to protect the youngest child, a boy of seven, who is reacting badly and refusing to go to school. The other child is a girl of fourteen, who seems to cope well.

The man expresses his guilt about the work situation and is anxious for advice, now that he has told you about the state of affairs. Although he seems honest in this, he stresses that he would not like colleagues to know about his family affairs.

Your basic aim is to:
- try to reduce his absences;
- help this colleague so that he can invest more energy in his work.

Step 1

Discuss with a partner how you will tackle the problem. Outline the main points below.

Step 2

Try to assess the following:
- What possibilities and different approaches exist for you to choose from?
- What values seem to be shaping your reactions?
- What are the risks involved in your preferred course of action?
- How will your colleagues react?

Write brief notes on these questions below.

Step 3

Role play the situation.

Discuss what made you act the way you did. Assess the connection between what you did and the preliminary questions.

Summary

1 The special contribution of the pastoral team to the success of the probationary teacher is examined. Stresses and conflicts are identified. The pastoral team will help with the adjustment problems of those who are in a marginal position in the profession. An outline programme which is activity-based is presented.
2 The general impact of stress on teachers is discussed. Some hints about dealing with the stressed colleague are provided.

6: Issues of special concern for the head of year or house

Group counselling

The words 'group counselling' intimidate some heads of year or house unnecessarily. Yet they accept individual counselling. There is nothing esoteric about group counselling. For the head of year/house it is an intensive form of tutorial work, focused on a particular problem, providing a group of pupils with the skills needed for more adequate coping. The principles of counselling, the values and techniques described earlier apply and should present no problem to the head of year or house. It is helpful to see group counselling as a carefully planned and structured learning experience, with certain advantages that must be considered.

1 It is more economical, allowing the middle management team to escape from some of the frustrations imposed by lack of time.

2 Pupils find it less threatening than individual counselling.

3 It allows the head of year/house to demonstrate his competence in tutor period activities.

4 Use is made of the fact that what is learned and practised in the presence of peers is more likely to transfer to other situations.

5 It provides opportunities for developing support and co-operation among participants.

I have written about group counselling (Hamblin 1974; 1983) and there seems no point in replicating earlier discussion. Some basic questions are answered below:

Size of group	From 4 to 8 members.
Sex of participants	There are advantages in single sex groups in the first five years of the secondary school.
Frequency of sessions	Once or twice weekly.

Duration of each session The normal period, unless blocks of time are allocated to faculties. If the latter conditions hold, thought has to be given to the problem of visibility of the pupil, and difficulties created for the teacher.

These are suggestions only. The head of year/house should consider what suits him best – there are no rigid prescriptions.

Group counselling offers an opportunity to close the curricular/ academic gap, if it focuses on achievement. Guidance for success is a neglected theme. Yet the pastoral heads wish to deny the perception that they are concerned only with pupils in trouble and troublesome pupils. The thrust should be towards success. Disruptive or withdrawn pupils benefit from group counselling but, even here, the weight of effort is directed towards acquiring more reward-bringing behaviours. Pupils from disadvantaged backgrounds desire success but do not know how to achieve it.

A unit of group counselling lasting 6 to 8 sessions has an impact which can be followed up by the form tutor. The objectives of each unit should be clear and known to the pupils. Targets must be clear. With pupils from deprived backgrounds, a paucity of planning skills has to be taken into account. Clear short-term goals are crucial, for these pupils must not only succeed but know they have succeeded. Success is concrete and meaningful tasks stimulate motivation. One can employ an old principle of remedial teaching, *viz* that the best ways of changing negative attitudes is to give new and interesting work pitched at a level slightly below current capacity.

Group counselling is not to be taken on hastily or without mutual support. Pastoral heads can form their own support and development group. Students at an advanced course have found it useful to consider the following ideas:

The development of guidance programmes which stimulate achievement

Motives can be divided into broad groups: those marked by the tendency to approach some activity or object; and those whose function is to help the individual avoid pain.

Therefore, an individual can have a tendency to undertake an activity which is expected to lead to success
or
a tendency to avoid undertaking an activity that is expected to lead to failure.

This over-simplified statement draws attention to the subjective nature of elements involved in achievement. A pupil can see a learning activity as exciting, meaningful, dull, rewarding, punishing or irrelevant. The main subjective elements involved are:
- EXPECTATIONS of success or failure
- COMPARISONS with others
- BELIEFS in the source of control as primarily lying within the individual or outside him in his environment.

Behavioural modification principles do not work when a pupil has no expectations of success or when he believes luck and chance determine what happens to him rather than his own efforts.

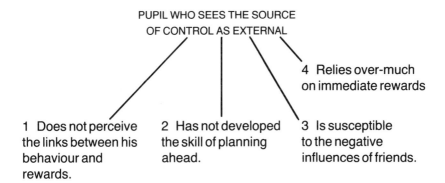

PUPIL WHO SEES THE SOURCE
OF CONTROL AS EXTERNAL

1 Does not perceive the links between his behaviour and rewards.

2 Has not developed the skill of planning ahead.

3 Is susceptible to the negative influences of friends.

4 Relies over-much on immediate rewards

Pastoral heads can then discuss ways of implementing the statement below.

These subjective factors can be explained to pupils as part of the guidance programme through taped extracts, cartoons and case histories, but all this will need to be accompanied by practical measures to develop the *skills* which are lacking in pupils. Ways of changing negative attitudes is to give new and interesting work, pitched at a level slightly below their current capacity in the subject field.

Pastoral heads should begin by extending their ideas about the way they can stimulate skills. Two examples are given, using the facts above. Both are concerned with self-management.

Example 1
Objectives (As given to pupils.) In this session we are going to look at ideas about success, and the way we can bring failure on ourselves. In this tape you will hear two pupils who are equally capable, but one has done very badly, whilst the other has done well.

185

Activity   A tape has been prepared. The failure makes excuses for failure. Friends are blamed: they kept calling round and had to be let in; then they forced him to go out, using emotional blackmail. The tape builds in the *implicit appeals* often used by such pupils, e.g. 'Well, I had to go out with them, didn't I? They'd turn nasty on me in school, and I couldn't have that, could I?' Then the successful pupil interrupts, pointing out that they both have friends, but that he has a Saturday job, which the other has not. The successful student goes on to illustrate how his time is managed. Other aspects of self-management are also stressed.

Application   Partners work on planning the use of time. (The pastoral head running the group would decide the exact task.) Precise targets are set, to be achieved in the interval before the next group session. Friend contracts to help friend.

Example 2
Objectives   (As given to pupils.) We can blame other people and refuse to take responsibility for our success. First, let us look at what we do. Consider this remark.
   'If you did all the teachers want you to do, you'd have no life of your own.'

Activity   Pupils are given a check-list of the twenty-four hours of the previous day. It is set out hour by hour, from midnight to midnight. They fill in what they did – sleeping, eating, enjoying themselves, working or just drifting. They then discuss in groups how they fared in use of time.

Application   The task becomes one of planning the next day so that they can get homework done efficiently and enjoy themselves.
   Pastoral heads might sharpen their ideas about *motivation for success in school*. The following simple notes could provide a structure for discussion which is a prelude to planning the content of the group counselling unit.

A basic assumption
Confidence and the desire for success can be fostered in pupils by appropriate guidance.

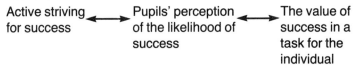

Two definitions

1 Confidence is the pupil's own estimate of his likelihood of achieving in a task. This simple statement is often neglected. Its implications should be explored.

2 Achievement is:

Active striving for success ⟷ Pupils' perception of the likelihood of success ⟷ The value of success in a task for the individual

Key points

1 The pupil's beliefs about the nature of the forces which cause success or failure in learning (his sense of being in control of his own destiny or of being the victim of forces beyond his control) are the crucial factors in creating the determination to succeed or the tendency to react by avoidance and minimal effort.

2 Two fundamental patterns of achievement behaviour seem to exist. (These of course are extreme types.) One is active and the other is passive.

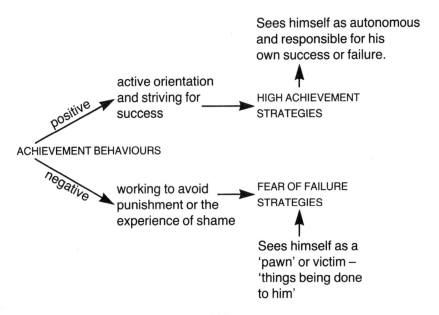

Sees himself as autonomous and responsible for his own success or failure.

active orientation and striving for success → HIGH ACHIEVEMENT STRATEGIES

positive

ACHIEVEMENT BEHAVIOURS

negative

working to avoid punishment or the experience of shame → FEAR OF FAILURE STRATEGIES

Sees himself as a 'pawn' or victim – 'things being done to him'

The pupil motivated with the desire to achieve tends to see failure as the result of insufficient effort, and so the cause of it is seen as lying within his own control. This view robs failure of undue threat and ensures that the pupil takes responsibility for his actions.

The pupil who believes the causes for failure lie outside himself (e.g. 'It's the teachers', 'It's the way they teach', 'The course is no good') is unlikely to assume responsibility for his own failures. This is the case, even when they say they 'lack ability', because this means there is nothing they can do about it.

It is to be remembered, however, that rewards have little impact on the behaviour of the pupil who believes that the world is dominated by luck and chance. Therefore the rewards he obtains have little to do with his own effort.

General introductory steps to increase achievement motivation

1 Avoidance strategies can be modified to some degree by:
   a Presentation of simple taped situations which demonstrate the ways in which pupils could shift the responsibility for success or failure to others or to forces outside themselves, e.g. blaming friends or the teacher. Discussions follow the tapes.
   b Discussion of the mechanisms of setting goals, followed by exercises in which:
      – pupils set clear goals in precisely delineated areas of learning for the next week;
      – they work with a friend to achieve these goals, each pupil assisting and reinforcing the efforts of the other.
   c Examination of beliefs about what causes success or failure. This can be done by taped excerpts which contrast the extreme positions or case histories which show the consequences of both types of belief, e.g. in the fifth year this could be related to examination success or failure. (See the example above.) Pupils should learn that the high achiever stresses that success is dependent upon:

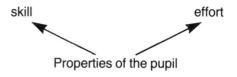

skill   effort

Properties of the pupil

Conversely, the low achiever stresses:

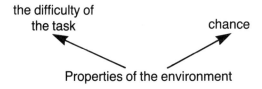

the difficulty of
the task

chance

Properties of the environment

To help pupils understand the significance of this is to help some of them begin to understand the self-defeating nature of their approach to learning or to reinforce the effective orientations of others.

2 We can also help those who are under-achieving deal with the fact that anxiety can cause a mechanical persistence, rather than a flexible, adaptive and vigorous attempt to master the task.

3 Bring out into the open 'pretence effort' or ritual minimal performance. To discuss such mechanisms is to make it difficult for them to operate. Underfunctioning pupils tend to exert sufficient effort to avoid punishment, but not enough to make them feel committed to the task. The outcome is that they run their lives on excuses.

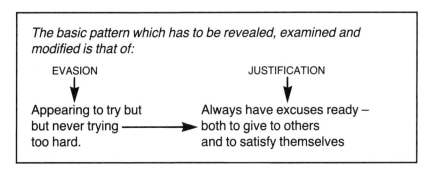

The basic pattern which has to be revealed, examined and modified is that of:

EVASION

JUSTIFICATION

Appearing to try but but never trying too hard. ⟶ Always have excuses ready – both to give to others and to satisfy themselves

The stimulation of achievement motivation

1 To try to bring the achievement of all pupils to the same level is manifestly absurd and would be to court mediocrity. There are minimal levels which all should reach, but each pupil must be encouraged to strive for individual excellence.

2 It is false to assume that failure *per se* is damaging to self-respect. PROLONGED FAILURE IS HARMFUL. Individual and rela-

tively isolated incidents of failure can be used constructively to stimulate analysis of the situation and suggest more viable ways of working.

3 The first general skill is to state clearly the objectives of each learning task – Davies (1976) shows that clear objectives can enhance achievement.

4 Pupils should then be encouraged to look at a task and break it down into small steps. (Making an amorphous and apparently unmanageable task reveal its structure puts the pupil in control.)

5 Pupils then contract with a friend to undertake the first step and proceed at their own pace. The friends support and reinforce one another.

6 Teach pupils self-management skills, e.g. how to break up homework periods and use self-testing and recall activities. Tapes of study skills can be used for this purpose. Exercises help pupils examine ways of approaching a learning problem. Sketches recorded on tape describing two ways of approaching a learning difficulty can be presented and pupils are encouraged to discuss which suits them. The sense of being able to make a choice is crucial.

SELF-DIRECTED LEARNING, INDEED, STUDY WITHOUT DIRECT SUPERVISION, AS IN HOMEWORK, IS EFFECTIVE ONLY AFTER PUPILS HAVE BEEN TAUGHT STUDY SKILLS

7 Pupils should be trained to evaluate and assess their own work in a systematic manner. A simple plan for this should be given to them. It should increase in complexity as the pupil progresses through the school.

Experience teaches that the taking-over of ready-made programmes for group counselling is a doubtful procedure. At the best, they will need considerable modification. Pastoral heads need to consult the heads of relevant academic departments, e.g. if the theme of the group counselling unit is the acquisition and improvement of social skills, the heads of RE and social education will have much to offer. Interesting ideas often come from the PE department, who know the pupils in a different context. Let me now expand this theme.

Group counselling should reflect the Newsome Report's insistence on relevance to life. This is laudable but confining, if interpreted too literally. Group counselling could give undue weight to dealing with pupils who are ·nuisances. Rather than contribute to positive mental health, based on striving for self-mastery, it could be socialisation for things as they are, not developing the critical, questioning attitudes which are necessary for success in a post-industrial society. This is not endorsement of omnipotence or egocentricity, but stresses the need for the pupil to act rather than withdraw, and to accept responsibility.

Group counsellors must therefore face controversial issues, e.g. intergenerational conflict, consciousness of harmful rather than beneficial features of school, and disruptive behaviours sustained by inner needs. Pupils offered group counselling tend to:
– have undeveloped communication skills and to present themselves badly;
– be wary of the unfamiliar, or what does not meet their preconceptions;
– be socialised into 'us against them';
– be concrete thinkers who find it difficult to abstract;
– find it difficult to take the standpoint of others.

As group counselling is made relevant to success these tendencies will weaken, but we still need to set problem-solving into a familiar context and to incorporate meaningful problems. Realistic acceptance of this need to be down to earth does not mean that pupils are to be tied to the immediate environment. Action should always lead to reflection. Teaching skill is employed to aid abstraction and to clarify principles, encouraging mature discriminations. Limited behavioural repertoires lead to the same response to different situations. The group counsellor helps participants discover ways of applying and extending what they have learned. Group counselling is a constructive attack on rigidities, black-and-white values and self-defeating behaviours. Assimilation and application of these principles are a pre-requisite for success. They are not sufficient, but they are necessary.

Truancy

I have discussed truancy elsewhere in depth (Hamblin 1978; Carroll 1977). The focus of the brief discussion here will be two-fold. How effective are the structural arrangements within the pastoral team for dealing with absenteeism? More important may be consideration of the question, 'What is there for some pupils when they do come to school?' To say there is necessarily something wrong with the individual rather than with the institution from which he absents himself is unconvincing. This topic brings our attention back to the early section on discipline and punishment. Perceptions of the nature of authority, and involvement in it, may be crucial. The work of Reynolds *et al* (1980) is helpful in addressing the problem.

The following outline analysis and suggested strategy will be of help in devising an approach.

The nature of truancy
Truancy can be seen as a product of a learned tendency to avoid challenge, a sense that control lies outside the individual, a belief that success is unobtainable and that school is not only uninteresting, but that teachers are, at best, uninterested in the truant.
Truancy and underfunctioning are linked in a way which suggests that an attack on the former should be associated with steps to remedy the latter.

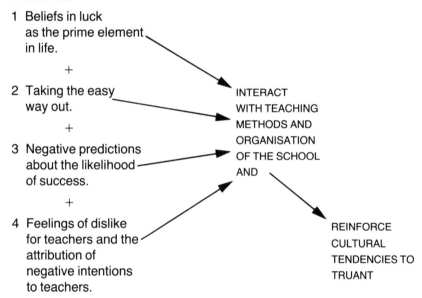

THEREFORE

1 Beliefs in luck
   as the prime element
   in life.

        +

2 Taking the easy
   way out.

        +

3 Negative predictions
   about the likelihood
   of success.

        +

4 Feelings of dislike
   for teachers and the
   attribution of
   negative intentions
   to teachers.

INTERACT
WITH TEACHING
METHODS AND
ORGANISATION
OF THE SCHOOL
AND

REINFORCE
CULTURAL
TENDENCIES TO
TRUANT

A strategy

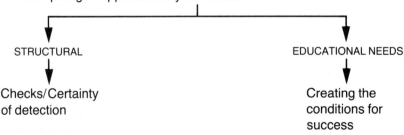

1 A two-pronged approach may be useful:

STRUCTURAL

Checks/Certainty
of detection

EDUCATIONAL NEEDS

Creating the
conditions for
success

2 *Structural measures*

S1 *Certainty of early detection*

    a Training form tutor to inspect the pattern of absences of pupils in their form.

    b Alerting the year- or house-head, who sees that EWO is informed and can take action early in the pupil's secondary school career.

    c Special surveillance of pupils who have truanted during their last two terms in the primary school.

S2 *Reception of truant back into school*

    a Avoidance of immediate harangues or punishment which erodes the pupil's self-respect.

    b Provision of support by form tutor:
        – catching up on missed work;
        – examination of difficulties in relating to his age group and to teachers;
        – provision of skills to cope with pressures, including invitations from friends and the blackmail of name-calling, etc.

    c Examination of the measures taken to help pupils cope with cumulative 'step-by-step' subjects after absence.

S3 *Establishment of a report system for persistent truants*

    a This must be consistently applied. It must not be possible for the pupil to escape the checking process.

    b It must not allow a pupil to learn to substitute selective absence from lessons for absence from school.

S4 *The development of a policy for working constructively with the EWO*

    a Decisions as to the type of case which should form the focus for the efforts of the EWO.

    The hard core and chronic cases may absorb undue attention, causing other pupils to learn they can truant successfully.

S5 *The examination of links between home and school*

    a The importance of building up positive links with parents as soon as the pupils enter the school.

    b Involvement of the form tutors in these links, thereby avoiding the 'swamping' of the head of year or house. Emphasis of the importance of the form tutor in parental contact can ensure the continuity of concern, if the form tutor stays with group for two or more years.

    c Arrangements to contact the father. Mothers are often in collusion with their children.

Curricular measures

C1 *Evaluation of teaching methods*

    a Appropriateness of teaching methods for pupils whose preferred mode of learning may be *visual* and *active* rather than simply visual.

    b Examination of the goals. Pupils who have the tendency to avoid challenge need signs of success. They do not plan ahead and are dependent upon immediate rewards. Therefore they need:

        i clear short-term goals

        ii structured learning situations which contain supports.

C2 *Adjustment of teaching methods and timetable*

    a The elimination of unnecessary fragmentation of subjects.

    b Less frequent changes of topic and more systematically planned opportunities for pupils to apply what they have learned.

    c The demonstration of the relevance of current learning to life after school – especially important in an age of growing long-term structural unemployment.

C3 *Measures for building up positive relationships with a smaller number of teachers*

    a This may mean timetable adjustments. Less able pupils may need consistency of relationships because they respond more strongly to the *context* of teaching.

> b Restriction of the number of adjustments they have to
> make to teaching styles may be a necessary part of the
> positive discrimination essential for their success in school.

Systematic exploration of the following questions will help the pastoral heads devise their own strategy.

1 What part should the form tutor play in the event of truancy?

2 Are staff conferences held to discuss the support for and control of students?

3 Is there an induction programme which provides positive skills and constructive attitudes for pupils entering their secondary school?

4 Are there positive links with outside agencies who may be consulted in cases of truancy? What agencies could be consulted?

5 Is the EWO seen as a supportive figure and link with the pupil's home?

6 Are group guidance and peer support used in school as resources?

7 Are school processes evaluated so that positive or negative factors tending to reduce or reinforce truancy are recognised?

8 Is there a policy for dealing with masked truancy, e.g. an effective reporting or spot-check system?

9 What steps are taken to deal with unpunctuality?

Coping with aggression

Pastoral heads should acquire a deeper understanding of aggressive behaviour if the current perceptions of their roles by pupils and by colleagues are to be modified. The aggressive behaviour of girls, already mentioned, is often a problem because unrecognised stereotypes influence our judgements and actions. Girls themselves have succumbed to the pervasive conditioning processes in society, accepting derogatory evaluations of their ability in certain areas of learning and believing in unreal differences between themselves and males. Pastoral heads need to examine these issues, but they also need to be aware of indirect and passive forms of aggression. The issues and indications of coping measures are given below.

This discussion is concerned with special problems of aggressive behaviour and with the indirect and less obvious forms of it which create difficulties for teachers. Indirect forms of aggression may well be a more serious problem than direct ones, rendering the teacher ineffective and lowering standards of performance within the class. The diagram below illustrates the complexity of aggressive action:

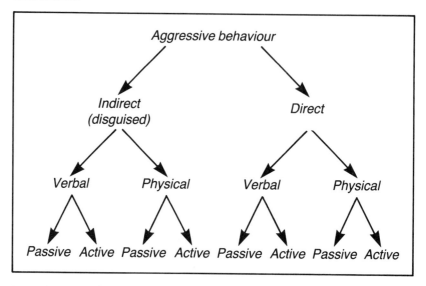

Not all of these forms will be dealt with here. For fuller discussion see Hamblin (1978).

We must also distinguish between:
ANGER and AGGRESSION. They are not identical.
Most aggression is instrumental, i.e. it is functional and purposive. Therefore we learn to look for the 'pay-off'.

Those who attract bullying
   1 Such pupils may be the real problem *but*:
      – The fact that they attract it, is not an excuse or justification for bullying. It merely underlines the fact that bully and bullied are in a particular social/emotional relationship.
      – It should not divert attention from the problems of those who bully and use direct physical aggression.
   2 Economy and humanity demand that we identify those liable to attract bullying, otherwise:
      – staff time is going to be wasted coping with incidents throughout the child's school career;
      – the pupil will acquire a negative identity, which will have serious long-run consequences;

- the personality factors which lead to the bullying may be reinforced.

3 Realism requires that we recognise the contribution of the individual to what befalls him.

THE INDIVIDUAL HAS TO ASSUME RESPONSIBILITY FOR THE RESPONSES HE CALLS OUT IN OTHERS – POSITIVE OR NEGATIVE.

Pastoral action not only recognises this, but provides the pupil with the *skills of coping and relating positively to others.*

4 *Analysis of problem*

1 From whom does the pupil attract bullying? This can tell us a great deal. We can speculate about the reasons for this.

2 WHY does he get bullied? Does he provoke by his mannerisms or his verbal responses? Does he provide entertainment for others by his tantrums? Does he boast or tell tales?

3 Is he different from his class or neighbourhood group? Is he effeminate? Late entry to puberty or an unusual quality of voice may be contributing to the situation. Does he hold middle-class values in a group where they are not acceptable or understood?

4 What is the pay-off? Is it gaining attention? If so, in what sense? From whom? From teachers, or in the hope of regaining the concern of parents?

5 What skills does the pupil need to acquire? Are these in the field of social interaction, learning to cope with demands in the classroom or self-presentation?

6 What is the contribution of the parents – especially the mother? Is she over-protective? Do parents foist unrealistic values on the pupil, which alienate him from peers? Have the parents taught the pupil to regard the less able and disadvantaged as inferior?

7 Are there certain personality mechanisms operating? Pupils may arouse jealousy in others by boasting about their possessions. They may tend to buy friendship through gifts and not understand why they are rejected or bullied.

The head of year or house will find it useful to diagram his analysis, checking the validity of the evidence. *Speculations must not be transformed into certainties without further evidence.*

Remedies when the pupil attracts bullying

1 Group guidance and pastoral help which is skill based. This implies that pupils are taught how to cope with teasing and how to make friends. Such activities are part of the normal programme of guidance.

2 Deliberate use is made of peer help. Friends are taught how to help one another and achieve success in school.

3 In form periods teachers make it clear that the school regards bullying with disfavour. Systematic building up of values which are against bullying should occur from entry to the school.

4 Private sessions should deal with the signs of deviance in the pupil who attracts bullying, e.g.
   – the tendency to take a 'teacher's pet' role;
   – signs of deviance which lead to 'attacks' on the school bus.

5 Parental consultation may be necessary, although it should take place before a crisis point has been reached.

Aggressive behaviour in girls

1 The fallacy of seeing aggressive behaviour in girls as greater today than previously stems from:
   – failure to see that it is the expression in its *direct form* which is becoming more frequent;
   – the different legitimacy accorded to violent and aggressive action;
   – the greater acceptance of violence coupled with the decline of inhibitory factors in recent years;
   – more rapid acceptance that nothing will be done unless the protestors display aggressive tendencies.

It is false to say females are more aggressive today. The balance of the forces which allow or inhibit the expression of aggression has been altered.

2 *Form*
   a Although in out-of-school situations there may be more direct, overt aggression, female aggression is mainly psychological. It includes:

- destruction of reputations and character assassination;
- innuendo and the erosion of self-esteem;
- reducing the victim to the status of a 'non-person' by talking about them destructively in their presence but refusing to accept – or apparently register – any protests or communication from them.

  b It seems realistic to state that female aggression in adolescence has a quality of ruthlessness. It focuses on the victim in a combination of psychological destructiveness and physical intimidation.

3 The basic themes emerging from my work on girls' aggression in school are those of *patronage* and *power*.

  Girls have acute sensitivity in these areas:
  - they react fiercely to 'being looked down on';
  - they refer to middle-class teachers as 'nags' and 'snobs', etc;
  - they use strong categorisations which they refuse to modify, e.g. snobs, but also exploit weaknesses.

4 The problem is complicated by their low expectations of what life has to offer – even jobs are seen differently by the less skilled female:

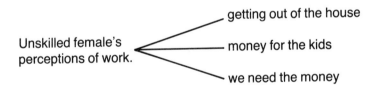

Unskilled female's perceptions of work.
- getting out of the house
- money for the kids
- we need the money

5 Some aggressive girls:
- have learned to be aggressive to protect themselves from undue demands at home, where they feel used by mothers at work and by their brothers;
- have learned aggressiveness in connexion with their sexual relationships and role, as a protest against male manipulation and lack of fundamental respect;
- react against male teachers who cope by using 'joking relationships', which they dislike;
- tend to assert their power by being provocative to male teachers and attempting to get them to overstep their professional boundaries.

6 *Remedies*
- Avoid any element of patronage – the sense of 'being looked down on' is the most frequent precipitating factor.
- Sarcasm should be avoided – these girls cannot forgive or forget it. Our inadequacies can lead us to resort to it and so make matters worse.
- Raise their level of aspiration through good careers work and study skills.
- Examine the school situation for signals of devaluation and discrepancies between responsibilities carried at home and those in school. Rectify them by giving responsibility in *acceptable* forms. Many 'difficult' girls are carrying out adult responsibilities at home, but feel treated as 'kids' in school.
- Use of pastoral curriculum periods to explore perceptions and modify attitudes.

The practical joker

1 *Why is the practical joker a problem?*
   - He is a skilled player of the game of indirect aggression.
   - His jokes often have hostile components, e.g. making others appear foolish.
   - It is an example of 'double bind' expressed behaviourally. He uses 'It was only a joke' as an excuse, whilst a complaint produces an injured look and 'He can't even take a joke'. Heads and tails – the joker wins.

2 *General guidance: What can be done?*
Guidance sessions should provide pupils with knowledge and the opportunity to discuss practical joking.

   The class should understand that practical joking of a severe type can be:

- an example of negative role-sending, i.e. part of the process of creating a scapegoat within the group;
- compensating the joker for his feelings of inadequacy;
- diverting attention from the joker to his victim.

3 *Individual work*
   - should teach simple techniques of
      - not responding in a way which lets the joker win;
      - responding with a smile and humour;
      - modifying behaviours which seem to involve teasing.

Indirect aggression

1 *General points*
   a Indirect aggression is a product of the *malaise* created by the irrelevant and demeaning identities sometimes provided by the school. This draws our attention to the bigger questions of the relevance of the curriculum, the appropriateness of teaching methods and the school's beliefs about what pupils can or should learn.
   b Passive aggression takes the 'tongue in cheek' approach. The façade hides the fact that there is no real compliance or active cooperation.

   It is often linked with negative attributions and predictions about the pupil's success and the motives of the teacher. When a class has developed this technique, there is little point in individual confrontations, for the aim is to turn the teacher into a 'nag' or unreasonable person. Homilies only reinforce the negative attitudes.

2 *Action*
   a Work from areas of strength, using study skills and the suggestions made earlier for raising the level of aspiration.
   b Use pupils' hobbies and interests in form tutor periods – a great deal of enthusiasm can be generated by this. Teachers' skills in making use of hobbies are still essential, e.g. roller-skating involves a number of complex physical skills which can be related to performance in PE.
   c Make the form base attractive – see that it reflects a positive identity for the form.
   d When teaching such forms, *consistently* reinforce anything positive – over a period of some months this can help them

move from a position of minimal response to more active involvement. Steadfastly refuse to be manipulated by them into the position where their negative perception of teachers is confirmed.

3 *Gossip and rumour*
   a This is a very strong form of indirect aggression, probably more commonly used by girls, but by no means confined to them.
   b Negative images are being purveyed of a particular pupil who attracts it – often by responding to the rumour in a way which pleases the originators.
   c Identify the opinion-leaders and assess the reasons for their dissemination of the rumour. Sometimes one can discuss the situation with them without making them feel attacked.
   d Produce a value climate in which such activities are regarded as immature and silly, avoiding dramatisation which adds importance to behaviours unworthy of attention.
   e Try to modify the situation by asking those involved to help deal with the problem. They sometimes feel they have started a process which has got out of hand. The aim is the practical one of allowing them to stop the process without losing face. Once this has occurred, it will be productive to examine the reasons why the rumours started.
   f The target of rumour will need help, often in two ways:
      – Integrating them with a group of friends, for often the object of the campaign of rumour is to isolate the victim from others, thereby increasing their vulnerability;
      – Alerting them to their attitudes and actions which alienate others.

A final point
A high degree of indirect aggression can be taken as a possible indication that there is something wrong with the educational organisation and pupil-teacher relationship within the school. It will need planned exploration and a search for remedies.

The pastoral team has to learn to function as a team, and also how to instigate less formal team-work as a response to problems and the stress they create. Certain individuals occupy an undue proportion of teachers' time; and certain classes develop negative identities as they pass through the secondary school. Staff-room taboos and the conscientiousness of the teacher inhibit staff discussion and analysis. Pupils may be using simple mechanisms for evading work or being aggressively passive, forcing teachers to hector. The behavioural patterns would be interrupted in the primary school, but the intermittent contact of teachers with classes in the secondary school allows it to flourish. Such situations can be rectified only by cooperation and a team effort by all – or the majority – of those who teach the class. The pastoral head and form tutor should be the spear-head for changing the situation, *but* it is a team effort conducted knowingly as a shared enterprise. Interested heads of year or house can follow up the materials given below by my chapter in Best *et al* (1980).

Basic points
Modification of the behaviour of pupils in classes described as disruptive demands a *team effort* and *careful planning*. A well-established and possibly rigid set of transactions will have grown up between teachers and pupils in such a class. This may have been reinforced by comments in the staff-room. A prerequisite for action is the modification of teachers' perceptions, and it may be helpful if a teacher of senior status is responsible for the exercise. Evaluation is essential. The group must decide how long the attempt will run before evaluation occurs. Certainly, the group must meet regularly to discuss progress. The endeavour must allow for the well-known 'Hawthorne effect', i.e. the positive response to novelty and attention.

Key principle

Parsimony is essential. Only the minimum actions and changes to secure the necessary modification of behaviour should be used.

Step 1: The first conference
1 This is an analytical and information-sharing exercise out of which should emerge the first step in a policy of *consistent* handling.

- There can be no real caring without control.
- Consistent handling is an aid to socialised behaviour, therefore it may be necessary to increase the uniformity of disciplinary demands on pupils. Too wide a range of variation can accentuate Machiavellian tendencies. Many pupils are adept at playing off one adult against another.

2 *The basic question*

NOT	INSTEAD
'How has the class become this way?' This could be time-wasting and the answers could be misleading.	'What functions does the disruptive behaviour serve?' 'What is the pay-off?' More productive questions.

3 Identification of points of breakdown, which differ from class to class and will include, amongst other things:
- entry and settling down;
- early stages of lesson;
- switch rules, i.e. how teachers instruct pupils to move from listening to an activity which applies what has been taught;
- short attention span, which makes it difficult to maintain the 'pay attention' rule for long periods.

4 Methods of teaching which yield results and rewards to which pupils respond.

5 Analysis of the structure of relationships within the class. This would probably include:
- opinion-leaders who influence others – either the 'stars' or the 'links' of a socio-metric survey;
- roles habitually taken up by certain pupils – clown, perpetual cynic, stirrer of others, practical joker, etc;
- factions and groups bound together by mutually supportive relationships and behaviour.

NOTE This analysis is a major factor in restoring power to the teacher in a constructive way. He is in control because he no longer reacts to the class as a unit but as individuals with whom he interacts in different ways.

Key questions
1 Which individuals tend to disrupt?
2 In what situations or under what conditions do they become disruptive?
3 Which pupils are positive in behaviour and attitude?
4 When and under what conditions do these pupils manifest their positive attitudes and behaviour?
5 What is the 'pay-off' for both positive and negative behaviours? (In relation to the latter, this might be evasion of difficult learning tasks, status increased with friends, etc.)

Principles
1 Our focus is on strengthening the positive as we control. Hence we eliminate sarcasm, negative signals and nagging.

A PUPIL CANNOT HAVE HIS REPUTATION HAMMERED DAILY INTO HIS HEAD WITHOUT SOMETHING HAPPENING TO HIS PERSONALITY FOR GOOD OR FOR ILL.

2 Classes of the type under discussion contain pupils who have been socialised to see the world in terms of 'us against them'. Our remedial strategies will take this into account, eschewing the tendency to 'get them before they get you', because it crystallises negative behaviour into long-term resistances.

Main steps

1 *Objectives*
  a To change the existing patterns of interaction between teachers and pupils to more productive ones.
  b To achieve consistency, not only of discipline but also of routine. This demands consensus amongst the staff about procedures, although it is unlikely to be complete, despite goodwill.
2 Change of the pattern of interaction is likely to be achieved when:
  – the 'pay attention' rule is reduced to the minimum;
  – when the sources of confrontations between pupils and teachers have been identified and are handled consistently by all who teach the class;
  – the amount of activity is increased as the 'pay attention' rule operates for shorter periods;

– the activities have *clear targets* and pupils *know* they have been successful. This emphasis on knowledge of results means immediate marking through self-checking activities and the return of marked books the next day. This can be done, if necessary, through the form tutor.

3 Timing of activities and a clear structure is essential, particularly in the subjects where breakdown in discipline seemed to occur frequently.

4 As such a class has acquired a negative identity within the school, it may be necessary to change the input from other teachers. This can be achieved by the deputy heads and others coming in more frequently – yet not too obviously – to speak to the teacher and making some favourable comments. A few outside visits, *clearly related to academic work and followed up on return to the school,* have also proved helpful.

5 The emphasis will be on reward – not on the occasional reward of praise for the individual pupil, which is self-defeating because it embarrasses him – but on the gradual weighting of interaction between teachers and pupils towards the positive. Negative behaviour can be dismissed as rather silly and an unworthy lapse, thus depriving it of much of its capacity to give status to those who indulge in it.

6 The help of first-year sixth or fifth-year students with the small group work or project has also facilitated change in attitude and the acquisition of new behaviours.

Techniques

1 Basically, anticipation and interruption of behaviour patterns coupled with positive use of the structure of relationships within the class.

2 Cooling off – not in an obvious way, but by changing the pupil's activity positively or changing the physical location of the pupil by asking him to do something simple, e.g. get a book that will help him.

This approach should come as early as possible in the behaviour sequence leading to the positive interruption of disruptive behaviours. It is at these points that teachers provide supports, displaying their professional skills as teachers rather than purveyors of information.

3 Investigation of waste of time – even if it is not a mixed-ability class, there is a spread of ability in particular subjects. Disruptive behaviour is sometimes associated with pupils who finish a task before the others but receive no positive reward for it. They may be also given unclear instructions about what to do when they finish.

4 Avoidance of confrontation – requires positive use of the opinion-leaders, building up the images of these significant pupils rather than 'cutting them down to size'. The image which we build up *over a period of time* is that they are individuals of whom the teacher has positive expectations and to whom responsibility can be given.

5 Change can be incorporated into the teaching method by such devices as a project in which two classes join together and two teachers work in cooperation. This changes the traditional situation of a teacher appearing for a short time, who, in isolation, deals with a class which knows its reputation. Another device is for another teacher who has something special to contribute to a topic to come in for a period and work with the teacher taking the class. The second teacher must have something to offer, otherwise the class could misinterpret this.

6 If projects are used, the class should be encouraged to mount and display its work. This, although it would not be stressed as such, creates the situation in which the pupils visibly demonstrate not only their ability to achieve something but their allegiance to the aims of the school.

7 The findings of the initial analysis should make teachers aware of their zones of interaction within the class and the way they react to certain individuals. They can then discuss how the situation can be modified – often there is little opportunity for this.

8 Some schools have found it helpful to use the sixth form with such classes. Often the sixth-form student will go to a great deal of trouble in preparing material for work with a small group as part of a project.

Commonsense

It should be obvious that it will be impossible to change a long-standing state of affairs overnight. Yet, in practice, we sometimes

behave as if this were not the case, looking for some instant remedy. The incomplete suggestions given here require:
- adaptation to the specific circumstances;
- constant monitoring;
- a sustained team effort over a period of some months.

Integration of the handicapped

The division of labour mentioned in Chapter 1 will allow one member of middle management to gain expertise in this field. Two accounts, both practical and sensitive, are those of Chapman (1981) and Hart (1981). Further reading is advisable, but my task is the limited one of alerting pastoral heads to key factors, encouraging them to develop their own reading and thinking. As carers, it behoves us to begin by looking at phantasies and emotional factors. They have to be considered in an enlightened and thoughtful way if we are not to perpetuate the view of the handicapped as eternal children, denying areas of maturity, including sexuality.

Issues include:

Stigma
Even balanced adults experience irrational reactions to physical or psychological defects because they evoke childhood reactions or have idiosyncratic significance.

Fallacies
Knowledge of the nature of specific handicaps is lacking or faulty amongst teachers. Therefore conditions are often seen as identical when they are not, e.g. educational subnormality and maladjustment.

Guilt
Guilt is normally a problem of parents, but the caring teacher may experience it if he feels unable to respond to a particular handicap or person. Without training, guilt may be produced by the complicated attitudes brought into school when the brothers and sisters of the handicapped pupil express resentment because he receives favoured treatment at home. Be clear that the handicapped pupil is far from helpless. He may indulge in devious manoeuvres to manipulate others.

Anxiety

Parental anxiety can be high. Self-blame is translated into anxiety, or questioning of the capacity and willingness of the teachers to cope with the problem. Pupil anxieties have to be considered – not only of the handicapped – but of his classmates.

Denial

This takes many forms. Parents may deny the reality of the consequences of the handicap, while the pupil may not be able to accept its permanence.

These notes now focus on broad issues of which pastoral workers should be aware. What are they? First, teachers rightly resent demands made without the provision of sufficient support and information. Next, the impact on teaching style is often under-played. Increased verbalisation and reduced use of the blackboard are necessary for meeting the needs of the visually handicapped. Teachers have to learn not to look down or turn away when speaking, if a partially-hearing adolescent is present. Peers have to be allowed to provide assistance, which can lead to control problems. The skill of constructive questioning of the handicapped to ensure they are following the lesson *without reinforcing their sense of deviance* is not easily acquired. When the tape-recording of lesson material is necessary, it is the rare teacher who does not feel some sense of threat.

Bluntly, integration, like comprehensive education will succeed or fail in accord with the planning and resources invested in it. Provision of resources is essential if the professional role of the teacher is not to be eroded. Ancillary staff – not teachers – must deal with dressing and incontinence. I am not uncaring, but caring involves setting limits to our task so that we serve pupils efficiently. Pastoral heads must consider the support they will give tutors and others through training within the school. The points which follow are based on the experiences of past students who have been closely concerned with the problem and who have coped successfully.

In-service training

A counselling approach is necessary. First, resistances must be examined. Teachers voice the following views which are not to be dismissed lightly:

- educational standards will deteriorate because integration demands too much of teachers already under stress and stretched to the limit;
- teachers are asked to become 'unpaid social workers';

– teachers will not be able to cope, and there will be a risk of accidents;

– classes, even if not disrupted, will be more difficult to control;

– they were not trained to cope with handicapped pupils or provide adaptations of the kind necessary.

Such anxieties must be brought into the open and given careful thought. Training gives:

a General knowledge of handicaps. The help of the educational psychologist seems crucial to achieve this.

b Skills of managing classroom situations. An analytic approach is necessary which examines:
   – the disabled/handicapped adolescent's behaviour;
   – the likely response of the peer group;
   – teachers' reactions.

c Recognition of the fact that teachers who work with certain pupils can be seen as being of low status. The phrase 'maladjusted teacher' is not uncommon!

d Pastoral care workers should train tutors to:
   – provide individual counselling for handicapped pupils;
   – create constructive awareness of areas of sensitivity for the pupil.

e Counselling explores:
   – pupils' feeling about their handicaps, *if* this is a problem;
   – social skills, remedying deficits;
   – the possibility that the adolescent is clinging to the hope that the handicap will magically disappear. Some are reluctant to come to terms with a physique that is with them for life and have mechanisms of denial;
   – family difficulties – manipulation of handicaps leads to poor sibling relationships;
   – identification with the peer group, which is especially difficult for the girl, who may be desperate to prove she is attractive. This opens her to exploitation. The handicapped adolescent has a real fear of life without marriage and sexual relationships;
   – low self-evaluation is accompanied by withdrawal. The handicapped adolescent cannot respond to signals of acceptance, indulging in 'touchy' behaviour or clowning.

A strategy derived from good practice

1 The stress is on similarities between the handicapped and other pupils rather than differences.

2 Discussion of readiness for integration is discussed thoroughly. If possible, the integration should occur at the usual age of transfer from primary to secondary school. It is difficult to enter the second- or third-year group when relations in a group have crystallised.

3 A planned introduction is necessary, e.g.

   i   After selection comes preparation of parents, which deals with their doubts and anxieties.

   ii The special school teachers are involved in this preparation as a matter of course.

   iii A visit to an open evening in February or March is helpful.

   iv Formal interviews of parents and child then occur.

   v   A week's placement at the new school in July is helpful.

   vi Formal placement begins in September.

   Parental fears can remain despite this preparation. It is crucial that parents have access to someone they trust to examine their anxieties. Without this, anxiety may be conveyed to the pupil after the stimulation provided by the novelty of the change has disappeared.

4 Entry probably should be at the beginning of the year and not during it. Tensions arise in pupil groups, and an entrant at a time of tension is likely to become a focus of attention or be put into a deviant role.

5 Teachers need the skill of taking active steps to increase integration, e.g.

   a   deliberating reinforcing interaction between the pupil and a few 'target' peers in the form;

   b   providing a peer model who gives a helpful guide by his behaviour – obviously the peer model should be a popular member of the class;

   c   incorporating the handicapped pupil into working groups as consistently as possible.

Practical points

1 Physical needs create problems that can lead to tensions. Lavatories obviously have to be adapted – a plinth and a sluice may be more appropriate than conventional arrangements. Staff attitudes to late arrival at class lead to deterioration of relationships. The handicapped pupil may have to be toileted. Welfare assistants may not realise the need to inform teachers when this occurs. Such minor factors can combine to make integration a conflict-ridden activity.

2 Careful thought must be given to positioning of blocks and ramps. Some pupils may need a table at the front of the class. Teachers will have to delegate responsibility – after careful thought – to pupils, once the initial arrangements have been made, if their teaching competence is not to be eroded. For example, another pupil or small group may be responsible for helping in practical lessons where mobility is necessary.

3 Welfare assistants are necessary and their presence in school is acceptable. More complex feelings exist about the two teacher roles often necessary:
   a a liaison teacher who works with staff and relevant agencies as well as with the family;
   b a support teacher who may be present in the class if the degree of handicap demands it.
The latter, however, may highlight the difference of the handicapped child or provide a source of threat for some teachers. Some cannot adjust to the presence of a colleague in the class. These issues have to be discussed fully, if smouldering resentments are not to exist.

4 Fire drills and safety procedures have to be adapted. The hearing-impaired adolescent has to be trained to stay in the middle of a line of classmates. Wheel chairs may have to be 'bumped' or brought downstairs by four pupils in emergencies; if setting exists, the whole year group has to be trained to do this.

5 Breaks and lunch-time present difficulties. Disciplinary problems centre on this. Other pupils can misuse the fact that the handicapped child has to remain in the classroom or library. The handicapped pupil can also misuse it by bargaining with pupils, if friends are allowed to join him.

A final note

Realism is essential. Sentimentality reinforces the sense of deviance of the handicapped. A guidance programme – applied in the context of the classroom – has to be devised by a member of the pastoral team. Individual guidance is necessary in which the skills are delineated and practised initially. Classroom teachers – possibly peers – are made aware of each step, and reinforce it, e.g. coping constructively with ill-timed offers of help.

Helping the pregnant adolescent

My discussion will be brief, because I wonder whether this task is part of the proper responsibility of the pastoral head. In other contexts I have been deeply concerned about this dilemma. We must limit our task: it is not infinitely expandable. But pupils trust teachers, and they look to them for help to cope with the emotional and developmental issues of their predicament. Guidance and counselling, after discovery of pregnancy, may be vital in preventing a later recurrence. The evidence from concerned agencies is that absence of counselling is associated with a greater likelihood of a subsequent pregnancy. However, I feel I should warn teachers that they should never send a pupil straight to the Family Planning Clinic or an equivalent agency. This is not cowardice: it is concerned realisation of our ethical responsibilities to important people in the life space of the pupil. It is better to ask the girl to go to her family doctor, who knows her medical history, and under the seal of confidentiality discuss the advisability of contraception carefully. This is respect for the individual, as well as proper maintenance of professional boundaries.

The person who has been approached should not take the pregnancy for granted on the statement of the girl. Tactful exploration may reveal that there is a need for confirmation. Anxiety may be responsible for a delayed or missed period. If there is evidence of pregnancy, and the responsibility of providing guidance and counselling is acceptable, the first step is to find out whether the parents know. If they are unaware of her condition, the girl's predictions about their reactions must be discussed. If she fears or is anxious about their response, ask:

a Whose reaction will be more severe – that of father or mother?

b Should the mother be told first?

c Should both parents be told together?

d *When* should they be told? Timing has to be considered carefully.

e *Where* should they be told – at home, in the GP's consulting room or perhaps at school?

Beware of making helpful offers to tell the parents. First, one has to consider their reaction. They could be angry or deeply hurt that their daughter's teacher has been told first by their daughter. To support a pregnant girl does not mean we absolve her from responsibility.

Girls often need to have a space cleared in which they think about what they will do. A major reorganisation of values and relationships will occur. Tension brings vulnerability to pressure. Time may be short, but some exploration is vital. Parents often focus on the problem without considering the wider values and emotional complications and seek abortion, regardless of the emotional issues. Three possibilities exist:

1 *The girl keeps her baby.* Sometimes this desire reflects immaturity or is an escape from reality. Despite knowledge of the stresses and messes of coping with a baby, she focuses on the image of an immaculate infant in a gleaming perambulator, who brings the admiration of passers-by. The baby is a curious doll substitute. In this unreal world the girl expects her mother to undertake the hard work of child-rearing. Mothers no longer will accept this, even in working class sub-cultures where this was the traditional solution to illegitimacy.

2 *She decides to have it adopted.* Precautions, regrets and dangers have to be explored. The danger of resolve weakening if the girl picks up and nurses the baby is one illustration. Even at this preparatory stage, the girl must realise that the child will have the right to know the natural parent when it is eighteen.

3 *She should have an abortion.* I will not enter into the ethics of abortion, but simply urge that the decision must be the girl's, and not reached hastily. I have met too many cases where hasty decisions – time is limited, of course – have led to guilt, depression and self-inflicted injury. Preparation and knowledge is essential, as the sensitive girl is profoundly upset by the mechanistic approach which often exists. The school nurse, if temperamentally suited, can be invaluable here. Girls sometimes feel intimidated by the impression of distaste given by doctors and nurses, whose orientation is towards preserving life, so that abortion, unless necessitated by urgent medical reasons, is obnoxious. Let me be emphatic that real care is given and that a professional stance is maintained. However, many girls sense the inner reservations. The conscience clause does not prevent this happening, because the nurse knows withdrawal would mean an increased burden for colleagues.

To counsel without considering the attitudes and feelings of the father would be limited. Parents of the girl may see him solely as a bad, exploitative person, and forbid all further contact with him. The boy may have deep feelings for the girl, intending to marry her or support the child. Young males can react strongly to the destruction of the child they helped create. Abortion then becomes an impediment to the continuance of a healthy, loving relationship.

Why did it occur? This facet of counselling may bring into the open issues of evasion of responsibility, vulnerability to emotional blackmail, disbelief in attractiveness to the opposite sex or a lack of self-respect which led to failure to take precautions.

Counselling is often needed after the abortion, but not provided. Yet in the more obvious trauma of a miscarriage we would be alert. The majority of girls need no special help, but a few react adversely. Interruption of a physiological process has consequences that are difficult to predict. A few girls experience the equivalent of a post-natal depression, whilst others seem to need a period of 'mourning' in which they work through complex feelings: they wonder about the characteristics of the lost child and what future it would have had.

Rarely, and only rarely, some experience a sense of violation or intrusion, usually linked with poor preparation for the abortion, and unresolved mental stresses. This, if strong, is a sign that specialist help is needed. The orifices of the body have been associated with deep phantasies for time out of mind.

Perhaps the major part of our endeavour will be that of helping the girl find success in school if she returns. It would be reprehensible to single her out and suggest that she is deviant. My remarks have been brief and merely offer guidelines when help is sought by the pupil, and the pastoral worker feels he should give it.

The following situations could form a focus for discussion by pastoral heads.

1 How will you cope if a fifteen year-old girl comes to you and says she thinks she is pregnant because she has missed two periods. Her story is that she went to a party at Christmas and drank to the point of insensibility. Her ex-boyfriend, who was there, later told her they had sex, but she cannot recall it. He says she was 'flopped out'. She refuses to go to the doctor or to have a pregnancy test because she is afraid her father might find out. He is a widower and unpredictably violent.
(A true incident, as are all the illustrations in this book.)

2 Girls come to you and say that Anna is pregnant. Anna is athletic, with the build of a champion weightlifter. She denies it angrily. The rumours persist, but again Anna vehemently denies the possibility. The headmaster intervenes and says you are not to interfere again. Anna is pregnant. Her parents hear

of the rumours and ask angrily why you did not contact them. They accuse you of negligence. So?

The family and performance at school

Post-war research has stressed the contribution of the family to success or failure at school. Banks and Finlayson (1973) demonstrate an association between underfunctioning in able pupils and parental mode of discipline. It is not so much the presence of parental interest and attitudes favourable to the school as the *way* in which they are expressed.

Interpretation and application of such research poses difficulties for pastoral heads. There are tendencies to:
- Simplify research, ignoring the careful qualifications made by the researchers.
- Ignore key variables such as gender or social class.
- Incorporate assumptions that are not submitted to critical scrutiny, e.g. that a child from a one-parent family is necessarily at greater risk than one from a two-parent family.
- Confuse correlation or a relationship of association with causality.

Pastoral heads should discipline themselves and train tutors to adopt the functional approach which asks, 'What has this pupil learned within the family which impinges directly on performance in school?' Note that this limits the responsibility of the teacher. We cannot modify home conditions or give extensive help to parents as this would conflict with our primary task, and the resultant diffusion of role reduces efficiency. We can, however, help the pupil react in a less costly way to adverse home conditions. The questions we ask are:

a Has he learned to predict failure? In such circumstances teacher exhortations become irrelevant.

b What behavioural reactions to frustrations have been learned?

c Does he perceive the world in terms of threat or as a dangerous place in which 'things are done to you'? This is not the same as 'get them before they get you'. The result is avoidance of trouble as the basis for interaction within the school.

d Has a view of the world developed in which control is seen as lying outside the individual? This creates a dependence upon others. The result may be at one extreme, 'The teachers are no good, they don't teach you properly here!' or some other form

216

of refusal to take responsibility for performance. At the other extreme we see the view that, 'The teachers *ought* to make you work, and if they don't, they're soft.'

e Are negative views of authority being transmitted, which result in the pupil bringing defensive attitudes into the classroom.

f Are pupils socialised within the home in ways which lead them to see school in almost solely restrictive terms of control? 'You'll have to do what the teachers say. You won't get away with it like you do at home.' Coupled with this are many statements which suggest that school is irrelevant to their future.

Regular monitoring of contacts with parents is an essential part of the middle management tasks within the pastoral system. Many parents are suspicious of files and reports. (I suspect that profiles will be no exception.) We must explain the purpose and operation of the system, drawing attention to safeguards, dispelling parental myths. Only the foolhardy would maintain a defensive or omnipotent position towards parents. But we may be unaware of the negative impression given by rules about access.

Parents need to be kept informed because they possess a voice which can help the development of the school. It has been said that parents do not wish for contact with the school or that they are disturbed by it. The argument suggests that they do not want it because they do not claim it. This may be a false position, for parents seem to want contact if they realise it is available and that benefits are involved.

Pastoral heads should keep open minds, investigating the nature of communication between school and home. Many communications from the school are excessively formal or contain implicit threat, e.g. about pupils' progress or by suggesting that the parent is being evaluated. Consumer research on what parents feel are appropriate reasons for visiting the school or writing to a staff member would be enlightening. Pupils may welcome home/school contact in the first two years and possibly in the third year, but in later years they interpret it as infringement of their autonomy. Life in school is a matter between themselves and their teachers!

Pastoral heads will obviously work towards:

- involvement of parents by better reports which invite co-operation and demand a constructive parental response;
- giving training about coping with homework;
- helping parents understand adolescent developmental problems, avoiding exacerbation;

– the provision of the skills of coping with pupil stress at O-level and A-level.

One member of the middle management team should gain deep knowledge of the mechanisms and processes within the family which shape behaviour and create identities. The symbolic environment created by the family is the basis for interpreting the world. Pupils learn fundamental things about power, motives, the nature of success and sources of satisfaction within the family. We can talk globally about social class, neglecting the fact that the family filters the values and perceptions associated with it, emphasising some, and discounting others.

I have written about the family in greater depth elsewhere (Hamblin 1973; 1978). Divorce and separation bring problems of fatigue and adjustment which fall especially heavily on the mother alone. Without assuming that stress in the one-parent family is endemic or inevitable, the following description of tensions may be helpful, particularly if discussion follows on ways of coping with such situations.

1 The mother may well have had experiences of violent or deviant sexual practices by the husband before divorce or separation occurred. This can lead to:
   – maternal restriction of social contacts;
   – negative feelings about men generally, resulting in the children feeling that goodness is a female quality and that masculinity is a bad thing;
   – anxiety about the protection of the daughter, which causes her to interfere when the girl gets a boyfriend;
   – frustration and ambivalence, which produce a stressful climate within the home.

2 Rigidity or inadequacy may prevent her from assuming the role of the father. If she is unable to do this, things get out of control. Some mothers alone tend to precipitate the crisis they fear by placing unrealistic restrictions on the children, which provoke rebellion.

3 The divorced father may manipulate the children as a means of punishing the mother. Again, tensions develop which can be brought into school.

4 Tensions may appear if the mother decides to remarry. The eldest son or daughter carves out a role which gives them autonomy and satisfaction. The anticipated loss of these benefits may precipitate behaviour difficulties. These are often most severe in the daughter.

218

5 Poverty and a restricted life style are the most common concomitants of fatherlessness. A mother alone lacks the opportunity to make do and mend or shop around. The impact on the children of this needs to be understood; otherwise the children feel the school is also rejecting them.

6 The difficulties of the father alone seem to be less severe, although the daughter may be handicapped by the lack of a woman in the home. This is especially true in the male-dominated household, when the only girl suffers from menstrual difficulties.

Unemployment creates stress within the family – understanding of family interaction becomes more urgent for the pastoral team. The implications go beyond the points made below, but they provide a constructive framework for study of the issues.

Relevant factors

1 We have seen that the family creates a symbolic environment through which meaning is given, to a large degree, to the events faced by its members. The world may be seen as threatening or unpredictable, or there may be over-emphasis on the importance of the evaluations of others. Prediction or assessment of the impact of unemployment have to take this family ethos or symbolic environment into account.

2 The reactions to unemployment will be influenced especially by:

a The father's security in employment.

b The moral value placed on work as part of a residual 'Protestant ethic'.

c Sex role stereotypes. The more rigid they are, the greater may be the difficulty in adjusting to the changes stemming from unemployment.

Main issues

1 *The father's reaction to the loss of significance* which is an accompaniment of unemployment is one source of difficulty. He may attempt to compensate for diminished authority by exercising additional controls over his son or daughter. In some cases, the family becomes an arena in which the father unwillingly provokes rebellion.

2 *The life style* which often develops with prolonged unemploy-

ment of the young person is another focus for conflict. Scrounging, late nights and 'sleeping on' become major issues.

3 Parents fail to recognise the *seriousness of depressive behaviour*. They often urge the unemployed young adults to go out and join friends rather than 'mope about'. The psychological difficulties of doing this, when one feels hopeless, are ignored, and the well-meant injunctions become a source of added pressure.

4 Many unemployed adolescents believe that adults will blame them for their plight and, in the words of many young people, 'want to put them down'. The redundant father is not necessarily more sympathetic to his son's/daughter's unemployment. He may express his own self-distaste or guilt through condemnation of his children, although he is aware consciously that they are as powerless to change the situation as he is. The anxious mother may further exacerbate difficulties – she is likely to become the focus of attack. This seems to exemplify the old adage that each man 'attacks the thing he loves'. Mother and child may become caught in a self-perpetuating cycle of hostility and recrimination.

5 Family relationships also show stress when *father and elder son are jobless, but the younger son or daughter has a job*. The employed adolescent can be provocative – often unwittingly – and cause tensions that are very real.

6 Female unemployment is now increasing more rapidly. Many girls who are unemployed feel they are trapped, and that there is a retrograde movement which will confine them to domesticity.

7 Tensions often develop within families when an unemployed adolescent wants to marry another unemployed person. Provident, cautious and forceful parents react sharply, creating a tense situation. The reality is that, as yet, we have done little to help young people cope with marriage in a situation where neither has had employment nor is likely to have. Parents focus on the issue of child-rearing, e.g. 'What sort of family is that to bring up children in?' Their reactions force the young adults into marriage or co-habitation as a counter-reaction.

A caution

1 We must not assume that the tensions outlined above are inevitable. Insufficient is known about the long-term effects of

220

unemployment in adolescence to make rigid statements. The disadvantaged may be better able to cope than those from other backgrounds. Disruption of expectations and the symbolic environment of the family may well be the crucial factor in determining the type and degree of stress which appears.

Implications

Pastoral heads will have to develop tutorial materials which anticipate the family difficulties associated with unemployment, providing pupils with the knowledge and skills which allow them to cope. I am not advocating passive acceptance but asking that the pastoral team should equip young people to maintain self-respect, build significant relationships imbued with responsibility, and actively strive for mastery of their environment.

Summary

1 Group counselling is introduced as a development and intensification of tutorial activities. Heads of year or house are encouraged to develop such small-group work, not only as an economical use of time but as a way of demonstrating their competence in the activities they ask tutors to undertake. Credibility is then enhanced. Such groups should focus on the positive, not solely on the negative; therefore the fostering of achievement motivation is stressed.

2 Truancy is examined through a strategy for the pastoral team which includes both structural and curricular considerations.

3 Aggression is treated in a manner which shows the types: active versus passive; direct versus indirect; physical or psychological. The need for carefully-planned team work which tackles the modification of behaviour of difficult classes is introduced. Ideas for mounting an attack on the problem are given.

4 The contribution of the family to school performance is examined and some ideas are offered for improvement of interaction and understanding. Associated topics of integration of the handicapped and helping the pregnant girl are discussed. Stress is laid, however, on the limits to the task of the teachers and the dangers of courting ineffectiveness through undue diffusion of roles.

7: Aspects of management of concern to the pastoral team

Management is a term that may seem to conflict with the warmth and humanity essential to good pastoral care. We have seen, however, that pastoral care is influenced by curricular organisation and the value climate of the school. It can be an activity more orientated towards static constraints than to caring and development. It may lack definition to the point of amorphousness. Doubtful assumptions about pupil and teacher may be present: the teacher may be seen as a quasi-social worker, and the pupil as possessing problems which he recognises and which he expects the tutor or year head to solve. In some schools pastoral care is restricted to the provision of 'emotional first aid'. In others, it is couched in developmental and preventative terms, yet the procedures negate the declared aims. All this makes management difficult, but that is not a reason for evasion of the task.

Monitoring is essential. To monitor pastoral care means collecting and comparing the standpoints of senior management, heads of department, heads of year/house, form tutors, pupils and parents. Discrepancies between them emerge, which explain contradictions and illuminate the causes of tensions. A combined Mannheimian and Lewinian position is held, in which we accept that behaviour is a function of the environment as perceived. For those who monitor, truth is propositional and all reality is necessarily multiple. Subject teachers may be tutors, but they see no connexion between their task and the activities of head of year/house. Teachers may see pastoral work as yet another imposition which does not take into account the realities of the pressures they face.

The dual nature of pastoral care has to be the basis for evaluation. It incorporates:

– a systematic, ordered and demanding programme of developmental guidance, providing the skills for academic, social and emotional success;

– constructive caring and coping with personal problems which impinge on behaviour and performance in school.

Those who monitor must beware of the fallacy of '*the* pastoral system' or '*the* school'. The pastoral system is not uniform within a school. Different levels and types of performance can be found in the same school, e.g. the head of one year may have training, using skills of leading tutors and developing materials to good effect, while other years operate disjointedly with sparse or negative communication as the norm.

Monitoring is a process of assessment based on perceptions and feed-back derived, ideally, from all concerned with the pastoral system. Monitoring of separate years may occur over a period of time, and once-for-all monitoring is obviously illogical. Monitoring will not provide clear-cut causal relationships, but will *suggest* possible links. It should act as an 'early warning system', indicating remedial action, e.g. detection of certain attitudes in the second year should lead to anticipatory or preventative action towards the end of the first year. Monitoring is concerned with factors which impede success. We are not only concerned with the success of the system in achieving its stated objectives but with the relative success of sub-populations, e.g. the gifted, girls, boys, or the less able. Monitoring should define and examine critical periods and tasks, e.g. transition from the fifth to the sixth year, which brings new intellectual and social demands, relating to peer groups and fending off anti-work pressures.

We must learn to separate description and judgement. The *descriptive* element of monitoring focuses on *what is happening,* e.g. emphasising the type of transactions between tutors and pupils in tutor periods, and pupils' perceptions of the role and functions of head of year. The *judgemental* element ascribes import to the above, looks at standards of performance and ways of raising them. The monitoring team has to ask, 'What is negotiable and what cannot be modified?', seeing that change in pastoral roles creates change elsewhere. Attitudes need to be assessed. It is legitimate to question what kind of pastoral care can occur in a classroom where the key principle for pupils and teacher is 'Get them before they get you'. Monitoring requires that attitudes are not seen solely as psychological attributes: they mirror social relationships in the school, and it is not too strong to say they *are* social relationships. Changes in attitudes bring related changes in interaction with pupils and colleagues. But let us not over-simplify. Behaviours towards pupils and performance of professional tasks may stem from the equivalent of sub-cultural pressures which have acquired an almost compulsive hold over the teacher. This means that there are no short cuts; that conflict cannot be evaded; that pastoral heads have to think in terms of processes and gradual development.

Monitoring is, therefore, a long-term process, which is tentative and adjusted to the needs of a school. If we are developing tutorial work which provides pupils with skills and which transfers into the classroom to give teacher and pupil greater role satisfaction, monitoring of tutorial interaction is an essential element of management. The obvious source of help is past and current studies of classroom climate and interaction. Stress has been placed traditionally on verbal behaviour, especially that of the teacher, whilst the contextual influences have been underplayed. Research has sometimes appeared to underestimate the importance of non-verbal communication which is often used by the teacher to modify his verbal messages. Pupils are attuned to these signals. Flanders (1965) gave attention to indirect types of influence, but the emphasis was still on verbal behaviours. We can ask whether:

1 The social climate of the classroom is a group phenomenon which impinges on all pupils in the same way?

2 The behaviour of the teacher is the most important factor in creating classroom climate?

3 Verbal behaviour reflects accurately other facets of a teacher's behaviour?

All these assumptions are questionable. They may or may not hold in a particular tutor group. Within the same tutor group pupils will experience different psychological climates, not only derived from individual definitions of the situation but from the time given to them by the teacher and from the amount and type of contact they have with him. We may see striking similarities between tutor groups. It will then be as important to explain the similarities as the differences. Particularly successful tutors and their work should be studied to provide data for all-round improvement of performance. Education has often concentrated too much on the characteristics of failures and insufficiently on those of successes.

Problems abound in the precise measurement of interaction, but even intuitive and impressionistic records allow development, provided that they have been submitted to rational scrutiny and their tentative nature kept in mind. Let us realise that our assessments of tutorial interaction are likely to be speculative, which is legitimate as long as we do not treat them as certainties. The search for evidence must be pursued vigorously, without falling into the trap of finding only what we want to find. Much of our monitoring is concerned with the acquisition of understanding of the latent functions of phenomena, e.g. conflicts about uniform, jewellery or hairstyle may be positive, offering opportunities for negotiation, or act as tension points which prevent pupils from expressing more fundamental grievances. Monitoring should be undertaken by all who are willing, allowing a new sensitivity to system forces which constrain the performance of both teachers and pupils or which facilitate satisfaction. Stimulation of active questioning is a by-product of monitoring. One finds that heads of year or house whose complaint is that tutors do not cooperate have never set out resolutely to stimulate questioning and a search for methods. My uneasy feeling has been that they desire an unthinking acquiescence from the tutor.

The gradual development of monitoring changes the level of involvement, if it is seen as a process of self-evaluation. Evidence of the autonomy of the teacher as a professional is inherent in self-evaluation. Staff development and job satisfaction is fostered by participation in assessment at a time when promotion opportunities are limited. Self-evaluation allows us to provide answers to ill-based criticisms of school made by those who do not understand the complexity of the issues.

Self-evaluation is a tool, but can be a trap if it becomes a blind justification of current procedures or reinforces divisiveness. Again, the pastoral team takes the long-term view. Inadequate preparation and explanation are patently counter-productive. Colleagues need not so much to be re-assured as to understand what self-evaluation is, relating it to themselves and the current and future course of their careers.

The first chapter provided the background for self-evaluation. I see it as a process in which there is continuous questioning of the validity of what is being attempted in pastoral care, coupled with an assessment of how what is achieved matches what we claim we do. Uniqueness of the school as a social system is kept in mind, but we do not let it become an excuse for poor practice. The simple approach laid out below has been helpful. It suggests, rather than prescribes, and certainly it is not a recipe for evaluation. A sequence is suggested in the framework, but the pastoral team may find it better to devise their own order of approach. Indeed, Step 7 could be tackled first as a way of orientating to the task. Monitoring and evaluation are on-going processes, therefore we return to questions and issues. From the beginning, we accept that it may be necessary to return and attack the issue from a new angle. We may want to impose a neatness or finality which is as silly as imposing on someone our definition of what their problem ought to be.

Step 1: Question

1 Each individual raises crucial questions about the factors which lead to successful performance and those which prevent it. Group discussion follows in which more stringent questions are raised:
e.g. 'We feel we have insufficient time, but are we using what time we have effectively?'

2 This draws attention to redundancy, i.e. the growth of unnecessary or unproductive routines which fully occupy people's time but which have never been submitted to careful scrutiny, e.g. much of the administrative work of head of year or house.

Step 2: Critical incidents

Critical incidents are examined, that is, tasks or situations in which success has far-reaching positive effects, e.g. successful teaching of the skills necessary to meet new demands at entry to the secondary school. Failure will have equally severe consequences. Perception of salient critical tasks will vary somewhat from school to school, although there will be considerable agreement between schools. Staff should, however, define the critical tasks for themselves in their own terms.

Step 3: Input

Characteristics of pupils, composition of teaching staff, current views held by pupils, parents, colleagues and governors are considered. The views of heads of academic departments must be closely scrutinised without assuming that they will be negative. Our aim is to make pastoral–curricular exchanges and interaction more productive.

1 *Role* — as *prescribed* in official documents or similar sources;
as *interpreted* by the role-holders;
as *expected* by others;
as *performed* by the holder.

No assumptions of uniformity should be made. The role of the pupil may vary on all or some of these dimensions at different age levels. There may be striking differences between first- and second-year tutors and those in the fourth and fifth years, if tutors do not move with their form groups.

2 *Resources*

What organisational 'back-up' and resources are available? This includes the less tangible elements of appreciation and support. What periodic stresses exist? Is there money allocated for pastoral materials?

3 *The views of role-holders about other role-holders*

e.g. Form tutor ───────➤ Head of year/house

Head of year/house ───────➤ Form tutor

Form tutor/Head of year/house ───────➤ Pupils

Pupils ───────➤ Head of year/house

Pupils ───────➤ Form tutor

This can be repeated with senior management. We can then identify and examine the significance of discrepancies and concordances.

4 The way in which role-holders *react* to problems and *explain* them.

5 The ideas held about the skills needed for performance of a particular role. (We have seen that there are fallacious ideas about the skills needed by the head of year/house.)

Step 4: Processes

Examination of 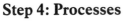 Essential tasks

Redundancy (as defined above)

Distorting factors (unwitting negative bias to tutor interaction with form tutor or head of year/house almost solely engaged in trivial administrative tasks or ineffective punishments)

Conflicts between roles

This may well be the most important and time-consuming step. It may have to be returned to at intervals.

Step 5: A job analysis

This gives greater precision to what has been done in Steps 3 and 4. The focus is on identification of:

1 *Procedural tasks*
  The maintenance and efficiency of routines for individual role-holders personally and generally within the organisation.

2 *Signal tasks*
  Actions which are a response to certain cues, i.e. signs of change in a pupil's attitudes to learning or behaviour. Changes noted by a number of teachers in the responses of a particular class.

3 *Problem-solving tasks*
  These include clashes between the recommendation of external agencies and what the school can do, or between the demands of pastoral and academic work.

Step 6: A skills analysis

This is concerned with *how* the job is done. The analysis should give direction to the school's in-service training programme. Staff should assess:

1 What are the skills needed for tutor work?
2 Are they present? What are the strengths and deficits?
3 What teaching skills are involved?
4 Are counselling and communication skills well developed and used effectively?
5 What overlap and differences exist in the skills of the form tutor, head of year/house and senior management? What skills need to be acquired or are insufficiently developed?

Step 7: Output

1 What is the contribution made by the pastoral system to the output of the secondary school?
2 What is the difference between output and specified objectives?
3 Do pupils and parents see the output as legitimate and relevant?
4 What needs to be added? Why?

The methods used will gradually develop. Pupils can be asked to describe the role of form tutor or head of year/house; decision-making exercises can be given which show to whom they would go for help and with which problems; open-ended sentences can be used as checks; suggestions can be garnered about activities and desired developments. Doherty (1981) describes this approach. The standpoints of pupils, tutors and heads of year/house can be elicited and evaluated. My desire, however, is to emphasise that the actual methods are not as important as the underlying thought and the presence of team-work. Group effort makes it more likely that we shall appreciate the multiple perspectives that relate to a particular problem or activity. To introduce tutorial work without examining the contrasting viewpoints is to create additional difficulties. To evaluate or monitor alone increases the probability that the evaluation will answer inappropriate questions or be misunderstood. The group involvement in evaluation creates awareness of the needs and purpose of training. Indeed, evaluation *is* a form of training, as stated in the Introduction.

People are easily intimidated by words like 'objectives' and 'goals', or confuse them with mechanistic forms of behaviourism which many behaviourists would reject. There is little point in a statistical structure in which a mass of data obscures poor thought and lack of planning. Attitude scales and questionnaires may contain bias or their validity may be suspect, but they remain unquestioned. It is vital that evaluation and monitoring develop gradually over several years, using only what is understood by those who evaluate.

Once this flexible viewpoint is taken, evaluators can select from various ploys other than those mentioned above or in Chapter 1, e.g.

- the balance between after-the-event and anticipatory or preventative effort can be examined carefully in each house or year group;
- incidents which are important can be selected and analysed to assess the implications for improving practice – conflict with parents and others, mishandling of situations, resounding success or satisfactory containment of potentially damaging or dangerous problems which are not fully resolvable, are included.

Inclusion of this illuminative analysis based on a wide selection of important incidents as described offers the possibility of organic growth. The concrete element of a real situation is useful, allowing the evaluators to see habitual patterns of behaviour and false solutions, and also to recognise ways in which more creative solutions can be generated. Awareness of 'blinkers' and of stereo-typed responses that limit insight and action is one of the benefits of incident analysis. The situation provides an anchorage which prevents people from escaping into platitudes and vagueness. New alertness to potentially destructive situations arises, increasing the team's sense of being in control. Attack on the mythologies that stifle initiative, deny potential and keep pastoral care at its current low level also result. Trainers were asked to deal with such defensive reactions as:

- 'We don't have time.'
- 'We do care, of course, but there is just so much to do.'
- 'You have to be an expert to cope.'
- 'It's not our job.'
- 'Anyway, we don't have very great problems here.'
- 'It might apply to some schools, but . . .'

A planned examination of situations teaches the team a great deal about attitudes, role confusions, frustration and misdirected energy, but also about unused potential. Suggestions are given below about the questions that can form the framework of analysis. Trainers should construct their own list.

Incident analysis: Basic questions

1 What was the intent of participants? What possibilities for conflict or co-operation existed?

2 Which aspects of roles became salient? What justifications for their positions were held by participants? What beliefs about authority and ways of behaving in this situation were present?

3 What frustrations came into being?

4 How was communication affected by participants' perceptions of the motives of one another?

5 What blocks to a positive outcome were present? What facilitated a successful outcome?

6 What priorities were held by participants helpfully or unhelpfully?

7 Who constituted the 'invisible audience'? Whose later judgements had to be kept in mind?

8 What were the implications of the outcome for future interaction?

9 How could the handling of similar incidents be improved?

This simple manual expresses constructive belief in the capacity of teachers to evaluate and train. As we have seen, the two processes are inter-related. The demand for self-evaluation requires a research orientation from teachers. The social-anthropological approach of Parlett and Hamilton (1972) evades the sterility of over-reliance on the psychometric approach to evaluation. This demands we take into account the viewpoints of all concerned, especially the learner. Danger lies in the indiscriminate collection of data or in the methods degenerating into a misleading anecdotal approach. Those who monitor could lose too much by blindly responding to vociferous malcontents or to those who value change for change's sake. They must also have the wit to see that individuals or groups of teachers who respond badly to proposals for innovation and evaluation are not inadequate.

The pastoral team is being steadily induced by the development of New Training Initiatives and pre-vocational courses to look at the relationship between the economy and what is achievable within the school. No crude determinism is postulated; but a transitional phase of de-industrialisation as we move towards a post-industrial society will influence pupils' perceptions of the school curriculum and teacher–pupil relationships. We may still be guided by an out-of-date perception of the life for which we prepare pupils. New questions will arise about the value and significance for pupils of current forms of education.

Values are insufficiently discussed by the pastoral team. Comprehensive schools have, to varying degrees, embodied the idea of egalitarianism. We need to deepen our questioning in a situation of demographic and drastic technological change. We could ask what function a pastoral system plays in a true community school which caters for all age groups. It is urgent for the pastoral heads to explore underlying assumptions and values. Daunt (1975) raises the question of whether we define the comprehensive school in terms of its intake or of how we treat that intake. This, in turn, raises searching questions:

- Does the comprehensive school merely delay selection? We hope it receives an unselected intake, but it still has to pass pupils on to systems of education and employment which are selective.
- But doing away with selection does not mean that equality of opportunity has been achieved.
- Is positive discrimination necessary? Daunt argues for 'equal value', i.e. that the education of all children is held to be of

equal value and that all children are equally valued, although treated differently.

Pastoral heads need to thrash out these issues, if helping is not to allocate deviant identities and signal inferiority. How can the helping endeavour avoid its own hidden curriculum of unwitting collusion with forces that give negative labels to those who find difficulty in meeting the demands of the school? Do we need to identify those who need compensatory action or should we admit to a type of egalitarianism which denies differences between individuals? If we accept the former, have we asked what the cost of accepting that compensation is? Evasion of such questions prevents escape from after-the-event provision of first aid to a more creative position.

It is imperative to estimate the value climate of the school, which can change in unnoticed ways. Stress in evaluation of effort rather than intelligence influences pupils in surprising ways. Ideological positions inherent in beliefs about the nature of intelligence and the influence of the home shape disciplinary judgements, cohering unnoticed into a blame frame habitually employed. Effectiveness of teachers is partially determined by the school organisation, which creates or limits opportunities. Teachers, like pupils, cannot show initiative, if the school does not encourage it. To assess tutors without reference to the institutional setting in which they operate is unrealistic. Reorganisation, redeployment and a history of ill-explained, unwilling change leads to self-protective resistance when further development is mooted. Behaviour depends upon the way the working environment is perceived – and it can be seen as manipulative. People then band together in ways which are backward-looking, defensive and personal rather than professional, future- and task-orientated.

Questions have to be raised about the pupil role. Pupils may have too little say in decisions – what is 'good' for them may be defined almost solely by adults. Receptivity to what is taught rather than thought may be stressed. We can examine their ploys for dealing with unpalatable conditions and demands. For them, lessons may be evidence of the tiresome idiosyncrasies of teachers which can be met only with evasion and are certainly not to be treated seriously.

Issues of deficit or irrelevance, as suggested, have to be closely examined. Pateman (1980) argues that accountability requires examination of levels of deprivation, some of which are not obvious. Second-level deprivation exists when pupils cannot do something, because the school does not teach it or make it available to them, but still appear satisfied. Accountability normally focuses on areas of traditional importance. The dimensions of the problems underlying equality of opportunity, sex role and learning, and recognition of minority rights and needs are only just emerging. Second-level deprivation therefore relates strongly to girls, but boys also suffer, e.g. family pressures which *condition* the children towards certain areas of ability to the detriment of others – second-level deprivation which creates a false self. Third-level deprivation exists when people are unaware of the social forces which shape perceptions and roles, so that they accept their place in the existing order as legitimate, perhaps unalterable. Alternatives are literally unthinkable. Some parents see PTA activity as not meant for them, largely because the possibility of participation in and influence on the educational process has never entered their awareness.

Management means bluntly facing the fact that there are different levels of efficiency in both curricular and pastoral areas. King (1973) provides a very useful framework, suggesting we can assess under the following headings:

---

1 *Activities*
  a Instrumental activities ⎫ i.e. the processes used in
  b Instrumental performances ⎭ transmission of *knowledge*
  c Expressive activities ⎫ i.e. the processes used in
  d Expressive performances ⎭ transmission of *appropriate modes of behaviour*

2 *Structure*
  i.e. organisation of activities
  a standardisation – the rules, procedures and routines
  b formalisation – the organised use of paper
  c specialisation – the influence of imputed abilities, age and sex
  d ritualisation – the use of symbols, emblems and ceremonials, such as assemblies and speech days.

It would be tempting to assume that the pastoral system is preoccupied with expressive activities and performances. The presence of a skills-based programme of guidance for success makes this a fallacy. Too great a weighting of the expressive probably indicates inefficiency or an out-of-date conception of pastoral care.

Used sensitively, King's work is helpful. Questions are raised about the activity of the school. Is it primarily concerned with social development, individual development, the transmission of knowledge and skills or moral training? Is there too heavy an emphasis on one aspect? Is the pastoral team taking a balanced approach? Much of the teaching in certain schools boils down to 'policing'. With less able or disadvantaged pupils the moral features ('If we all behaved like this . . .' or 'I cannot let this go unchecked because . . .') constitute a significant part of the interaction between pupils and teachers. The alleged moral features of classroom interaction take precedence over the cognitive. The cognitive seems to function, albeit weakly, as a justification for the methods of control. I am convinced that this perpetuates disadvantage because it distracts from the learning task and reinforces the orientation towards trouble found in such groups.

We must also critically appraise the nature of power and responsibility. Mention of this occurred in Chapter 1. Power can be coercive, remunerative or normative. Coercive power creates alienation. Reward power of the usual type is affected by the contraction of schools, whilst normative and traditional power is being eroded by technological change. Nothing is simple. Many apparently constructive management strategies function badly because they conceal the fact that, although delegation is stressed, people are given the tasks without a professional level of responsibility or the power to deal with problems appropriately. They then feel insecure and withdraw. Pastoral teams must identify these issues.

In stressing negotiation as the basis for development, there may be an unacknowledged hope for consensus. But in a complex organisation consensus will be only partial. Some kinds of opposition may have to be over-ridden in the end. The nature of the opposition which is acceptable, the way in which tensions are resolved and the manner in which power is exercised are matters for debate and evaluation. Let us go back to Daunt, who argues that the head has to take final responsibility. He has to maintain a balance between departments and other interested groups – including the pastoral heads – struggling for scarce resources, especially time and money. He can be seen as manipulative or as a scapegoat but, if decision-making were handed over to staff, would it, in fact, be less authoritarian? Would the strongest pressure group win? There is no evidence that the pressures of peers are less constricting than those from other sources. Pastoral heads will be failing if their monitoring does not bring these processes to the forefront of the debate.

234

Personality

It seems fitting that this manual on pastoral care should end with a few thoughts on personality. I sometimes fear that the individual and his well-being is in danger of being forgotten in discussion of pastoral care. Certainly, I have had to take myself to task about this. It is curious that in an age of technology, Dionysian man with his immediacy of gratification and desire for sensation may be in closer alignment with life than the prudent and planning Appolonian. Technology opens up new opportunities for enjoyment and vitality, allowing people to live more fully. But there seems to be a major division between theories of personality. Some suggest that, if a person is to be socialised, gratification of basic needs is not sufficient. He must experience frustration, coming to terms with it and with those who frustrate him. Freud (1935; 1938) stresses the need for frustration and sublimation of instinctual drives. Inside the person are deep instinctual urges which need to be controlled and allowed only socially valuable forms of expression. Aronfreed (1968) argues that children have to learn to behave in a socially adaptive way, acquiring inner controls through anxiety, and inhibiting impulses. The other approach sees self-realisation as a goal to be sought. Workers who take this stance postulate the existence of an inherent growth process, which, if not hampered or distorted, inevitably leads to creative living and gives satisfaction. It is assumed that these 'self-fulfilled' modes of living make positive contributions to society.

The truth is probably not contained in one approach; both have something relevant to say. The point is that the pastoral heads should debate these matters with their tutors. Maddi (1972) is one of the writers who distinguish between Lockean and Leibnitzian views of personality. A general indication of the two standpoints is given below, although it obviously leaves out much.

The Lockean view

a The child is seen as a *tabula rasa* or blank sheet. The mind is seen as active only when stimulated. It is conceived as passively receiving the impression of experiences. This leads to the old dictum that there is nothing in the mind that was not first in the senses. Not only is a passive mind moulded by external circumstances postulated, but early experiences are seen as more fundamental than later ones. Later impressions conform to earlier and deeper ones. Later complex ideas are seen as combinations of earlier simple ones.

---

b Integrity of personal development therefore depends upon the consistency of childhood training and of early events which mould the child and determine his responses.

The Leibnitzian approach

The mind is inherently active, manipulating experience in accord with its own nature. Behaviour is not the result of past experience, but is partially the product of the pulls from within. (We may need to question our assumptions about determinism emanating from early experience. Certainly, the orientation in pastoral work in the Leibnitzian tradition is that the focus of effort will be on what the pupil can become, rather than stressing what he has been subjected to in the past as a cause of current behaviour). The Leibnitzian approach has much in common with that of White (1959), who argues that the hallmark of humanity is an inbuilt tendency to explore the environment and strive for mastery. Human beings are basically motivated by an intrinsic need to deal effectively with their environment.

It might be enlightening to consider what might happen if the pastoral heads tend to one viewpoint, and the academic heads to the other. (It might be self-deception to assume that the pastoral heads would take the Leibnitzian approach!) If the contribution of these conceptions of the nature of learning and personality to methods are not examined as part of curricular and pastoral development much will be lost. These ideas must not be dismissed: they are germane to innovation and practice in an age where pupils dismiss much of the curriculum and school as irrelevant. Tensions and dilemmas often relate to these apparent oppositions. If we are to link the pastoral and the curricular then it is sensible to examine the issues below. Questions for debate are:

a *Imposed development or unfolding?* This reflects the issues of moulding or shaping versus untrammelled growth, i.e. the potter or gardener versus the wild plant; rewards and reinforcements which shape behaviour and emphasis on socialisation against provision of the appropriate conditions for growth. This dilemma applies to:
  i Moral development. Reliance upon external checks or surveillance, or controls from within?
  ii External versus internal sources of self-evaluation.
  iii Authoritarian, or humanistic conscience?

b Socialisation or self-actualisation?

   i Let us note that self-actualisation does not maintain that the individual will always realise his potentials. It does stand in the tradition that the final cause, inherent in man, is striving to realise his essential qualities.

   ii The Lockean tradition sees the mind as inert, acting only because it is stimulated by both internal and external sensations. Freud argues that the ego is a product of tensions produced by instincts conflicting with external social reality. Against this, Kelly (1955) would argue that even the young child forms constructs with which to anticipate future events and *interpret* his environment.

   iii Determinism or emphasis on potentials?

   The current emphasis is often on the importance of the early years. The Leibnitzian approach recognises that constitutional factors and environment influence the probability of future outcomes, but do not determine strictly those outcomes. We must always distinguish between possibilities and the use made of them. The individual can, however, decide on his own lifestyle and also decide the meaning of earlier experience.

   iv Integration of personality.

   The Lockean tradition sees integration of personality as dependent upon the consistency of childhood training and early moulding. Those educating in the Leibnitzian tradition place the locus of conflict between the person and his environment.

We should beware the easy erection of opposites because they could be deceptive, e.g. reward and punishment may not be the extremes of a continuum, but independent systems organised through very different principles. More cogently, the 'either/or' approach should be avoided. The normative fallacy which implies that one or the other is necessarily best is dangerous. Debate and examination are crucial elements – educational method has to include both the viewpoints. The 'mix' can be decided only by those involved in the situation.

Implications are present in these approaches about cognitive processes. Freudian theory has been described as a reductionist theory of cognition. Talking is seen as a series of cue-producing verbal responses, each word is a response to the previous one, and a stimulus to the succeeding one. For Freud, thinking is procrastination poised between impulse and action. Taken to an extreme, creativity is reduced to aim-inhibited libido which is given expression through phantasy. For the Leibnitzian approach, the intellect is active, initiates and is the driver, rather than being the driven. Again, caution is necessary, for both views may be valid, and are not mutually exclusive.

The Lockean view makes man an object to be studied in the same way as other objects are studied, i.e. through a reductive-analytic method which identifies the elements involved and the relationships existing between them. The other approach takes a holistic approach and sees man as pro-active. In simple words, where he is going rather than where he has been determines his behaviours. Education, like therapy, should help the individual live more satisfactorily *now*, look forward positively to the future, and, if necessary, reformulate the meaning of the past.

A key point:

In an age of change, discussion in schools about learning, pastoral care and the curriculum should look at the issues set out above. Without this, change may be abortive because the deeper issues are ignored.

Self-fulfilment theories

1 Theories of self-fulfilment, e.g. Allport (1955), Maslow (1962) and Rogers (1961), have had considerable effect on educational practice. No attempt is made in this brief discussion to produce an outline of these works. Senior pastoral workers should consider them and the validity, or otherwise, of the points made below.

2 These theories assume that all the inherent potentialities of man are in the service and enhancement of life. No destructive tendencies are envisaged. Negative expressions are 'distortions of man's true nature'. The negative self-image, if present, is a product of interaction with others. Only when the potentialities have to be expressed distortedly through environmental pressures is behaviour destructive to oneself and others.

3 The inadequate statement made above is sufficient to draw attention to certain points vital to educational development:

   a Self-fulfilment theory is demanding. Achievement of potentials, rather than ease or comfort, are the primary aims. Tension inevitably increases as the person strives to be the best he can be. He has a choice between experiencing anxiety as he strives, or guilt and shame at a later stage in life.

b A genetic blue-print is probably implied, but unfortunately this cannot be specified in theories.

c A major question is the link between deprivation and achievement of potential – especially deprivation early in life. Yet creative people exist who have been severely deprived early in life. It is illuminating to ask if frustration of survival needs leads to abandonment of self-actualising behaviour or loss of creative endeavour. But what of John Bunyan in Bedford Gaol and the creative thinking of Bettelheim in a concentration camp?

4 It is commonplace to talk about people having defences. Two extreme viewpoints exist. Freud sees defences as an essential and necessary accommodation to social demands. Rogers sees defences as leading to a damaging constriction of life. In educational terms this asks to what degree can we foster trust and openness, and to what extent must we produce caution and reserve? If we have a social responsibility, how does this conflict or agree with the implications of self-fulfilment approaches to personality?

5 Allport (1955) defined maturity as:
(Allport's points are *italicised* in the sections below. The comments are mine).

a *Specific enduring extensions of self.* In what should students invest themselves? Questions of values enter into this. Is part of pastoral work concerned with the clarification and inculcation of values? But where does education end and indoctrination begin?

b *Dependable techniques for warm relationships with others.* This brings problems of providing models and overcoming the legacy of backgrounds where pupils have models of exploitation, aggression and indifference. How can such techniques be supplied when the student <u>may</u> be going through a period of cynicism and mistrust or is gaining identity by opposition?

c *Stable emotional security or self-acceptance.* This gives recognition to the fact that truly responsible behaviour stems from self-respect, but complications exist. A discrepancy between actual and ideal self seems to be essential for development. Promotion of the desire to work for standards of excellence is part of the pastoral effort. Quicke (1978) argues that Rogerian approaches could reduce into acceptance of the *status quo*. This would be a distortion, but the possibility cannot be ignored. Pastoral management implies looking at what is built into the transactions between pupils and the school, analysing the weighting of forces promoting self-respect, passivity, achievement and responsibility.

d *Habits of realistic perception.* This should occupy a more important place in tutorial work than it does. Tutor activities, if poorly constructed, can reinforce self-indulgence, and fail to encourage pupils to question their perceptions of self and others. This is a major contribution to the intellectual, social and emotional development of pupils when well done.

e *Skills and problem-centredness.* Insufficient attention can be given to the key skills of coping with frustration, audience anxiety, loss of face or a sense of helplessness. The intellectual component can be under-estimated. Pupils need to have the opportunity to solve behavioural problems and verbalise their coping strategies. Whilst this does not guarantee they will apply the learning to life, it makes it more likely. (Perhaps we should ask if there is a danger of pastoral care being determinedly anti-intellectual.)

f *Self-objective, applying insight and humour.* This provides a counter-balance to external and self-set pressures. It exemplifies the need to teach pupils about the forces which impinge on them negatively, maintaining a sense of personal responsibility in the faces of these pressures.

g *A unifying philosophy of life.* This is part of the school's endeavour in creating the truly morally educated person. But what contribution is made specifically by tutors and the pastoral system?

A final note

Current discussion of the pastoral/academic divide may be helped by consideration of these issues. In examining issues in a rapidly changing society and school system we may concentrate on effects, whilst the causes – undoubtedly multiple – may lie in matters such as these. It would be enlightening to ask what the above discussion touches on which is crucial to our task of equipping pupils to take up a responsible role in society.

Outline

1 The need for involvement of staff in a continuous process of monitoring is highlighted. The approach advocated is a gradual one in which latent as well as manifest factors are understood. The systematic comparison of perceptions and viewpoints of senior management, heads of year or house, academic, department heads, tutors and pupils is regarded as essential data.

2 Analysis of important incidents is seen as a tool to be developed by the pastoral team, which offers helpful insights.

3 A final section examines the relationship between personality and learning. Questions are raised to which no easy answers can be given. Earnest debate on these issues is seen as leading to the constructive integration of the pastoral and curricular, showing that pastoral care is not condemned to take a permanent anti-intellectual stance.

References

Allport, G. (1955) *Becoming*, New Haven, Conn: Yale University Press.
Aronfreed, J. (1968) *Conduct and Conscience: The Socialisation of Internalised Control Over Behaviour*, New York: Academic Press.

Balogh, J. (1982) *Profile Reports for School Leavers, Schools Council Programme 5*, London: Longman.
Banks, O. and Finlayson, D. (1973) *Success and Failure in the Secondary School*, London: Methuen.
Berkowitz, L. (1980) *A Survey of Social Psychology*, New York: Holt, Rinehart and Winston. (2nd Edition).
Berne, E. (1966) *Games People Play*, London: Deutsch.
Best, R., Jarvis, C. and Ribbins, P. (1980) *Perspectives on Pastoral Care*, London: Heinemann.
Best, R., Ribbins, P., Jarvis, C. and Oddy, D. (1983) *Education and Care*, London: Heinemann.
Blackburn, K. (1983) *Head of Year, Head of House*, London: Heinemann.
Bloom, B. (1976) *Human Characteristics and School Learning*, New York: McGraw-Hill.
Bradbury, M. (1981) Development of an Activity for Pastoral Care and Tutorial Periods, in Hamblin, D. *Problems and Practice of Pastoral Care*, Oxford: Blackwell.
Buss, A. (1980) *Self-Consciousness and Anxiety*, San Francisco: Freeman.

Carroll, H. (Ed.) (1978) *Absenteeism in South Wales*, Swansea: University College of Swansea Faculty of Education.
Cave, R. (1970) *Partners for Change*, London: Ward Lock.
Chapman, L. (1981) Integration of Handicapped Pupils into the Comprehensive School, in Hamblin, D. (Ed.) *Problems and Practice of Pastoral Care*, Oxford, Blackwell.
Conger, J. (1973) *Adolescence and Youth*, New York: Harper and Row.
Crites, J. (1968) *Vocational Psychology*, New York: McGraw-Hill.

Daunt, P. (1975) *Comprehensive Values*, London: Heinemann.
Davies, I. (1976) *Objectives in Curriculum Design*, London: McGraw-Hill.
Davison, A. and Gordon, P. (1978) *Games and Simulations in Action*, London: Woburn Press.
Docking, J. (1980) *Control and Discipline in Schools*, London: Harper and Row.
Dockrell, B. (1982) Profiles in Preparation, in *Profiles*, London: Further Education and Curriculum Review and Development Unit.

Dockrell, B. and Hamilton, D. (1980) *Rethinking Educational Research*, London: Hodder and Stoughton.

Doherty, K. (1977) An evaluation of a pastoral care system of a comprehensive school in South Wales, Swansea: Unpublished M.Ed. Dissertation, Department of Education, University College of Swansea.

Doherty, K. (1981) A Framework for the Evaluation of Pastoral Care, in Hamblin, D. (Ed.) *Problems and Practice of Pastoral Care*, Oxford: Blackwell.

Dunham, J. (1978) Change and stress in the head of department's role, *Educational Research*, 21, No. 1, pp. 44–47.

Dunham, J. (1980) An exploratory comparative study of staff stress in English and German comprehensive schools, *Education Review*, 32, No. 1, pp. 11–20.

Dweck, C. and Licht, B. (1980) Learned Helplessness, in Garber, J. and Seligman, M. (Eds.) *Human Helplessness*, New York: Academic Press.

Eggleston, J. (Ed.) (1979) *Teacher Decision-Making in the Classroom*, London: Routledge and Kegan Paul.

Elms, A. (1969) *Role Playing, Reward and Attitude Change*, New York: Van Nostrand Reinhold.

Erikson, E. 1968 *Identity*, London: Faber and Faber.

Evans, M. (1982) *A Study of the Perceptions of Pastoral Care Held by Pupils and Teachers*, Swansea: Unpublished M.Ed. Dissertation, Department of Education, University College of Swansea.

Ferri, E. (1971) *Streaming: Two Years Later*, Slough: N.F.E.R.

Flanders, N. (1970) *Analysing Teaching Behaviour*, New York: Addison-Wesley.

Freud, S. (1935) *Beyond the Pleasure Principle*, New York: Boni and Liveright.

Freud, S. (1938) *The Basic Writings of Sigmund Freud*, New York: Random House.

Garber, J. and Seligman, M. (Eds.) (1980) *Human Helplessness*, New York: Academic Press.

Goffman, E. (1959) *The Presentation of Self in Everyday Life*, New York: Doubleday Anchor.

Gross, N., Giacquinta, J. and Bernstein, M. (1971) *Implementing Organisational Innovations*, New York: Harper and Row.

Hamblin, D. (1973) *Communication Within the Home*, Occasional Papers, Division of Clinical and Educational Psychologists, British Psychological Society, No. 3, pp. 115–124.

Hamblin, D. (1974a) The Relationship of Depth Psychology to Moral Development, in Collier, G., Tomlinson, P., and Wilson, J. (Eds.) *Values and Moral Development in Higher Education*, London: Croom Helm.

Hamblin, D. (1974) *The Teacher and Counselling*, Oxford: Blackwell.

Hamblin, D. (1978) *The Teacher and Pastoral Care*, Oxford: Blackwell.

Hamblin, D. (1980) Adolescent Attitudes Towards Food, in Turner, M. (Ed.) *Nutrition and Lifestyles*, London: Applied Science Publishers.

243

Hamblin, D. (1980) Strategies for the Modification of Behaviour of Difficult and Disruptive Classes, in Best, R. *et al* (Eds.) *Perspectives on Pastoral Care*, London: Heinemann.

Hamblin, D. (Ed.) (1981) *Problems and Practice of Pastoral Care*, Oxford: Blackwell.

Hamblin, D. (1981) *Teaching Study Skills*, Oxford, Blackwell.

Hamblin, D. (1983) *Guidance: 16–19*, Oxford: Blackwell.

Harding, J. (1983) *Switched Off: the Science Education of Girls*, London: Longman.

Hargreaves, D., Hester, S., and Mellor, F. (1975) *Deviance in Classrooms*, London: Routledge and Kegan Paul.

Hart, M. (1981) Integration of Handicapped Pupils into Ordinary Schools, in Hamblin, D. (Ed.) *Problems and Practice of Pastoral Care*, Oxford: Blackwell.

Holland, R. (1977) *Self and Social Context*, London: Macmillan.

Kandel, D. and Lesser, G. (1972) *Youth in Two Worlds*, San Francisco: Jossey-Bass.

Kelly, G. (1955) *The Psychology of Personal Constructs*, New York: Norton.

King, R. (1973) *School Organisation and Pupil Involvement*, London : Routledge and Kegan Paul.

Laing, R., Phillipson, H. and Lee, A. (1966) *Interpersonal Perception*, London: Tavistock.

Lickona, T. (Ed.) (1976) *Moral Development and Behaviour*, New York: Holt, Rinehart and Winston.

Maddi, S. (1972) *Personality Theories*, Illinois: Dorsey Press.

Mansell, J. (1982) A Burst of Interest, in *Profiles*, London: Further Education Curriculum Review and Development Unit.

Marland, M. (1980) The Pastoral Curriculum, in Best, R. *et al*, *Perspectives on Pastoral Care*, London: Heinemann.

Marland, M. (1981) (Ed.) *Information Skills in the Secondary School*, London: Methuen.

Maslow, A. (1962) *Towards a Psychology of Being*, Princeton, N.J.: Van Nostrand Reinhold.

Moreno, J. (1946) *Psychodrama*, Vol. 1, New York: Beacon House.

Newbold, D. (1977) *Ability Grouping: The Banbury Enquiry*, Windsor, N.F.E.R.

Oliver, R. and Butcher, H. (1968) 'Teachers' Attitudes to Education', *British Journal of Educational Psychology*, Vol. 38, pp. 38–44.

Ormerod, M. and Duckworth, D. (1975) *Pupils Attitudes to Science*, Windsor: N.F.E.R.

Partlett, M. and Hamilton, D. (1972) *Evaluation as Illumination*, Occasional Paper 9, Edinburgh: Centre for Research in the Educational Sciences.

Pateman, T. (1980) in Bush, T., Glatter, R., Goodey, J. and Riches, C. *Approaches to School Management*, London: Harper and Row.

Patton, M. (1982) *Practical Evaluation*, Beverley Hills: Sage.

Quicke, J. (1978) Rogerian Psychology and Non-Directive Counselling in Schools, *Educational Research*, Vol. 20, No. 3, pp. 192–200.

Reynolds, D., Jones, D., St. Leger, S. and Murgatroyd, S. (1980) School Factors and Truancy, in Hersov, L. and Berg, I. (Eds.) *Out of School*, Chichester: Wiley.

Rubenowitz, S. (1968) *Emotional Flexibility – Rigidity as a Comprehensive Dimension of Mind*, Stockholm: Almquist and Wiksell.

Rutter, M., Maughan, B., Mortimore, P. and Ouston, J. (1979) *Fifteen Thousand Hours*, London: Open Books.

Schools Council Committee for Wales (1983) *Profile Reporting in Wales*, Cardiff.

Spivack, G., Platt, J. and Shure, M. (1976) *The Problem Solving Approach to Adjustment*, San Francisco: Jossey-Buss.

Stott, D. (1966) *Studies of Troublesome Children*, London: Tavistock.

Sugarman, B. (1973) *The School and Moral Development*, London: Croom Helm.

Sumner, R. and Warburton, F. (1972) *Achievement in Secondary School*, Windsor: N.F.E.R.

Taba, H. (1962) *Curriculum Development: Theory and Practice*, New York: Harcourt and Brace.

Taylor, J. and Walford, R. (1972) *Simulation in the Classroom*, Harmondsworth: Penguin.

Tyler, L. (1965) Minimum Change Therapy, in Adams, J. (Ed.) *Counseling and Guidance*, New York: MacMillan.

Tyler, L. (1969) *The Work of the Counselor*, (3rd Edn.) New York: Appleton Century Crofts.

Wall, W. (1948) *The Adolescent Child*, London: Methuen.

Wankowski, J. (1973) *Temperament, Motivation and Academic Achievement*, Birmingham: University of Birmingham Educational Survey and Counselling Unit.

Ward, L. (Ed.) (1982) *The Ethical Dimension of the School Curriculum*, Swansea: Faculty of Education, University College of Swansea.

Watkins, C. (1981) Adolescents and Activities, in Hamblin, D. *Problems and Practice of Pastoral Care*, Oxford: Blackwell.

Watts, A. (1983) *Education, Unemployment and the Future of Work*, Milton Keynes: Open University Press.

White, R. (1959) Motivation reconsidered: the concept of competence, *Psychological Review*, 66, pp. 297–333.

Woods, P. (1975) Showing Them Up in Secondary School, in Chanan, G. and Delamont, S. (Eds.) *Frontiers of Classroom Research*, Slough: N.F.E.R.

Young, T. (1972) *New Sources of Self*, New York: Pergamon.

Index